T0376742

Lean for Banks

Improving Quality, Productivity, and Morale in Financial Offices

Bohdan W. Oppenheim
Marek Felbur

CRC Press
Taylor & Francis Group
Boca Raton   London   New York

CRC Press is an imprint of the
Taylor & Francis Group, an **informa** business

A PRODUCTIVITY PRESS BOOK

CRC Press
Taylor & Francis Group
6000 Broken Sound Parkway NW, Suite 300
Boca Raton, FL 33487-2742

First issued in hardback 2017

ISBN-13: 978-1-4822-6084-7 (pbk)
ISBN-13: 978-1-1384-6392-9 (hbk)

Visit the Taylor & Francis Web site at
http://www.taylorandfrancis.com

and the CRC Press Web site at
http://www.crcpress.com

Contents

List of Figures

List of Boxes

Preface

Banks are among the most popular service industries. Banking has biblical roots and is thus one of the oldest professions. Over the centuries, tens of thousands of banks have served billions of customers of all ages, cultures, and economic systems. One would think that after such vast experience bankers would be able to perfectly and efficiently perform their daily work. Not so. Most banking institutions suffer from fairly basic inefficiencies such as problems and frustrations arising from poor productivity and work quality; inefficient planning; inadequate coordination and communication; insufficient preparation of people, processes and tools; uneven workflow; excessive bureaucracy; reactive rather than proactive management; mistakes and rework; and general lack of enthusiasm.

This is not a unique fault of bankers; it is the fault of a modern civilization that places higher premiums on quick profits than on long-term streamlining of work. In their defense, banks operate under myriad local, state, national, and international rules and laws and also follow their own regulations intended to ensure client data safety and security that are not conducive to efficiency.

Few traditional (non-Lean) banks are aware that they have vast reserves of productivity. Typically, both managers and staffs in such banks work extremely hard and often work overtime. Their intuition tells them that the system has no reserves left and that is as Lean as can be. The knee-jerk reaction is to blame the frantic pace on excessive amounts of work and shortages of employees. The solution is usually hiring more employees, but this often has the opposite effect. More people make the system even more difficult to manage, more convoluted, and less efficient.

Fortunately, an excellent solution exists. This book describes the application of the Lean and Six Sigma paradigm (Lean for short) to bank operations. Lean originated in auto production at Toyota and soon expanded to many other industries, some of which did not involve manufacturing. The paradigm has been used in the areas of administration, government, health-care delivery, supply chain management, education, project management, product development, engineering, systems engineering, defense work, and enterprise management. We know with absolute certainty that Lean brings significant improvements and applies to any type of work in any industry, nonprofit or government organization, in any country, and in any economic and political system.

Soon after Lean is deployed in a serious way, organizations can achieve a higher quality of work in a shorter amount of time, *with nobody working harder, and everybody working smarter.* Employees transition from fighting crises to increasing both customer satisfaction and bank competitiveness. Work becomes more predictable, stable, and pleasant. It soon becomes truly shocking to both management and staff how much work can be accomplished in the same amount of time and with the same resources, simultaneously improving productivity, quality, cost, work morale, and customer satisfaction. The effects of Lean can be dramatic: up to doubled productivity in the entire system; process times cut by 50% to 90%; the number of errors reduced by 50% to 90%; development time for new bank products reduced by half; loan approval time cut by 90%; modest capital investments (only training); dramatically better human relations at all levels; and, most importantly, vastly better customer satisfaction and bank competitiveness. Banks pioneering Lean already report these figures. But Lean does not stop there. Lean is like an onion: as we peel off the "skins of waste," we discover more waste and more opportunities to improve.

When faced with stiff competition, traditional companies brutally cut costs, usually by massive layoffs, and by overworking the remaining employees and suppliers. Without addressing underlying systemic problems, these cuts simply eliminate needed resources and therefore slow the operations. This causes more frantic work pace, loss of quality, and decreasing customer satisfaction. When this happens, additional customers and profits are lost, resulting in even more cuts and more layoffs. This spiral of failure can easily lead to collapse.

In contrast, Lean focuses on recovering productivity reserves by waste elimination. This in turn leads to lower costs, higher quality, and increased customer satisfaction. Lower operating costs enable banks to keep employees on the payroll because they will be needed as customer satisfaction attracts more business. During the Lean deployment period, the employees can address those improvements for which they never had time, contributing to better productivity and quality. The success spiral is achieved without layoffs.

One of the most pervasive myths in the banking industry is that higher quality requires higher costs. This may be true in the superficial sense of marble floors in front offices, but is totally wrong in terms of the cost of operations. Lean demonstrates that a high quality of operations is actually the least expensive improvement. In Lean, we avoid the high costs of mistakes, errors, defects, rework, delays, frustrations, and subsequent crises, and focus instead on making operations better and better.

Employees love Lean because Lean is people-centered. Everyone in a Lean organization is motivated to solve problems rather than hiding them in the traditional workplace culture of fear, naming, blaming, and shaming. Employees see sense in the work allocated by managers and trust that the managers make good decisions. In turn, the managers earn trust and respect by training and mentoring employees, inspiring them to reach their full potential (just like superb teachers do).

The banking industry seems to be one of the last Lean frontiers, delayed no doubt due to the severe 2007–2011 crisis and subsequent massive layoffs in the industry. However, pioneering banks are rapidly implementing Lean. In this book, we describe the banks and financial institutions that have more or less mature Lean deployments. They all report significant, often dramatic, improvements in productivity and quality.

In Chapter 2, we contrast an ideal bank to a dysfunctional bank. Our interviews with bankers in the United States and Europe revealed that practically all banks suffer from many, if not all, of the maladies of the dysfunctional bank. In several interviews, when we mentioned the "ideal bank," experienced bankers responded with sarcastic laughter. We disagree. This book will demonstrate that an exciting journey toward the ideal is possible. We invite all readers to join us on that journey.

Bohdan W. Oppenheim and Marek J. Felbur

Acknowledgments

The idea for this book was born during a sail to Santa Catalina Island off the coast of California. While chatting about the applications of Lean Thinking in different work domains, Bohdan Oppenheim, one of the authors, and Dr. Jacek Lipiec, a faculty member at the Warsaw School of Economics, agreed that Lean wisdom could easily expand into the banking industry. Dr. Lipiec contributed a number of editorial ideas to this book and planned to add several chapters focused on the important interaction of Lean and social obligations of banks. Regretfully, long-term professional duties prevented him from doing so and he advised the other two authors to proceed without him and not delay the book. Dr. Lipiec's intellectual modesty made him refuse to be listed as one of the authors; he claimed that his contributions were not significant enough to deserve it. We hope that eventually a second edition of the book enriched by Dr. Lipiec's important chapters will be published, and that his name will grace the list of authors.

The authors will always remain indebted to Toyota Motor Corporation for inventing the Toyota Production System (TPS) and to Dr. James Womack, formerly at the Massachusetts Institute of Technology (MIT) and later at the Lean Enterprise Institute, for reinventing a Western version known as Lean Thinking and popularizing it beyond Japan. Without these contributions, this book could not have been written.

Bohdan Oppenheim, one of the authors, has been associated with the Lean Aerospace Initiative (LAI) consortium in a variety of ways almost from its creation. He is immensely grateful to his LAI colleagues, particularly Dr. Earll Murman, initially a mentor, later a co-researcher and coauthor, and always a friend, for his support. This book uses several quotes and illustrations from the successful introductory course on Lean and Six Sigma named EdNet Lean Academy™ [Lean Academy, 2008] developed by the LAI network of universities. Drs. Murman, Hugh McManus, and Eric Rebentisch of MIT led the course development and Oppenheim served as a lead instructor in several courses.

This book was inspired by and uses several quotes and illustrations from two exciting books on Lean healthcare: *Lean Hospitals* by Mark Graban and *On the Mend* by John Toussaint, MD and Dr. R.A. Gerard. Both books are extremely important because they clearly and successfully describe the evolution of Lean Thinking from manufacturing to a non-manufacturing (healthcare) domain. However, no fault of the present book must be blamed on Graban, Toussaint, or Gerard.

The authors are immensely grateful to all the numerous friends and colleagues, too many to list here, at several banks and financial institutions who shared their wisdom and experiences with banking operations and we thank those who shared their comments after reading the book draft. Several names deserve particular recognition: Michał Wolak of Lean Action, Krzysztof Nieć of Bank Zachdni, and Wiktoria Gromowa.

The authors are grateful to Azade Bateni, research assistant in the Graduate Systems Engineering Leadership Program at Loyola Marymount University, for the skillful and patient preparation of most figures in the text and for performing background research.

The authors are grateful also to Stephanie Nicolard, a graduate student at Loyola Marymount University, for her professional help in proofreading and editing the entire manuscript. Any remaining imperfections are our fault and not hers.

Last but not least, the authors are grateful to Joselyn Banks-Kyle, our very friendly, helpful, and skillful project coordinator, and to Iris Fahrer, the book's project editor at Taylor & Francis.

Bohdan W. Oppenheim and Marek J. Felbur

Chapter 1

Introduction

Banking is one of the oldest professions. Over the centuries, tens of thousands of banks have served billions of customers of all ages, cultures, and economic systems. One would think that after that vast experience, bankers would be able to perform their daily work perfectly and efficiently. Not so. Almost all banking institutions suffer from fairly basic inefficiencies related to poor productivity; insufficient planning; inadequate coordination and communication; training failures; ineffective processes, tools, and workflow; excessive bureaucracy; mistakes and rework; and general frustration of staff.

These inefficiencies are the products of our society, not the unique faults of bankers. The business climate places higher premiums on quick profits than on long-term streamlining of work. In defense of banks, they operate under myriad local, state, national, and international rules and laws and also must adhere to their own regulations intended to protect client safety and security. Under the weight of all these restrictions, many employees wonder that banks are able to function at all.

Few traditional banks are aware that they have vast reserves of productivity. Typically in such banks both managers and staff work extremely hard, often overtime. Their intuition tells them that there are no reserves left in the system—that the system is "as Lean as it can be." The knee-jerk reaction is to blame this frantic pace on excessive amounts of work and insufficient employees. The apparent solution is to hire more employees, but this often has a negative effect. A system with more people becomes even more difficult to manage, more convoluted, and less efficient.

Fortunately, an excellent solution exists. This book describes the application of the Lean Thinking and Six Sigma (Lean for short) paradigm to bank operations. Lean originated in car production at Toyota. In the 1990s, it came to the United States and other Western countries, first in manufacturing, where it has established itself as the new paradigm, and soon expanded to many other industries—some having nothing to do with manufacturing such as administration and government [Carter, 2008], government finance [Reagan, 2011], healthcare delivery [Graban, 2009], supply chain management [Bozdogan, 2004], education [Emiliani, 2004], project management [Oehmen, 2012], product development [Ward, 2007], engineering [Murman, 2002], systems engineering [Oppenheim, 2011], defense work [LAI], and enterprise management [Jones, 2006]. We now know with absolute certainty that Lean applies to any type of work, in any industry, nonprofit or government organization, in any country, and in any economic and political system. Lean can be applied to any human activity because it is grounded in the commonality of human behavior. G. Convis, the president of Toyota's Kentucky plant, offered the following description of Lean [with small edits made for consistency with book text]:

"Lean system is an integrated and interdependent system involving many elements. I like to think of it as a triangle, where one side is philosophy, one side is technology, and the other side is management. Cradled in the middle of the triangle is what Lean is really all about—people. Human development is at the very core of Lean. It is often overlooked, as people seize on the more tangible aspects of Lean … The philosophical underpinnings include a joint work floor, customer-first focus, an emphasis on people first, a commitment to continuous improvement, and a belief that harmony with the environment is of critical importance. The managerial culture for Lean is rooted in several factors, including developing and sustaining a sense of trust, a commitment to involving those affected by first, teamwork, equal and fair treatment for all, and finally, fact-based decision making and long-term thinking … One of the fundamental concepts of Lean is the 'customer-first' philosophy. Typically, organizations think of the customer only in terms of the person or institution who buys the final product or service. In Lean each succeeding work activity is the customer. Every employee knows his or her dual role: being the customer of the previous activity and the suppliers to the next activity downstream" [adopted from Convis, 2013].

Soon after Lean is deployed in a serious way, organizations can achieve higher qualities of work in a shorter time, with no one working harder and everyone working smarter. Employees transition from fighting crises to increasing both customer satisfaction and competitiveness. Work becomes more predictable, stable, and pleasant. It soon becomes truly shocking to both management and staff how much work can be accomplished in the same amount of time and with the same resources, simultaneously improving productivity, quality, cost, work morale, and customer satisfaction.

The effects of Lean can be dramatic: up to doubled productivity in the entire system; process times cut by 50% to 90%; errors reduced by 50% to 90%; development time for new bank products reduced by half; approval time cut by 90%; modest capital investment (only for training); dramatically better human relations at all levels; and, most importantly, vastly better customer satisfaction and company competitiveness. Banks pioneering Lean reported these figures. But Lean does not stop there. Lean is a journey toward excellence and it never ends. The farther we travel on this journey, the more eager we become to do even better. We use the term "Lean Thinking" to emphasize that Lean is indeed an ongoing thinking process and not just a checklist to complete.

When faced with stiff competition, traditional companies brutally cut costs, usually by massive layoffs, head-count reductions, and by overworking the remaining employees and suppliers. Without addressing underlying systemic problems, these cuts simply eliminate needed resources and therefore slow down the operations. This causes more frantic work pace, loss of quality, and decreasing customer satisfaction. When this happens, customers and profits are lost, resulting in even more cuts and more layoffs. This spiral of failure leads easily to collapse.

In contrast, Lean focuses on recovering productivity reserves by eliminating wastes. This focus in turn leads to lower costs, higher quality, and increased customer satisfaction. Lower operating costs enable banks to keep the employees on the payroll because they will be needed as customer satisfaction attracts more business. During the Lean deployment period, the employees can address improvements they never had time to implement, contributing to better productivity and quality. The success spiral occurs without layoffs. In fact, Toyota, "the most Lean company," had no layoffs for most of its history until the economic crisis of 2008. Most other car makers experienced cycles of boom and bust, with corresponding increases and decreases in employee numbers.

One of the most pervasive myths in the banking industry is that higher quality requires higher costs. This may be true for superficial factors such as marble floors in front offices, but is totally wrong in terms of the cost of operations. Lean demonstrates that a high-quality operation is actually the least expensive. In Lean, we avoid the high costs of mistakes, errors, defects, reworks, delays, frustrations, and subsequent crises, and focus instead on making operations better and better. Graban [2009] states: "Lean is a quality initiative. It isn't a cost cutting initiative. But the end result is, if you improve quality, your costs will go down."

The kernel of Lean Thinking is Lean culture identified as *respect for people*. Respect does not mean that people are always friendly and pleasant to each other or that interactions are always free of conflict. In Lean organizations, *respect* means that everyone is treated as a creative human being with the potential to significantly contribute to the workplace—not a scared, intimidated robot. Employees love Lean because Lean is people-centered. People are not divided into order givers and order takers. Everyone in a Lean organization is motivated to solve problems rather than hiding them in the traditional culture of fear, naming, blaming, and shaming. In a Lean bank, we make both work progress and work imperfections visible, thus motivating workers to eliminate problems fearlessly, urgently, and efficiently. Employees see sense in the work allocated by managers and trust that the managers make good decisions. In turn, the managers earn trust and respect by training and mentoring employees, inspiring them to reach their full potential (as superb teachers do). In Lean, managers become leaders and workers become proud and creative assets of the bank. The culture develops teamwork, a sense of trust, honesty, openness, fair treatment, and long-term focus.

The banking industry is one of the last Lean frontiers, delayed no doubt because of the severe economic crisis of 2007 through 2011 and resulting massive layoffs. However, pioneering banks such as Bank of America are rapidly implementing Lean. In Section 3.4, we discuss the banks and financial institutions that have relatively mature Lean deployments: AXA, Banco de Crédito del Perú, Bank of America, Bank of Montreal, BNP Paribas, Capital One, Department of Financial Services of Gwinnett County Government, Eureko, HSBC Holdings and HSBC Securities in Dubai, the Royal Bank of Scotland, and SWIFT. They all report significant, often dramatic, improvements in productivity and quality.

Lean basics are not difficult to learn. A book such as this one provides sufficient guidance to get started. Significant successes from Lean occur early in the transformation. The required investment is small—limited to the costs of training employees and engaging one or more Lean expert—and no risks are incurred. This book is an invitation to all bankers at all levels to join this exciting Lean journey and travel to the vastly superior and more satisfying world of Lean banks.

1.1 Banking Activities Addressed in This Book

This book is about improving the normal daily operations of a bank typically performed in the so-called "back offices," and to some degree, the work of tellers and supervisors in front offices, although this work has already been perfected in most banks to a high-quality routine. In short, this book discusses *how to do the work*, not *what work to do*.

Besides the front office, all main branches of banks usually have the following departments operating in "back offices." The departments may have different names in different banks, and some departments may be consolidated in smaller banks, yet they perform basically similar generic work, as follows:

- Corporate Management (developing and executing general strategy)
- Service of customer accounts and securities
- Sales of financial services
- Risk (analysis of credit, loan and transaction risk)
- Vindication (collection of unpaid obligations)
- Legal and Auditing (verifying that bank complies with all laws, rules and regulations)
- Accounting (accounts payable, accounts receivable, general ledger, internal and external reporting)
- Human Resources (employee hiring, record keeping, well-being, training and skill improvements)
- New Product (studies of competitors' performance, benchmarking, development and testing of new bank products, actuarial analysis)
- Advertising and Marketing (analysis of markets; also includes public, shareholder, and international relations; and lobbying)
- Front Office (walk-in and phone customer service)
- Information Technology (responsible for all hardware, software, networks, terminals, phones, data safety and security, fraud prevention, physical security)

- Legal (analysis of legality of transactions, compliance with laws)
- Chief Analyst (tracking trends in employment, inflation, Gross Domestic Product [GDP], growth rates, exchanges of currencies, etc., and performing macroeconomic forecasts. Some better banks compete in the media on the accuracy of their forecasts)
- Technical Expertise (responsible for valuation of security assets, compliance with national and international export controls, sanctions and embargoes)
- And numerous external consultants in all areas related directly and indirectly to bank operations.

In large banks, each of the above functions may be split into numerous subdivisions, constituting a very complex organizational chart. Bank branches usually just service local accounts and customers. However, large banks may perform some main office work in branch offices as well.

Back office departments perform both unique and routine daily work, essentially creating, processing, transforming, and securing information and knowledge related to all bank transactions, clients, and processes. As in other office-type industries, the work is performed and managed by humans using normal human skills, education, and emotions, with heavy reliance on computers. In that sense, Lean can be applied just as easily to banks as it can apply to other office organizations.

However, when deploying Lean, we must be sensitive to the distinct needs of banks. They must provide exceptional security and safety of client and bank data, physical security of vaults and offices, and fraud prevention. They face heavy burdens of laws and regulations, risk stockholders' capital as a matter of daily routine, and maintain electronic banking systems that must serve millions of clients 24/7 with extreme robustness, resilience, and reliability.

This book is about the application of Lean Thinking to the daily work in back offices of banks. Our goal is to simultaneously streamline work processes, increase work quality and productivity, increase satisfaction of external customers, and most emphatically improve human relations on which the other successes depend. While we focus on the back offices because the productivity reserves usually hide in those offices, we must not ignore the front offices. They must ensure that every customer who walks into the bank is served quickly, completely, and gracefully. If that kind of service is lacking, the first focus must be on the front office.

This book is not about a grand financial strategy; invention of new financial products; mergers; investments; loan policies; leveraging; liquidity; Glass–Stieglitz, Sarbanes–Oxley, or other major regulations about "too big to fail" philosophies; lobbying; FDIC rules; decisions about hedge funds and derivatives; or market segmentation decisions made in executive offices (although top management must understand, endorse, and support the Lean transformation). Those activities are left to the experts in finance, economics, international and national monetary and financial policies, and politics. Instead, this book is about how to improve the daily work in bank back offices. This work involves about 90% of bank employees and generates 90% of costs.

1.2 Intended Audience

We created this book as an entry-level text on Lean for all levels of bank employees: back-office workers, first-level supervisors, middle and higher level managers, and corporate executives. We hope that all bank employees can easily understand Chapters 1 through 6. Only Chapters 7 and 8 address advanced Lean concepts. The book is also intended for all levels of students at schools that teach banking skills—short courses intended for tellers, college courses in advanced banking operations, and continuing education for bank managers and line employees.

In creating an entry-level book, we tried not to overburden the readers with excessive details. This book does not contain a single mathematical formula. Some topics such as quality assurance and continuous improvement have evolved to university-level courses and are the subjects of entire libraries of excellent textbooks for all levels of readership. We cover them only briefly. A few pages are sufficient to give our readers enough understanding to prepare them for active participation in Lean deployment activities under the mentorship of an expert and also whet their appetites for more advanced reading. For readers who seek more knowledge, we have recommended additional literature.

Not all of the contents of this book will apply to every bank. Banks vary hugely in size, number of branches, employee distribution, clientele, loan portfolio, wealth, economic impact, sophistication and automation of operations, policies, and many other parameters. At one extreme are JP Morgan Chase, Bank of America, and Goldman Sachs—sophisticated giants with economic impacts dwarfing many countries' economies that can afford advanced operations. At the other end, we have small, local cooperative banks involving basic operations. The authors tried to cover common ground between these extremes.

Some examples given in the book will appeal to small local banks and may appear too simplistic for a giant bank. Other processes (e.g., the Lean Product Development Flow (LPDF)) will likely be more attractive to larger banks and may be of little use for a small community bank. We count on the common sense of the reader to decide which elements apply to his or her bank.

No one should feel threatened by Lean. If properly implemented, Lean does not lead to layoffs or firings. Lean will not destroy bank discipline or demoralize workers. Lean will free employees from the stress of frantic work and frequent crises to give them more time to serve their customers better. This book describes in easy language how to organize bank operations better, increase work productivity and quality by working smarter and not working harder, make fewer mistakes and decrease rework, reduce the time spent waiting for data or people, utilize work time more creatively, turn employees into creative problem solvers, reduce daily frustrations, elevate jobs from mundane and repetitive to creative and pleasantly challenging, and most importantly increase the satisfaction of bank customers and in turn enhance bank competitiveness and market share.

We have used several foreign, mostly Japanese, words in the text because they have become established parts of Lean practice; therefore, we have adopted them in this book. They are explained in the text and are written in *italics*. Also, the glossary at the end of the book explains the terms.

1.3 Organization of the Book

An excellent mental gateway to Lean Thinking is to contrast an ideal bank with perfect productivity in its normal daily work to a largely dysfunctional bank that attempts to carry out the same work but suffers from all sorts of problems related to productivity and quality. We enter that mental gateway in **Chapter 2**. The remaining chapters describe the amazing Lean approach of moving a bank away from the dysfunctional and toward the ideal.

This book could not have been written without the huge progress made in various applications of Lean by other authors. **Chapter 3** contains a brief history of Lean and a review of relevant literature sources. We also review available reports on the deployment of Lean in banks and financial institutions. The reader who is eager to move directly to practical Lean knowledge can skip this chapter without much loss of continuity.

Chapters 4, 5, and 6 present Lean knowledge: fundamentals, tools, and deployment in banks.

In **Chapter 4**, we introduce the simple yet elegant Lean Thinking basics. We focus on three concepts that are fundamental to the understanding of Lean: value to the customer, waste in our work, and the process of creating value without waste, which is captured into the so-called Six Lean Principles. These concepts have proven themselves in all work domains in all cultures on all continents. In virtually all developed countries, companies and organizations have applied the concepts with remarkable success. We devote a significant amount of text to discussions of waste because **eliminating waste** is a basic requirement for a Lean operation.

In **Chapter 5**, we present the Lean tools that we believe are particularly valuable to banks. For the convenience of our readers, we have compiled the tools in one chapter. There are simple, profoundly important tools such as **visual controls**, and more complex tools such as **continuous improvement** and **quality assurance** that have merited entire bookshelves in bookstores and graduate-level courses. As noted above, our intent is to provide readers who are new to Lean with enough knowledge to be able to participate in Lean deployment projects with help from mentors.

Chapter 6 explains how to deploy Lean. We recommend the initial steps, advanced steps, and subsequent activities on the journey to Lean. The focus is on practical steps and on the most important asset of any bank: people. We have tried to make the steps as easy to deploy and user-friendly as possible. We describe the various phases of employee reactions to Lean changes that may occur, and offer advice on drawing people into the new system to make them creative, effective, and enthusiastic participants.

Chapter 7 is intended for readers who already have some experience with Lean. It covers the best Lean-inspired bank practices for organizational leadership, culture, communications and coordination, general management, project management, process management, continuous improvement, hiring, planning, supplier relations, and metrics. The practices are called **Lean Enablers**. The authors have adopted the practices to banking from two large worldwide projects spanning 2006–2012 and focused on improving large and complex technological and weapons programs. The projects[*] involved about 30 experts and 300 practitioners, and two professional societies: Project Management Institute and International Council on Systems Engineering (INCOSE).

Chapter 8 is intended for bank employees who work on projects. It presents a super-efficient generic process called **Lean Product Development Flow (LPDF)** [Oppenheim, 2004] for planning and executing projects such as a development of a new bank product. LPDF promotes predictable progress of work as if it moved along an assembly line. The only prerequisite is that a project have no *unknown unknowns* so that the participants can develop detailed plans. The process was created for the space satellite industry, but has since been utilized for project management in all domains. It is ideal for bank projects, which typically involve 5 to 30 people for several weeks or months. LPDF exemplifies the ultimate workflow with the shortest possible delivery time, maximum concurrency, and high quality. Because all participants operate with a common rhythm, the creation of value is super-efficient.

The final chapters are dedicated to literature references, authors' biographies, and a glossary. We used several numbered text boxes; they are listed just after the Table of Contents. Important quotes and statements are set in vignettes.

---

[*] One of the authors (Oppenheim) was honored with two Shingo Awards, the INCOSE 2010 Best Product Award, and a Fulbright Award for this work.

Chapter 2

Ideal versus Traditional Bank

2.1 Ideal Bank

Imagine a bank where all employees:

- **Do the right work:** They work only on tasks that create legitimate value for external or internal customers (present or future). All work is well understood. The staff is prepared for contingencies. Only "known unknowns" occur. The bureaucracy is streamlined. The personnel eliminated all tasks and reviews executed only because "we always did it this way." All tasks and procedures have been tailored to eliminate unnecessary steps. Forms, document requirements, and computer interfaces are user-friendly and simplified.
- **Do the work right:** The employees are well trained and mentored to execute each task perfectly every time (as we call it in Lean: "right the first time") to satisfy each internal customer and create value for external customers.
- **Know the customer:** Before starting a non-routine task, each employee knows his or her internal customer (often not the supervisor) and coordinates the work content and outcomes to deliver what is needed on the first attempt.
- **Flow the work:** The sequential tasks in a process or project are successfully executed in order without waiting, rework, or backflow. The flow is continuous from the first task to the last. The entire focus is on creation of value. The work does not slow or stop when crossing departmental boundaries or bank branches.

- **Proactively coordinate:** People coordinate and communicate pro-actively in real time as needed to enable the flow of value-added work rather than working reactively after a problem is found.
- **Make the full status of work fully visible to all:** The work is made visible to indicate who is doing what, when, and how it is pro-gressing (subject to all security regulations, of course). Any problems are identified as soon as they appear and treated as opportunities for immediate improvements.
- **Implement superb quality of operations:** Employees are so well trained that they understand the work, processes, and tools, and the needs of their internal and external customers perfectly. They execute tasks "right the first time," with consistently predictable and robust out-comes, cost, effort, and completion time. In the rare event that a mis-take occurs, the employee at fault catches it immediately and corrects it on the spot so that defective work never travels beyond his or her work area. Problems are analyzed for root cause, corrected with permanent fixes, and prevented from recurring. The processes are equipped with sufficient warnings and alarms that it is practically impossible to make a mistake. The processes are so predictable that bank services can be quoted to customers competitively and reliably, earning good profits along the way. All staff members think creatively about how to do the work better the next time.
- **Work in the spirit of teamwork and respect:** There is no "blame and shame" culture. Problems are blamed on a system that needs improvement, not on employees who are captives of the system. Employees are free of fear; they work in teams and share feelings of openness, honesty, respect, and enthusiasm. No rivalry exists between team members; they compete as one team with external competitors. Every employee goes home at night feeling satisfaction about a job well done. Employees smile spontaneously and naturally.
- **Assign an "owner" to each job:** Every project and process has an "owner" who is responsible, accountable, and has authority to ensure successful and timely completion. No task is an "orphan." Employees are empowered to make decisions in their own areas of work.
- **Align with true leaders:** The bank has a culture of competent and experienced leadership. Leaders plan and manage the work while leading employees to new challenges. Managers motivate and engage large numbers of people to work together toward a common goal. They define and explain the goal, pave a path to achieve it, and assist

subordinates by removing obstacles. Team spirit dominates. Each leader is an experienced and competent banker with a spotless reputation and great people skills.

■ **Grow competitiveness:** The team of employees continuously improves bank operations, lowering costs, shortening process times, serving customers better, making the bank more competitive, and focusing on growth of market share and reputation.

Who would not love working for a bank that operated on such principles?

2.2 Dysfunctional Bank

Now let us look at the other extreme: a severely dysfunctional bank. It is almost a "negative" image of the ideal bank.

■ **Busy work:** Everyone works at a frantic pace without making visible progress. There appears to be a chronic shortage of staff; the operation never has enough people to do jobs well or on time. Work assignments are unclear, poorly understood, and inadequately executed. Every task appears unique, special, and difficult, and involves endless meetings, decision loops, and approvals. Processes are nonexistent or function poorly. The staff is never prepared for contingencies; anything out of the routine is perceived as a crisis. "Unknown unknowns" occur constantly. Bureaucracy is rampant; business and procedural units create too many complex, unneeded, and self-serving regulations. Massive numbers of documents, reports, and forms are created for no evident purpose. A significant number of tasks appear unneeded but they continue to be executed because no one bothers to eliminate them. Documents and forms are complex and difficult to complete; no one finds time to simplify them. The computer network functions poorly, computers crash, and software and databases are difficult to use. People spend inordinate amounts of time looking for things in computer and paper files. Everybody waits for everybody else and blames everyone around. Because of the chaos, high-level managers impose more and more controls hoping that they will clean the system, but the controls only increase bureaucracy and the work slows. Employees are overwhelmingly frustrated and exhausted.

■ **Defects and rework are constant:** Employees make mistakes and often create defective work; even worse, they repeat their mistakes and find ways to make new ones. Wrong forms are used; forms are lost; incomplete financial data is generated and passed along. Wrong interest rates are quoted. Mistakes in customer files are common. Like an iceberg that is 8/9 submerged but potentially destructive, the reworks and delays represent only a small portion of the overall damage to competitiveness and reputation.

■ **Management reactions:** To prevent mistakes, meticulous controls and tedious inspections are imposed, and massive rework is required, often on overtime. Supervisors are frustrated that employees make frequent mistakes. Employees are frustrated with supervisors' unreasonable demands and the result is mutual mistrust. Managers constantly find problems with work but do nothing about it but "blame and shame." Some mistakes are never caught. They grow in criticality until they explode in the form of a crisis. Heroic actions are then needed to handle the crisis—if it's not too late. Penalties and possibly lawsuits may result. Massive frustrations swarm like dark clouds. Massive finger pointing may escalate to involve the person who made the mistake, his or her supervisor, managers and executives, internal and external customers, and regulators. The company never has enough time to find the root causes of mistakes, devise mistake-proof processes and standards, train employees to levels where they no longer make mistakes, or learn from past problems. Consistently inefficient banks lose customers, market shares, and profits; implement layoffs; and close branches.

■ **Who needs this work?** Managers assign work to employees who complete it and generate results but no one knows who uses them. The division of responsibilities among departments is confusing and causes friction and duplication of effort.

■ **Waiting, stoppages, backflow, and torturous progress:** Work does not flow. The entire bank is "stove-piped" by rigid territorial boundaries. No one understands the required sequence of tasks. As a result the work starts and stops and its path appears almost random. Huge amounts of time are wasted on waiting for decisions and approvals. Excessive decision-making and approval levels slow the work progress, impair proper coordination, and create redundancies. The lack of coordination causes mistakes that require rework, inducing seemingly endless and frustrating loops of approval–rejection–rework–reapproval–waiting.

- **Poor coordination and communication:** The entire culture is reactive rather than preventive. People do not coordinate and communicate proactively. Work is done in an uncoordinated disjointed manner, requiring frequent rework and correction. Problems tend to grow in hiding until they reach crisis proportions and heroic efforts are needed to correct them.
- **Work progress is invisible:** It is difficult to see who is working on what task. Progress is difficult to see and assess.
- **"Blame and shame" culture:** Lowest level staff members are blamed for all problems. Middle managers blame lower level managers, and so on. Problems are blamed on employees and never on the system that is "good enough." People are blamed for not following procedures; ineffective procedures are never blamed. There is no teamwork, and individuals are made to compete with each other. No one volunteers bad news unless directed to do so. Managers command fear but not respect.
- **"Orphan" jobs are idle:** No one feels responsible for a process from beginning to end. When a task stops, all progress stops. Because stops are unnoticed, deadlines are missed and the result is a crisis. Some processes die without anyone noticing. Employees are not empowered to make decisions and managers waste time constantly answering trivial questions.
- **Autocratic and bureaucratic management:** The bank has bureaucratic and authoritarian managers but no leaders. People do only as ordered and no more. The knowledge and skills of experienced employees are ignored. No one works to fix systemic problems. Managers are not known for their people skills. Bonus structures appear arbitrary; promises are not kept and rewards are not based on objective evaluations of measurable achievements.
- **"Half-baked" products are released to the market:** The bank has no time to create and thoroughly test new products and the existing products become obsolete and/or uncompetitive. The new products are released before they are ready and thus require expensive corrections and clarifications, and they usually fail in the marketplace. Both employees and customers perceive that bank competitiveness is deteriorating.

2.3 Lean Challenge for a Real Bank

Where is your bank situated between the ideal bank presented in Section 2.1 and the dysfunctional bank described in Section 2.2? Every banker must address this question honestly if his or her bank is to survive and thrive amid stiff global competition.

Our interviews with bankers in the US and Europe revealed that most banks suffer from many, if not all, of the maladies listed in Section 2.2. In several interviews in which we mentioned the "ideal bank," experienced bankers responded with sarcastic laughter. Modern banks employ highly educated and motivated people, many of them brilliant. Why then do the problems occur? The traditional system of work organization with an authoritarian and stove-piped culture is to blame. As M. Graban points out:

> "Toyota achieves extraordinary results with average people working in a brilliant system, while most organizations get mediocre results by hiring brilliant people to fight their way through broken systems. Just imagine the potential of combining brilliant people with a brilliant system."
>
> **Mark Graban, 2009**

As noted in Chapter 1, the good news is that a powerful remedy is available. A well-established body of knowledge called Lean Thinking is directly applicable and available to the field of banking with only minor adjustments. This knowledge is focused on moving from the maladies of Section 2.2 toward the ideal described in Section 2.1. Even though Lean has started penetrating the banking industry only recently, a number of banks have already achieved good results. We list the banks and some of their Lean accomplishments in Section 3.4.

At first, it may be difficult even for experienced bank managers to see the operational similarities of banks and other organizations. Professionals in all fields think their work problems and frustrations are unique and entirely specific to their organizations, situations, times, clients, managers, employees, or processes. Hopefully this book will demonstrate that most of the "unique" problems are actually generic and can be eliminated with the Lean skill set. Of course, certain small implementation details are unique to the banking industry and even to individual banks and their branches. However, the overall approach is sufficiently general and proven to be applicable to all banks and financial institutions.

In Chapter 3, we sketch the fascinating history of Lean—a concept that originated in Toyota factories and took the world by storm. Lean has demonstrated extraordinary successes in manufacturing, product development, high-level technology, engineering, project management, healthcare, administration and government, and, increasingly, banking.

Chapter 3

The Amazing History of Lean*

A dwarf standing on the shoulders of a giant may see farther than a giant himself.

Didacus Stella

Soon after the end of World War II, Taiichi Ohno, vice president for technical operations at Toyota traveled to the United States to study how automobiles were built there. Americans were said to "leave their mothers' womb behind the wheel," and regarded as authorities on automobiles in those days since they had no competition after the devastation of the war.

After spending considerable time in Detroit, the executive returned to Japan to report to S. Toyoda, his CEO, that the US car manufacturing system was so wasteful and inefficient that only rich America could afford such a system. In contrast, the Japanese were "too poor. If we were to implement it [US auto manufacturing], we would go bankrupt in no time. Instead, we need to develop a vastly more efficient system. Let me work on it" [adapted from Ohno, 1988].

Ohno's observation catalyzed the development of the most efficient and amazing work organization system in the history of human civilization. He worked on his project tirelessly for almost 30 years. The system has had several different names over the years: Just-in-Time (JIT), then Toyota Production System (TPS), and now in Western countries it is known as Lean. The production system started in Toyota factories in Japan and has become the established standard in competitive factories over the world. In the 1980s and 1990s, mostly in the US, we learned that applying a bit of mental flexibility to Lean can bring extraordinary results to a variety of work environments. Indeed, as mentioned earlier, Lean is now used with huge success

---

* [Oppenheim, 2011]

in a large number of industrial domains. Banking remains one of the last frontiers, but strong Lean pioneering work is already evident.

As Oppenheim [2011] describes:

> The term *Lean* as an industrial paradigm was introduced in the United States in the bestselling book *The Machine that Changed the World: The Story of Lean Production*, published by the MIT International Motor Vehicle Program [Womack et al., 1990], and elegantly popularized in their second bestseller *Lean Thinking* [Womack and Jones, 1996]. The authors identified a fundamentally new industrial paradigm based on the Toyota Production System. This paradigm is based on relentless elimination of waste from all enterprise operations, involving the continuous improvement cycle that turns all front-line employees into problem solvers. Lean strives to meet customer demands at minimum cost as quickly as possible while ensuring high-quality work and defect-free products. Lean is driven by a unique management culture of respect, empowerment, openness, and teamwork.
>
> Factories adopting Lean observed direct and dramatic improvements in both operations and profits. Womack and Jones [1996] described six manufacturing case studies that demonstrated reductions of cost, lead time, and inventory of up to 90%, with simultaneous improvements in product quality and work morale across a wide range of company types and sizes. More dramatically, lead time and cost reductions on the order of 30% to 50% were realized routinely after only a few days of implementation on the factory floor, by simple rearranging of machines into the flow [LEI, 2007]. After the multi-year earlier attempts to improve productivity based on the Total Quality Management (TQM), Concurrent Engineering (CE), or Six Sigma initiatives, this was a revelation. Within a few years, Lean production has become the established manufacturing paradigm pursued by all competitive factories.

3.1 Do Not Displace Good Old Knowledge with New; Integrate It

It is not unusual to see companies apply a sequence of management paradigms one after another with minimal effect. When a given paradigm appears to fail to produce greater profits in a short term, it is declared a "fad" and the company moves on to the next "flavor of the month" program.

Such outcomes are guaranteed in companies that pay only lip service to every new approach typically consisting of a speech by the CEO, a short workshop for managers, promotional materials for employees, then a hope that by osmosis or a miracle the entire operation will follow the new path. Busy with the frenzied daily work and frequent crises, no one at any level has any chance to learn and implement the new system properly. As expected, it fails to produce the expected miracles, is pronounced a "fad," and eager consultants replace it with a new approach. After all, who wants to take responsibility for a failed implementation improvement program when it is easier to simply blame the program and move on to the next one? This sequence describes the fate of TQM, CE, Reengineering, Management by Objectives, and many other systems that were consigned unfairly to the "failed" pile.

The authors disagree with this approach. Most of these paradigms contributed some good ideas to the knowledge and practice of management. Throwing away an entire system because a new idea came into fashion is naïve and destructive. If each new idea receives only lip service, the system will never change. What is needed instead is an intelligent integration of the old and the new to enable constant evolution, improvement, and growth. In this spirit, let us briefly review some of the recent management improvement systems that built the foundations for Lean.

Lean Thinking, or Lean as it is called in this book, is an evolutionary industrial paradigm incorporating elements from earlier paradigms of Total Quality Management (TQM), Concurrent Engineering (CE), and Six Sigma. Let us briefly review these earlier ideas.

3.2 A Bit of History: From TQM to Concurrent Engineering, Six Sigma, and Lean

3.2.1 Total Quality Management (TQM)

In 1980, after numerous announcements, NBC TV in the US aired a special two-hour program titled *If Japan Can, Why Can't We?* The documentary opened US eyes to a new Total Quality Management paradigm sweeping industry by storm [NBC, June 24, 1980] as a response to recent dramatic losses of US automobile and electronics markets to Japan. Led by W. Edwards Deming [1982], TQM was an attempt to adapt successful Japanese industrial management methods to US industry. The strong message of TQM was that the pursuit of higher quality is compatible with lower costs. Inexpensive, high-quality automobiles and consumer electronic goods imported from Japan made this notion self-evident to US consumers but not necessarily to US industry.

TQM emphasized a *total* approach to quality by integrating management with processes and tools and developing business strategies focused on customer satisfaction. It promoted continuous improvement of all processes and popularized improvement tools such as bottom-up employee suggestion systems, quality circles, quick reaction *kaizen* teams, and process variability reduction using Statistical Process Control and Design of Experiment. TQM emphasized the importance of corporate culture based on respect for people and employee empowerment as prerequisites for continuous improvement, and relied heavily on self-motivation of employees. Designing quality into both products and processes and preventing defects rather than relying on final inspections to find and correct them are critical factors.

TQM received strong support from the US government including its Department of Defense [DoD, 1988]. After Japan announced the W.E. Deming Award, the Department of Commerce initiated the Malcolm Baldrige Award in 1987 as a motivational recognition of the best US companies in the categories of manufacturing, service, and small business (later expanded to include education, healthcare, and nonprofit and government institutions). The award is based on points scored in the TQM elements listed above.

In 2000, the International Standards Organization (ISO) issued a quality standard denoted ISO 9000:2000 that captured many TQM elements (the pros and cons of ISO certification for banks are reviewed briefly in Section 3.2.5).

The application of TQM to US industry yielded mixed outcomes. While quality improved, especially in the auto industry, profits did not increase proportionately. Quality improvements alone failed in many companies that tried TQM [Paton, 1994]. The earlier pessimism in the manufacturing industry continued and contributed to the subsequent export of nearly 70% of commercial manufacturing operations to cheaper labor countries.

The lack of widespread business success made TQM vulnerable to criticism and opened the door to new ideas. *Business Week* [Byrne, 1997] declared TQM a "dead fad," blaming its "lack of teeth" in implementation. While the TQM term is not used widely today, most of its key elements have endured and are integral to Lean Thinking [Murman et al., 2002].

3.2.2 Concurrent Engineering (CE)

Although *engineering* appears in the name, the concepts apply to any operation including banking. In the late 1980s, the CE industrial paradigm became popular and was proposed as a way to shorten the weapons system acquisition cycle [Winner et al., 1988]. CE promoted simultaneous and integrated planning of all product phases in an effort to replace the traditional slow, disjointed, serial effort that was inefficient and required lots of rework.

Multifunctional teams, sometimes called integrated product teams (IPTs), were important components of CE. The teams included representatives from all phases of a project, all participating departments, and major vendors. CE, when effectively implemented with workforce training, led to dramatic reductions in project rework, costs, and schedule times [Hernandez, 1995]. TQM and CE made important contributions to major new aircraft products such as the Boeing 777 and the Cessna Citation X in the 1990s [Haggerty and Murman, 2006]. As with TQM, CE principles are embedded in current day Lean Thinking [Murman et al., 2002; McManus, 2004].

3.2.3 Six Sigma

In the early 1990s, TQM evolved into another quality initiative called Six Sigma, arguably with "better teeth." According to Wedgewood [2007], "Six Sigma is a systematic methodology to home in on key factors that drive performance of a process, set them at the best levels, and hold them there for all time."

Originating at Motorola Corporation and relying on rigorous measurement and control, Six Sigma focused on systematic reduction of process variabilities from all sources: machines, methods, materials, measurements, people, and environment [Murman et al., 2002]. Like TQM, Six Sigma aimed to achieve predictable, repeatable, and capable processes and defect-free work by building elements to exacting specifications. Unlike the motivational TQM, Six Sigma achieves the goal via data collection, statistical analysis, and rigorous training of leaders.[*]

Lean and Six Sigma both appeared in the post-TQM mid 1990s as competing process improvement approaches. Six Sigma, identified with Motorola and subsequently with General Electric, gained investor visibility and popularity. Lean, identified with Toyota, was incorrectly seen as applicable only

---

[*] Six Sigma uses some *Ju-jitsu* terms. Belts of various colors designate different levels of training and experience.

to high-volume manufacturing applications. While Six Sigma focuses on a disciplined top-down approach to eliminating all forms of variation, Lean focuses on value streams and relentless elimination of waste through optimizing flow. Lean relies on Six Sigma to eradicate impediments to flow.

In fact, the basic principles of the two approaches are totally synergistic. Because of this synergy, many organizations adopted a blended version of the two bodies of knowledge and crafted them to meet their specific needs by early 2000. Names such as Lean Six Sigma, Lean Sigma, and other less obvious combinations appeared. Today, most organizations have harmonized Lean and Six Sigma.

Six Sigma was not free of problems; its implementation often involved a costly bureaucracy that led to the *waste of measuring waste.* It was criticized for being too top-down and for displacing two other critical continuous improvement tools of TQM: the small quick-reaction *kaizen* response and the bottom-up employee suggestion system that Toyota credits for half of its success [Oppenheim, 2006]. Six Sigma may also have been prone to suboptimization by focusing too narrowly on process improvements that may not have been needed. Murman et al. [2002] described this deficiency as "a focus on *the job being done right,* but not necessarily on *the right job.*" Lean, the next step in this industrial evolution, provided an integrated focus on *the right job* and *doing the job right the first time,* while also promoting the management culture necessary to meet both objectives.

In addition to the above-mentioned paradigms that became integral parts of Lean, we mention two others because of their popularity in banking: Management by Objectives and the ISO 9000 quality standard.

3.2.4 Management by Objectives

In the second half of the twentieth century, many banks adopted a management paradigm formulated by Peter Drucker [1954] and called Management by Objectives.* It encourages employee empowerment and involves employees in goal setting. Goal clarity is stressed and most goals are stated in financial terms. Elaborate computerized management information systems monitor each employee's progress toward meeting the goals and note any deficiencies such as customer complaints. Bonuses were linked to meeting goals. Every employee and department is supposed to know what is

---

* Much of the material about Management by Objectives was adopted from an excellent article in Wikipedia: http://en.wikipedia.org/wiki/Management_by_objectives.

expected. Non-performing employees are coached, then admonished, and eventually replaced. The system is basically directive.

Like Lean, Management by Objectives emphasizes the clarity of work assignments and roles along with employee empowerment. However, they diverge in a number of other areas. W. Edwards Deming [1982] argued that goals tend to be set arbitrarily, often capriciously, without solid understanding of the work system, productivity reserves, capacities, wastes, and opportunities. When focused on meeting goals rather than on continuous improvements, a company has few incentives to change. All changes are implemented from above because line employees are too busy trying to meet their goals.

Deming also stated that setting work targets encourages people to meet the targets by any means necessary, leading to lack of teamwork and poor quality. In contrast, teamwork is a critical part of Lean. The emphasis of Lean is on understanding and optimizing work processes and tools, developing employees to their full potential, and motivating them to be creative problem solvers in the never-ending process of continuous improvements.

3.2.5 ISO 9000

The ISO 9000:2000 (or briefly ISO 9000)* is a formal global certification-based quality management system defined by the International Standards Organization and available through national bodies. It is a popular program in banks.

ISO 9000 is *intended* to help organizations satisfy the needs of customers and other stakeholders while meeting statutory and regulatory requirements related to their products. The standard deals with the fundamentals of quality management systems. *At the time of this writing*, well over a million organizations worldwide have been certified, making ISO 9000 one of the most widely used management tools in the world today. The intended benefits include:

1. A more efficient, effective operation
2. Increased customer satisfaction
3. Reduced audits
4. Enhanced marketing
5. Improved employee motivation, awareness, and morale

---

* Much of the material about ISO 9000 was adopted from an excellent article in Wikipedia: http://en.wikipedia.org/wiki/ISO_9000.

6. Facilitated international trade
7. Increased profit
8. Increased productivity
9. Facilitated standardization

These advantages can be significant if an organization's starting point is low on the quality scale since ISO 9000 can then be expected to help "clean up the original mess." The ISO 9000 standard requires an organization seeking certification to publish a quality manual detailing adopted standards and procedures.

ISO does not certify organizations. Numerous certification bodies audit organizations and issue certificates to successful organizations. Many countries have formed accreditation bodies to authorize certification. International agreements among the various accreditation bodies ensure that their certificates are accepted worldwide.

Two types of audits are required to meet the standard: internal audits by a specially trained staff followed by external audit by a certification body. The process of review and assessment is intended to verify that a system works as it is supposed to; determine where it can improve; and correct or prevent problems identified. The certificate must be renewed every three years.

The debate on ISO 9000 effectiveness centers on whether the certification yields a good return on investment. In Europe, ISO 9000 certification is often required to do business. Numerous studies claim significant financial benefits from ISO 9000 certification [e.g., Corbett et al., 2005; Heras et al., 2002; Naveh and Marcus, 2006; Sharma, 2005]. However, we find no proof of direct causation between the ISO 9000 certification and increased profits. Heras et al. [2002] suggested that the improvement is partly driven by the fact that ISO 9000 certification is pursued by better performing companies.

A common criticism of ISO 9000 and the related ISO 9001 is the amount of money, time, and documentation required for registration. Dalgleish [2005] cites the "inordinate and often unnecessary paperwork burden" of ISO. Wade [2002] argues that ISO 9000 is effective as a guideline, but that promoting it as a standard "helps to mislead companies into thinking that certification means better quality … [undermining] the need for an organization to set its own quality standards." To paraphrase Wade, reliance on the specifications of ISO 9001 does not guarantee a successful quality system.

The present authors suggest that in many cases, ISO 9000 certification is like passing a driver's license—almost anyone who wants one can get it after some nominal effort. A license is needed to drive on public roads;

certification is required to conduct commerce in many regions. A driver's license ensures minimum skills but does not guarantee excellence in driving or safe practices. Certification does not guarantee excellence or quality. In contrast, the world-class Lean system is like a world-class car race: best drivers; best vehicles; best support system; perfect preparation, training, and teamwork. All participants are obsessed fanatics who work hard to win.

In summary, the quality and scope of ISO 9000 implementation depend on the organization seeking certification. The scope can be very broad, including all products and processes, or very narrow, for example, limited to a single product. Quality can be high if management requires it or mediocre and superficial if management uses certification only as a marketing tactic.

While the authors fully support ISO 9000 certification because it tends to "clean up" operations and improve customer satisfaction, we also include a word of caution. ISO 9000 alone does not guarantee world-class operations. Any bank can become certified with only nominal effort. The level of quality achieved can be superb or modest, depending on the motivation, ambitions, and expertise of the bank leaders. Since only modest efforts are sufficient for certification, most organizations achieve only modest improvements and tend to remain at that level. The modest improvements alone are worthwhile if a bank starts from a low quality level. In contrast, Lean Thinking is the race to the top league, with dramatic improvement potential and dramatic results even on the first attempt.

3.2.6 Relationship of Lean to Other Improvement Strategies

Lean incorporates many TQM, CE, and Six Sigma principles and practices. Like TQM and CE, Lean focuses on preventing defects, Deming's continuous improvement cycles, and engaging front-line employees as problem solvers in process improvement. It goes beyond TQM and CE to adopt a value stream focus, connecting tasks and processes into the flow of value-adding effort and a relentless pursuit of waste elimination.

While Lean, TQM, and CE all focus on process improvement, Lean also streamlines the flows between processes. Sharing with Six Sigma a data-driven approach to eliminate process variations, Lean favors a bottom-up improvement strategy and relies less on formalized qualifications of improvement experts. As with the other improvement paradigms, successful Lean implementation depends on committed leadership and an enterprise-wide approach across all functions. Lean surpasses the TQM, CE, and Six Sigma approaches to adopt a holistic value stream methodology and relentless waste elimination.

The value stream represents the linked end-to-end activities necessary to create the work products, systems, and services for internal and external customers. Waste encompasses all activities that do not directly contribute to customer value. Wastes often occur between value-added activities, for example, when people wait for data or data waits for people. Lean strives for optimum total flow without blockages and unplanned rework. Toyota's "father of Lean" wrote:

> "All we are doing is looking at the time line from the moment the customer gives us an order to the point when we collect the cash. And we are reducing that time line by removing the non-value-added wastes."
>
> **Taiichi Ohno, 1988**

Since Lean combines a number of practices known by other names such as Six Sigma, Quality Management, Concurrent Engineering, and others, we must consider which practices can be called Lean legitimately. The criterion we use for classification is very simple:

> If a practice promotes value, reduces waste, and can be described by the six Lean Principles, it is called Lean and adopted here.

In this book, we will continue to use the Lean nomenclature, not to exclude Six Sigma and other approaches, but to treat the new Lean discipline as an integrated body of knowledge based on Lean, Six Sigma, high-performance work systems, and other process improvement approaches.

3.3 Evolution of Lean to Other Industries

The successes of Lean in repetitive production led to a popular misconception that Lean does not apply to *one-off* applications such as service industries, engineering, or banking. In those areas, the deliverables and work contents are indeed one-off, unique to the time, situation, or customer, but many processes and individual tasks should use repeatable logic based on best professional practices. Such established processes exist in all professions for most applications as a result of long professional experience and lessons learned.

In this sense, Lean should apply to banking as much as it applies to other business types. Indeed, the basic principles of Lean Thinking apply to all work areas. Lean has been applied to diverse work environments such as manufacturing [e.g., Womack and Jones, 1996], product development [e.g., Ward, 2007], engineering [e.g., Murman et al., 2002; McManus et al., 2007], supply chain management [e.g., Bozdogan, 2004], systems engineering [Oppenheim, 2011], project management [Oehmen, 2012], healthcare [e.g., Graban, 2009], education [e.g., Emiliani, 2004], administration and services [e.g., Carter, 2008], and enterprise management [Jones, 2006; LESAT, 2001]. This book fosters the application of Lean Thinking to banking.

3.4 Literature on Lean Banking

The earliest explorations of Lean application to banking appear in the German literature (never translated into English to our knowledge) [Uhle, 1993; Bonölken and Wings, 1994; Müller, 1994]. These books appeared before Womack's formulation of the Lean principles in 1996. We mention the books to ensure completeness and congratulate the authors for their pioneering work. However, we must note that Lean has advanced significantly beyond the scope of these books.

To the authors' knowledge, few publications in the English language have focused specifically on the application of Lean to bank operations and no book dedicated to the use of Lean in banking has been published as of this writing. Most source materials come from the Internet. They lack rigorous peer reviews and some are clearly promotional. Nevertheless, we list them to provide evidence that a number of pioneering banks and financial institutions have deployed lean with significant success.

Lasater [2004] includes a case study of Bank of America's Lean Six Sigma deployment success that started in 2001 and is summarized here. Ken Lewis, the then CEO of the bank, took on the first Green Belt project, setting the expectations for other company employees and providing strong support for

Lean Six Sigma. All Lewis's direct reports were assigned Green Belt projects with specific goals:

- Increased customer delight with problem resolution
- More precise control over payments to suppliers
- Increased productivity of new hires via training
- Elimination of significant travel expenses
- Enhancement of enterprise e-mail governance to improve productivity
- Reduction of potentially biased credit-risk assessments
- Elimination of significant numbers of electronic information subscriptions
- Increased associate retention in key areas
- Increased collections by reducing abandoned inbound calls
- Improved ability to detect and prevent fraud at banking centers

Bank of America achieved impressive results. Lasater [2004] cites the following accomplishments:

- Missing items on customer statements reduced 70%
- Defects in electronic channels (ATMs, online banking) decreased 88%
- Mortgage application time reduced 15 days
- Non-credit losses including fraud driven down 28% on a per-account basis while number of accounts increased by more than a million in 2003 alone
- Same-day payments improved 22%
- Deposit processing improved 35%
- Cumulative financial benefits exceeded $2 billion by the end of 2003
- Customer delight metric increased 25% across the company in 2003

Overall, the magnitude of benefits was similar to results for manufacturing organizations.

Reagan [2011] reported a comprehensive application of Lean in the Department of Financial Services of the Gwinnett County government in Georgia. While the government entity is not a bank, many of its processes are similar to bank operations. Reagan reports the successes:

- Taxpayer processing time cut in half
- Staff motion reduced 67%
- Defective return forms eliminated
- Tax appeals processing rate increased 220%
- Processing steps reduced from 14 to 6

Jenkins [2011] described several enlightening interviews of bankers and executives of various financial institutions about their Lean deployment experiences. They uniformly reported significant benefits from Lean implementation. The banks and institutions that reported such results include the Royal Bank of Scotland, Eureko, SWIFT, Banco de Crédito del Perú, and BNP Paribas.

Go Lean [2013] is a website describing Lean Six Sigma successes in several banks and financial institutions: AXA, Bank of Montreal, Capital One, and HSBC Holdings. Malhotra [2011] described a successful Lean deployment at HSBC Securities in Dubai. All these cases deal with normal back office banking operations. The Lean benefits at these institutions are so significant that they should remove any doubt that Lean offers a better way of performing bank operations.

3.5 Recommended Lean Resources

Over the past 25 years, a rich body of Lean literature demonstrates its power in improving organizations. This section reviews a number of key educational resources recommended by the present authors. While they do not deal directly with banking operations, they can be used to complement the present book to advance Lean education and implementation in banks.

3.5.1 Lean Enterprise Institute

Lean Thinking [Womack and Jones, 1996] is the seminal classic that started the Lean movement in the US. The book is a crystal clear and attractive formulation of the Lean principles in the context of production applications. After it became a bestseller, Dr. Womack created the nonprofit Lean Enterprise Institute [LEI, 2013], which publishes a wealth of general-purpose books and ebooks on various aspects of Lean—too many to list here. They cover Lean knowledge from fundamentals to advanced practice; how-to manuals for value stream mapping and flow and pull planning; Lean processes and tools: A3 forms; *gemba, hoshin kanri, kaizen, kanban,* and other topics. While most of these books were written for production environments, readers of this book should find them easy to understand and adaptable to bank operations.

3.5.2 Lean in Healthcare

Lean Hospitals: Improving Quality, Patient Safety, and Employee Satisfaction [Graban, 2009] is, in our opinion, the best book on transforming Lean Thinking from one domain (manufacturing) to another (healthcare). Much of the text applies to banks as well. *On the Mend: Revolutionizing Healthcare to Save Lives and Transform the Industry* by Toussaint and Gerard [2010] describes a Lean deployment that the authors led in possibly the most difficult of all environments: a large healthcare organization (ThedaCare in Wisconsin). Doctors and nurses originally met the effort with strong preconceived notions that were often opposite to Lean. (In that sense, a bank environment is a similar challenge.) After working with medical professionals for many years and achieving notable success, Toussaint captured his rich experiences with Lean deployment in *On the Mend*. We cited some of his experiences that could be related to banking environments in this book.

3.5.3 Lean Advancement Initiative and EdNet Lean Academy™

In 1993, the Massachusetts Institute of Technology (MIT) started a consortium named the Lean Aerospace Initiative (LAI)* consisting of US defense industries, the Department of Defense, and MIT in a leading role. LAI's mission was to develop Lean knowledge and practice in aerospace and later US Army and Navy technology programs, product development, and enterprise transformation. Over the next 20 years, LAI published numerous studies on these subjects, specializing in Lean enterprise transformation. Its activities significantly matured and expanded the applications of Lean beyond factory environments [LAI, 2013].

Until 2003, membership was available only to military entities and military contractors. In 2003, LAI formed an educational network of universities named LAI EdNet whose mission was to develop and deliver an effective course on Lean and Six Sigma basics for new hires, college students, and industry employees.† EdNet has since grown to 120 universities worldwide. Its course was named EdNet Lean Academy™. Over the next nine years,

---

* The original name was the Lean Aircraft Initiative. The consortium was renamed after aerospace companies joined it, and renamed again to Lean Advancement Initiative after the US Army and Navy became members. The LAI acronym and web page were retained. LAI was closed in 2013 but its publications remain online.
† Loyola Marymount University of Los Angeles, the employer of the first author, became the charter university of EdNet.

the Lean Academy™ trained 45 instructors including one of the authors (Oppenheim), and offered 60 short courses to 1,800 participants.

The course constantly underwent improvements and revisions [Murman et al., 2014]. It was formulated to serve all domains, although some of the slides use examples from production applications. A special version of the course was developed for healthcare use. The latest version of the course materials is available to the public for nonprofit education [Lean Academy™, 2008]. The course is not intended for self-study; course slides are recommended for instructor-led basic training of bank employees in the fundamentals of Lean and Six Sigma and require only minor additions relevant to banking operations.

3.5.4 *Toyota Production System (TPS)*

Taiichi Ohno, the creator of Lean at Toyota, described TPS in his book titled *Toyota Production System: Beyond Large-Scale Production* [1988]. He begins with the fascinating history of TPS and the motivation "to catch up with America," then describes in detail the integrated Lean Thinking culture, processes, and tools. The book contains invaluable lessons on human relations and Lean processes that apply to banking as much as they apply to automobile manufacture.

3.5.5 *The Toyota Way*

Another book with a fascinating description of the Toyota culture is *The Toyota Way* [Liker, 2006]. The author framed the extraordinary cultural aspects of the Toyota organization into 13 principles of Toyota (not to be confused with the six Lean Principles cited in this book).

3.5.6 *6S*

Experts on Lean tend to agree that implementation of Lean in a bank should start by cleaning the bank office and computer spaces, employees' desks, storage areas, and archives, and developing orderliness habits. The simple but powerful method of 5S (later renamed 6S) is well suited to these tasks. 6S involves six sequential phases of implementing orderliness. We describe the method briefly in Section 5.1. For more detailed self-study, we recommend an easy-to-follow book titled *The 5S's: Five Keys to a Total Quality Environment* [Osada, 1991].

3.5.7 Lean Enablers for Banking and Lean Product Development Flow (LPDF)

In this section we adopt two Lean products from the defense industry to banking operations. The first is a set of **Lean Enablers for Banking** (discussed in detail in Chapter 7). Lean Enablers consist of the 130 best work practices based on Lean Thinking adopted for banking from the authors' years of work in aerospace applications. The Lean Enablers deal with 10 categories of bank management activities: leadership, culture, communications and coordination, general management, project management, process management, continuous improvement, hiring, planning, and suppliers.

The second Lean product is **Lean Product Development Flow (LPDF**, covered in Chapter 8). It is a holistic process for planning and executing well-defined projects. While most daily bank work involves loans and financial transactions, banks also engage in projects such as developing new products, services, and capabilities. LPDF is a super-efficient method for handling small well-defined projects. It was developed for smaller projects in satellite applications, but the first author learned that LPDF became popular and effective in general office applications, so we adopted it to the banking environment. Readers interested in the products presented in Chapters 7 and 8 will find much more information in Oppenheim [2011].

Chapter 4

Critical Lean Concepts: Value, Eight Wastes, and Six Lean Principles

> All we are doing is looking at the time line from the moment the customer gives us an order to the point when we collect the cash. And we are reducing that time line by removing the non-value-added wastes.
>
> **Taiichi Ohno, 1988**

What is Lean?* The word is not an abbreviation. It is customarily written with a capital L. It simply means *without fat*. In the context of work, it means an operation is streamlined, optimized, and without waste.

The seminal *Lean Thinking* book [Womack and Jones, 2006] states: "Lean thinking is lean because it provides a way to do more and more with less and less—less human effort, less equipment, less time, and less space—while coming closer and closer to providing customers with exactly what they want." This definition does not mention work quality explicitly, but Lean is very concerned with both quality of work and quality of the end product. Quality permeates all aspects of Lean as illustrated by several "catchy" phrases:

---

* This chapter was adopted from *Lean for Systems Engineering, with Lean Enablers for Systems Engineering*, B.W. Oppenheim, 2011.

- Do more with less [Womack, 2006]
- Work smarter, not harder
- Do the right job right [Murman, 2002]
- Do the job right the first time [Murman, 2002]
- Operate Just-in-Time
- Create value with minimum waste
- Organize work by elimination of waste from all activities

These simple statements may appear to be slogans and some readers may have "an allergy" to slogans. However, these statements clearly represent profound characteristics of good work.

Womack wisely used the *Lean Thinking* title instead of *Lean Management, Lean Methods*, or *Lean Tools*. Lean is a state of mind. It simultaneously integrates people, processes, and tools. The TPS, which we call Lean is often depicted as the Toyota Triangle (Figure 4.1). Graban [2009] describes it as an integrated and balanced approach combining technical tools (what we do), managerial tools (how we manage), and philosophy (what we believe), starting at the center with people and human development. The total system represents the organizational culture.

Three concepts are fundamental to the understanding of Lean Thinking: **Value, Waste**, and the process of creating value without waste, captured into the so-called **six Lean Principles**. While they apply to all domains,

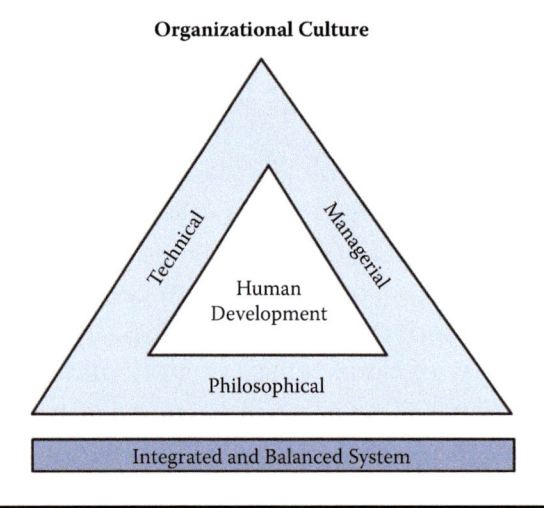

Figure 4.1 Toyota triangle [Graban, 2008].

they are covered in this chapter in the general context of bank operation. The concepts are explained in a self-contained style to free readers from the need to consult other sources. Readers who are new to Lean will benefit from reading the classic by Womack and Jones [2006].

4.1 Customer and Value

In Lean, two concepts are closely interconnected: customer and value. The entire Lean effort focuses on delivering needed value to each customer. The value may be a product, service, or both. The "customer first" philosophy permeates all aspects of Lean. Many organizations think of customers only as individuals or institutions that buy their final products or services. Lean designates them external customers. Internal customers are employees of a Lean organization.

> "Each succeeding work activity is the customer to the previous activity and every employee has the dual role: being the internal customer of the previous activity and being the supplier to the next activity downstream."
>
> **Gary Convis, 2013**

Each internal or external customer defines the value of the needed work. At its simplest, work value is what the customer says it is, considers important, and (if a customer is external) is willing to pay for or (if a customer is internal) is ready to accept the product as created and add value to it.

> Value is what the customer says it is and considers important. If the customer is external, value is what he or she is willing to pay for. If a customer is internal, value is defined as his or her readiness to accept a product or service as created.

In all cases, without exception, value has four characteristics:

Four Value Characteristics

- Quality and features that meet or exceed customer expectations
- Low price to external customer or low cost to internal customer
- Short lead time (time from order to delivery of value to customer)
- Nice service—a critically important if somewhat intangible characteristic

---

Bank products offered to external customers can be divided into standard and custom-made categories. Standard services and transactions are designed by the bank and offered and marketed to all present and potential customers. Examples are various types of checking and savings accounts, electronic banking services, standard mortgages, credit lines, and loans. The bank determines the values of its standard products based on its understanding of the market and validation by customers.

Custom-made products are designed for specific customers. An example is a large multi-currency corporate credit line that requires special handling. The external customer defines the value of a custom-made product within the portfolio of services of its bank.

The value to each internal customer is determined by that customer. When a certain value is to be created repeatedly, its definition should be captured into a standard procedure or checklist; otherwise the value will be considered customer-defined and unique.

However, we must stress that employees in traditional organizations often fail to see that what appears to be a unique activity is actually a routine process that should be perfected and standardized. Only the data flowing through a process is unique every time it is generated. The ability to distinguish unique activities from routine work that can be standardized can help uncover significant productivity reserves.

The "Value is what the customer says it is … [and] is willing to pay for" sentence may be unclear. In simple applications, the customer states what he or she needs and the supplier makes and delivers it, hopefully satisfying or even delighting the customer. This works well for a simple transaction such as buying ice cream—the customer sees what he or she is paying for. The value issue becomes more challenging when a bank designs a complex new product or completes a transaction that potentially may serve huge populations. It is critical to define and deliver the values of such transactions perfectly. One small mistake in the planning of a transaction that may serve millions of clients may ricochet into a stream of trouble with potential to destroy the bank.

Due to the high level of such risks and the complex regulations involved, banking projects often fall into the category of "complex systems." In such systems, the external customer usually cannot understand or define all details of the value received. The customer judges value only on the basis of the end service, and remains unaware and uninterested in all the complex transactions that must function perfectly in the background. Therefore, in a Lean banking context, the responsibility for capturing value includes both the portion visible to the customer and the segments handled by bank employees. In short, when defining value, we must think not only of external bank customers but also about all other relevant stakeholders.

4.1.1 Stakeholders and Value

In the banking industry, the number of stakeholders often reaches thousands or millions of individuals in numerous communities—customers, employees in all offices, regulators, lobbyists and politicians, accountants, shareholders, lawyers and courts, unions, and others. The various stakeholders insist on different aspects of value that relate to their interests, often in conflict with each other.

These differences make the capturing of value of complex bank operations a genuine challenge. Yet, the value capture must be done perfectly or subsequent transactions or projects will suffer delays, added costs, frustrations, and, in extreme cases, failure or worse. The banks that routinely create great value achieve customer satisfaction, employee satisfaction, competitive recognition, and increased growth and profits.

It is critical that every individual involved in value capture focus on capturing the final result with complete competence, wisdom, experience, and consensus. Final value definition must be crystal clear, unambiguous, and complete. It must encompass clear requirements and specifications and represent real customer needs and use scenarios that remain valid for an entire product or service life cycle. If a bank fails to understand the value of the work about to be performed, costly rework and even failure are almost certain. This rule applies to all activities—small single-person tasks and complex team activities.

4.2 Waste

Some bank work creates value; other work is waste or generates it. The ability to separate the two types of work and identify and eliminate waste is a critical Lean skill. The literature contains several definitions and descriptions of waste.

> "Waste is anything other than the minimum amount of resources (employee time, space, materials, equipment), which are absolutely essential to create value for the customer."
>
> **Shoichiro Toyoda, Former President, Toyota**
>
> "Waste is any problem that interferes with people doing their work effectively."
>
> **Mark Graban, 2006**

Waste in manufacturing is easy to see: a stopped machine, huge batches of product, or piles of rusting parts. Some wastes in a banking environment are also easy to recognize, for example, poorly organized data storage that requires excessive document retrieval time, errors that require rework, and waiting for data, approvals, and other items. Some forms of waste are more difficult to recognize. This section is intended to make waste easier to see.

The amount of waste in traditional organizations including banks is staggering. Waste is everywhere—more than anyone could imagine. Lean studies revealed that waste constituted 60% to 70% of work time in the best organizations and up to 90% or more in poorly managed operations. Even 100% of waste is possible in certain cases, for example, a bank's attempt to create a new product that fails in the marketplace or a new process that does not perform and must be abandoned.* All the work, materials, and funding used to create a failed product or process ultimately become waste. Examples of wasted resources include the direct salaries of the employees working on the failed product, prorated salaries of their managers, prorated costs of infrastructure, taxes, security, energy, and many other obvious and hidden factors.

---

* As explained in Chapter 8, Lean promotes efficient trial-and-error approaches and early exploration of possible options and risks during development of new products and processes. Most of these efforts are not wastes. The 100% waste discussed here refers to poorly designed products that need to be abandoned.

When we honestly calculate all costs involved, the price of failure is huge. The amounts of waste quoted may sound unbelievable to a newcomer to Lean. Hopefully, all readers will be convinced of the high cost of waste after reading this book.

Unless the waste is removed, work progress appears to be exceedingly slow and tortured, even when employees work frantically. While it may appear that more people need to be hired, staff additions rarely help over the long term. Lean offers a simpler solution: *uncover huge productivity reserves in the system by removing waste.*

In Lean Thinking we classify all work activities into three categories as defined in Box 4.1 [Womack and Jones, 1996; LAI Lean Academy, 2008]:

- **Value-added (VA) activities**
- **Necessary non-value-added activities (NNVA) or necessary wastes**
- **Non-value-added activities (NVA) or pure wastes**

Bank employees should not assume that every task they perform automatically adds value simply because "it's always done" or because a manager ordered the activity. Employees should question whether a task is absolutely necessary for value creation or whether a task is needed by someone else in the chain of value creation. If a given activity has no internal customer, it is a waste and should be eliminated. But the worker must not be eliminated. As noted earlier, Lean focuses on uncovering productivity reserves by eliminating wastes, thus reducing costs and service time, improving quality, and increasing customer satisfaction. These achievements will bring in more business. Employees freed from unneeded tasks will now be needed to serve the new customers.

No person whose regular work was determined to be waste and eliminated should be laid off. He or she should be assigned immediately to a value-adding activity.

Quality inspection is categorized as a NNVA. Ideally, work should be perfected to the level where it is right the first time and every time, and defects should be impossible. Can this goal be achieved? Of course it can.

BOX 4.1 VALUE-ADDED, NON-VALUE-ADDED, AND NECESSARY NON-VALUE-ADDED ACTIVITIES

VALUE-ADDED (VA) ACTIVITIES

To be value-added, an activity must satisfy three conditions simultaneously:

1. Transform information (or material) or reduce uncertainty. The activity cannot be just an unnecessary bureaucratic task that creates no value.
2. The external customer must be willing to pay for the product or service. The equivalent in a complex situation is that the customer would approve of the activity if he or she understood the technical details. An internal customer must be willing to accept the work product and be ready to add value to it.
3. The activity is done "right the first time."

NECESSARY (OR REQUIRED) NON-VALUE-ADDED (NNVA) ACTIVITIES

NNVA activities do not meet the value-added definition, but cannot be eliminated because they are required by law, bank regulation, contract, current technology, or other mandate. However, these activities should be reduced as much as possible or eliminated over the long term. Examples are the effort by a manager who does not trust the quality of work performed by his employees and feels compelled to inspect it; or the effort of sending a document copy to a regulatory agency.

NON-VALUE-ADDED (NVA) ACTIVITIES (PURE WASTE)

NVA activities consume resources but create no value; they are pure wastes. Examples are working on an unneeded document, waiting for data or data waiting for people, and defects that require rework. All NVA activities should be eliminated aggressively as soon as possible.

Consider an example: We do not hear about nurses who drop babies on hospital floors. This is not because the nurses were ordered by quality inspectors not to drop babies. The nursing characteristics of motivation, care, and intelligence prevent the defective actions. However, until the zero-defect goal is achieved and sustained, an organization must perform quality inspections that constitute NNVA activities. Section 5.2 describes Lean practices for quality assurance in banks.

The ability to identify and remove waste is a critical skill in Lean Thinking. Taiichi Ohno [1988] classified waste into seven categories. Originally, the categories were developed for production environments but were soon adopted by several authors to non-production work including professional and service environments [Morgan and Liker, 2006; McManus 2004]. The latest trend is to add an eighth category: wasted talent and enthusiasm. Box 4.2 summarizes the eight wastes in the banking context.

BOX 4.2   EIGHT CATEGORIES OF BANKING WASTES

Waste	Banking Examples
1. Waiting	People waiting for information or decision; information or decision waiting for people
2. Rework, defects	The killer *re's*: Rework, rewrite, redo, reenter; incorrect pricing of product or service
3. Overproduction of information	Creating information that was not requested; producing more output than needed by next process
4. Unnecessary movement of people	Need for employees to move to gain or access information; manual intervention required to compensate for lack of process
5. Unnecessary movement of information	Excessive information distribution Excessive hand-offs
6. Overprocessing of information	Refinements beyond those needed
7. Inventory of information	Retaining more information than needed; inadequate 6S activity[a]
8. Waste of talent and enthusiasm	Ineffective management that turns creative and enthusiastic employees into passive and frustrated minimalistic robots

[a] See Section 5.1 in Chapter 5 for description of 6S.

We now address each waste individually. We describe each waste, present one or more examples, and include a text box containing (1) suggestions for identifying and removing the waste, (2) assessment of how easy or difficult it is to remove, and (3) its status as controversial or not controversial.

4.2.1 Waste of Waiting

Waiting is usually the largest category of waste.* It includes all situations in which employees are unable to work on assigned tasks because the required data or documentation is not yet available, or is incorrect, or is ready but the person assigned to the task is not available. In both cases, the work of creating value for that particular customer is idle and value creation is interrupted. Simply put, no value creation is occurring.

Let us now make a profoundly important statement about Lean operation: it is *not* true that bank time is not wasted when people waiting for other people or for data spend the time working hard on other assignments. This thinking is totally incorrect. What matters is that the value creation in their value streams is stopped, making customers unhappy. Such waiting actually leads to frantic work that produces poor results overall. All bank workflow should be executed to create value for internal and external customers—not to keep employees busy. The cost of the value is proportional to the time spent creating it. When a workflow is idle, its customer is forced to wait for his or her value, and no customer enjoys that. Furthermore, all direct and indirect costs (salaries and benefits, management costs, infrastructure and energy, taxes, security, and other expenses) continue to accrue during waiting time. All these unnecessary costs arising from waiting by internal and external customers make a bank less competitive.

> Waiting is always a waste. Thinking that no bank time is wasted
> if employees work hard on other assignments while they wait is
> incorrect. It leads to frantic work, huge costs, and poor results.
> All bank activities should be aligned to create values for customers,
> not keep employees busy.

The five following examples illustrate frequent cases of waiting in banks. Box 4.3 contains guidance on identifying and removing this waste type, and whether the removal is or is not controversial.

---

* In some large organizations (not banks), wait constitutes 82% of employee work time [Oehmen, 2012].

Example 1: Waste of waiting for data—This wait is common in banks. An employee assigned to perform a task opens the case file and notices that the input data for the task is missing, incomplete, or incorrect. The employee sends requests for the missing data to appropriate colleagues and then waits until it arrives (or, worse, rejects the case and sends it back to the originator). Measurements indicate that for every unit of value adding work, at least two units of time are wasted on such waiting [LAI].

Example 2: Waste of waiting for risk decisions and approvals—Risk analysis is one of the most critical aspects of a well-functioning bank, but it must be performed efficiently with minimum waiting and information churning. Short decision time is an important aspect of bank competitiveness. Often, a loan or credit application is denied only because a minor piece of information was missing from an application package. The denial requires that the entire loan or credit application be redone, causing a frustrated customer to wait.

Instead, when a risk department employee notices that information is missing on an application, he or she should contact the person who handled the application or contact the customer immediately to request the missing data. Upon receiving it, the employee should make a risk decision promptly to minimize the lengthy second loop of the application process. Unnecessarily prolonged loan and credit approval cycles lose potential customers and frustrate other bank stakeholders. In addition, in some banks, risk decisions are arbitrarily made by a single individual. The lack of processes and guidelines makes the bank appear capricious and less competitive.

Example 3: Waste of waiting in long approval sequences—In many banks, even noncritical decisions are subject to several levels of approvals. Many approvals are bureaucratic; managers often sign documents without looking at them after the documents spend days or weeks in the manager's in-box queue. Some managers consistently reject cases without telling employees what to do to gain their approval.

In one aerospace company, an approval sequence involving seven managers took six months on average. Upon learning of the delay, a top executive issued the following order: "From now on all you [expletive deleted] approving managers must meet in one conference room for concurrent approving sessions once a week. Bring whomever you need and ask any questions you need, and then approve or disapprove the given case, so that the longest approval sequence would not exceed one week." The measure was radical but effective!

We are not suggesting that all complex cases can be reviewed and approved or rejected in that style. However, every effort should be made to

1. minimize the number of sequential approvals
2. concurrentize the approvals
3. treat each approval or disapproval as a high-priority item to be issued the same day the case is presented for approval
4. train employees to do work "right the first time" so that approvals rather than rejections become the norms.

Example 4: Waste of waiting due to excessively sequential work— When several tasks (e.g., in a project sequence) must be executed, it is always wise to ask which tasks may be executed concurrently rather than sequentially to cut overall project or process time. Of course, this requires good planning of all the tasks, with their inputs, outputs, and control points coordinated, to enable the creation of information just before it is needed by each task.

Example 5: Waste of waiting due to inefficient approval system— Assume a proposal to introduce new bank regulation is sent to several departments for consultation. Instead of synchronous consultation (a meeting of stakeholders who must approve or reject the decision), various parties submit remarks independent of each other and uncoordinated in time. The remarks then are re-circulated to all parties. As a result various versions of the edited regulations circulate uncontrolled among all stakeholders several times. Remarks are made about remarks, text changes travel back and forth among parties, and the time to gain approval grows to grotesque lengths, often months. If all stakeholders were asked to submit edits and meet promptly to agree on the final form of a regulation, the process could take days instead of months.

BOX 4.3 HOW TO REMOVE WASTE OF WAITING

Definition: People waiting for information or decisions, or information or decisions waiting for people.

Ease of waste identification: The waste of waiting is self-evident (people wait for data or approvals, or data waits for people, implying that someone is waiting for the data). Finding the waste is easy. Simply locate the waiting person and ask. Most people forced to wait for something they need will gladly discuss their frustration.

Is the removal of this waste controversial? No. Receiving what is needed faster is always a positive outcome.

Is the removal of this waste difficult? This waste is moderately difficult to eliminate and requires better planning of the process in which the waiting is discovered. Where waiting is necessary (e.g., waiting for a risk decision) the waiting time should be as short and predictable as possible. Involved parties should work in parallel and in coordination. The plan to eliminate waste may involve more timely allocation of the people to do the work, better procedures and guidelines, and better coordination of tasks in a given process. In addition, the several following easy steps can reduce waiting in a process.

- Immediately after completing a task, the results (file, e-mail, document) should be passed on to the next person in the process rather than waiting in a batch in someone's in- or out-box.
- Observe the logjams and gaps in the process and balance the flow so that every involved person will spend about the same amount of time on the task as the person who precedes or follows him or her. This makes the flow of work more predictable, almost like a production line.
- For maximum efficiency, organize the people (and their tasks and laptops) as a work cell, around a conference table, sitting in the order of tasks. If such processes are to be executed routinely, move their desks into one room, arrange in the order of tasks, to minimize walking and enable the "moving line" type of processing. We describe this powerful work cell organization in greater depth in Section 5.9.
- Do not batch documents from different cases. E-mail, upload, or deliver each case to the office where it is needed as soon as it is ready. If printed materials must be sent across town or across the country, scan them and send them by e-mail as soon as they are ready. If scanned versions are not practical, use the fastest possible delivery means, even if it is expensive, because the time of the people waiting for the documents is dramatically more expensive than even the most expensive delivery method.

4.2.2 Waste of Defects and Rework

A critical aspect of Lean is the ability to execute a process or task right the first time. The tools that serve that purpose include excellent capture of value proposition; effective procedures, standards, and checklists; coordination and communication with internal customers before starting work; training, mentoring, and learning from past mistakes; and error-proofing devices.

If we fail to execute a task right the first time, the internal customer receiving the output will reject it, causing rework and waiting wastes. Each time we hear a *re* word (redo, reenter, rewrite, etc.), we know that someone made a mistake and now the bank must spend money and time to correct the work.

In bank operations, most errors are not caused by recklessness or incompetence. Most are caused by an inefficient system and uncontrollable circumstances that lead employees to make mistakes or fail to prevent them. Most rework results from an incomplete, ambiguous, or inaccurate understanding of value in requirements and specifications, ineffective work standards, poor communication and coordination, lack of training and mentoring, or the pressure to deliver an unrealistically high rate of outputs. This waste is particularly frustrating to employees. Supervisory instructions—"Next time be more careful!"—are useless if a system is error-prone. Blaming the person rather than the system is unfair and will foster resentment.

Frequent work defects require massive inspections that are categorized as necessary non-value-added (NNVA) waste. The inspection is necessary because the existing processes are imperfect and open to errors. As we implement "right the first time" operations, the costs of inspections, rework, and waiting decrease while quality increases.

We must remember that quality inspection is rarely perfect. We never have enough time to catch all errors. Some sneak through to customers who always find them! We all can cite examples of checking and rechecking a document and still missing some mistakes. Relying on a final inspection is an expensive and imperfect means of creating quality. Quality assurance is covered in Section 5.2.

Example: Incorrect pricing of bank products and services—A sloppy, uninformed pricing of bank services and products can cause massive profit losses. A bank will lose customers (and profits) if its prices are too high and lose its profit margins if its prices are too low. When the pricing is determined to be defective, the analysis must be corrected and results re-published, which costs money. Box 4.4 contains guidance on identifying and removing this waste type and controversial or non-controversial status of removal.

BOX 4.4   HOW TO REMOVE WASTE OF REWORK

Definition: Many tasks could have been done right the first time with proper understanding of value, adequate information, effective training and mentoring, planning, coordination, and care. The failure to implement those measures produced defects. (This waste does not refer to planned iterations, e.g., prototyping or testing new software or product by trial and error, which is a frequent and perfectly normal developmental procedure.)

Ease of waste identification: The waste from defects and rework tends to be obvious. Most people hate having to redo a task because someone found fault with it.

Is the removal of this waste controversial? No.

Is the removal of this waste difficult? Removal is not difficult but requires solid commonsense efforts as described below.

- Prepare effective standards, checklists, and procedures that describe necessary steps in an easy-to-follow manner.
- Train and mentor the employees to do the work.
- If a task is not routine, identify the internal customer who is to receive the outputs and proactively coordinate the work (value, scope, formats, etc.) with him or her to enable "right the first time" execution. Remember: the internal or external customer is the only judge who decides whether the process or product is done right. If the internal customer seems to make unreasonable demands, both sides should negotiate, on the basis of value. Appeal to a manager should be the last resort.
- If a question arises during a task execution, the employee should seek an immediate answer from the internal customer, supervisor, or expert in the bank.
- Before starting work on a task, all tools, specifications, and information should be available. If any item is missing, inadequate, or unsatisfactory, correction or replacement should be requested immediately. Employees should think proactively rather than reacting after a problem occurs.

> ■ Each employee in the bank should be trained to have "two jobs": (1) execute assigned tasks and (2) perform quality inspection on the results. "Partial credits" allowed in schools do not carry any weight in a bank. A Lean operation has a binary judgment system: value is or is not created.
>
> ■ Each worker should have easy access to knowledge sources: internal customers, expert managers and mentors, tool or IT experts, and anyone else who can help the employee do the right job right the first time.

4.2.3 Waste of Overproduction of Information

This type of waste occurs when we create information that is not needed by anyone, or is created in excess of what is needed in the next process. Box 4.5 contains guidance on how to identify and remove this waste type, and whether the removal is or is not controversial.

Example 1: Wasteful process not needed by anyone—A manager in a bank reacting to a temporary crisis ordered a certain task to be done, intending it to be done only once. He forgot to advise staff that the task would not be needed after the first implementation. Soon after that, the manager left for another job. By then the task was completed routinely even though no one in the bank needed the output. The result is overproduction waste. All bank staff members should always ask who needs an output or document. If the question has no answer, the task or document should be declared a waste and eliminated.

Example 2: Waste of completing a form with difficult-to-obtain information—Every reader will recognize this waste. At one time or another, we have all needed to fill out complex forms seeking obscure information ("shoe size of great grandmother") that is never needed, is impossible to find, or would require an inordinate amount of time to locate. Every bank form should be reviewed periodically to determine the real need for the information requested. If no one uses the information, eliminate the item from the form immediately. If the information is needed only in rare instances, the circumstances should be explained in the form instructions. Otherwise allow the user to leave the field blank and train the employees who use the form to accept the blank field and not be bureaucratic.

BOX 4.5 HOW TO REMOVE WASTE
OF OVERPRODUCTION OF INFORMATION

Definition: Creation of information that is not needed by anyone or exceeds what is needed by the next process.

Ease of waste identification: Identifying unneeded information is easy: if we cannot find an internal customer for the task output, the task is a waste. Asking the internal customer how much information is needed and identifying excess is easy too, provided the information supplier and the internal customer coordinate the transaction.

Is the removal of this waste controversial? Overproduction waste may be controversial. People doing the work may argue that what they do is not waste and is "really good for the bank." Identifying unneeded tasks is easier than finding work that exceeds the requirements of the next process. In the former case we simply ask the internal customers if they indeed need the task since we suspect it is a waste. The answer to the question before Lean training may be, "We don't need it immediately, but do it just in case." After Lean training, the answer will be, "We don't appear to need it now, so don't do it. If we need it later, we will ask for it." Clearly, training is critical for removing this waste.

Is removal of this waste difficult? It is not difficult if we approach the problem in the right way. Every employee assigned a non-routine task should identify the internal customer and coordinate task scope and details (outputs required, format, etc.) before starting the work. That way the employee understands how much work is needed to create value, and performs only that amount. In many cases, an experienced bank manager must be called to judge whether a work scope is correct or excessive.

Consider the magnitude of this waste. If the information needed to fill a box on a form requires an hour of searching and the form is used daily by ten bank employees across branches, each hour costs the bank a minimum of $100 per person and the annual cost can be measured easily in six digits.

Example 3: Waste of overdissemination—This waste involves sending information to too many people. We all curse the overwhelming number of e-mails we receive. Most office e-mail traffic represents overuse or abuse of "carbon copy" notation. Each e-mail interrupts and delays work (the interruption is also a waste because of the mental effort required to re-focus on the work) and requires a time-consuming decision: Should the e-mail be saved as important? Deleted? Answered now? Answered later?

Our unscientific study of e-mails indicates that the average employee wastes an hour daily on unwanted messages. Multiplying the one hour daily by the number of work days in a year by the number of employees by the average salary is a huge number! Phrased another way, one hour spent reading unneeded e-mails daily represents 12.5% of a nominal daily work day of eight hours. If by some magic we could reduce that by half, the equivalent would be a quick hire of an additional 6.25% trained employees to do the bank work—a significant boost in productivity *at no cost*.

That "magic" is available: a memo from a top manager to all employees instructing them how to use and how not to abuse the carbon copy feature when e-mailing. The memo may take an hour to write but it will yield an enormous increase in productivity. This is Lean Thinking at work!

Example 4: Waste of sending a volume when one number is requested—Often a simple number (perhaps a statistic from last year) is needed in some process and an employee calls the relevant department to request it. "On its way" is the response. What arrives is a cartload of file folders and boxes containing reports the recipient (who needed only one number) must sort through to find what he or she needed. A waste! The creator of the reports would know where to find the number, so the total work time spent would be dramatically shorter than the time spent by the recipient unfamiliar with the report. In Lean, everyone works smarter, not harder.

Example 5: Waste of "reinventing the wheel"—Few bank processes or products are so totally new they need to start with fundamental research, as if it were scientific research. Most of our daily work involves reuse and adaptation of known processes. It is almost always faster and cheaper to tailor an existing process to current needs than start by redesigning the entire process. Senior employees at many banks have comprehensive knowledge of the operations. Asking them for help maybe a powerful shortcut to the solution and can also reduce bank cost and work time. Lean means decreasing time to create value!

4.2.4 Waste of Unnecessary Movement of People

This waste is caused by unnecessary movement of people during task execution. Banks should reduce excessive walking required to get

---

**BOX 4.6   HOW TO REMOVE WASTE
OF UNNECESSARY MOVEMENT OF PEOPLE**

Definition: Unnecessary movement of people during task execution.

Ease of waste identification: This waste is usually obvious. A spaghetti chart is recommended to detect this type of waste.

Is the removal of this waste controversial? Not at all. People enjoy the convenience of proximity to co-workers.

Is the removal of this waste difficult? No; the removal simply involves relocating the workstations (cubicles or desks) of the people who must interact often to a common area.

---

work done. Box 4.6 contains guidance on how to identify and remove this waste type, and whether the removal is or is not controversial.

Example 1: Wasteful movements caused by poor allocation of office spaces—A good office plan should place the people who interact often in nearby offices or cubicles to minimize time required to walk from one location to another (walking is good for blood circulation but excessive walking wastes bank money). Face-to-face communication is always better than electronic messaging.

An excellent tool for discovering this waste is known as a "spaghetti chart" of the bank floor area showing the employee walking patterns. If the chart reveals a maze covering the entire floor, the layout is probably less than optimum. Clusters of lines centered on specific work areas usually indicate a thoughtful work cell layout. Figure 4.2 illustrates both types of traffic patterns.

Example 2: Proximity of manager's office to his employees—In Section 5.11 we discuss *gemba*, the management practice of frequent walking through areas where employees perform work. This is done not to control the workers; the intent is to see where employees may need help and find opportunities for system improvements. The present Lean practice is to locate the office of each manager near his or her staff work areas rather than in a remote location. This enables the manager to visit work areas quickly and easily.

Example 3: Human intervention when a process stops—Suppose a bank process extends over two departments. It flows efficiently through the

Motion Study Chart (Spaghetti chart)

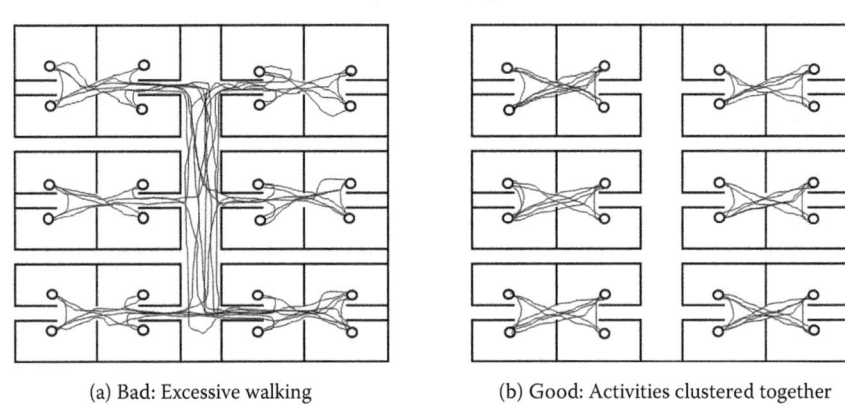

(a) Bad: Excessive walking   (b) Good: Activities clustered together

Figure 4.2 "Spaghetti" charts. (a) Poor office layout. (b) Efficient office layout.

first department, but when it crosses to the second department, it receives a low priority. The manager of the first department then must walk to the second department and beg a colleague for speedier processing. Even though this manifests as the waste of unnecessary movement of people, it is actually the waste of waiting. If this scenario is repetitive, the two managers should meet to negotiate a speedier solution. Possible solutions may involve increasing the priority of the process in the second department, better planning across both departments, shifting the responsibility for the entire process to one department or combining the two departments into one.

4.2.5 Waste of Unnecessary Movement of Information

This type of waste tends to be notorious in large banks that are geographically widespread. Unless information paths are planned and defined precisely, information often bounces back and forth between the main office and the branches unnecessarily, wasting time and resources. Another frequent manifestation of this waste type is information hand-off. Box 4.7 contains guidance on how to identify and remove waste from unnecessary movement of information.

Example: Excessive hand-offs—Hand-offs can be destructive to information flow for several reasons. We all played the "telephone game" when we were children and remember the useless information conveyed to the last kid in a series of verbal hand-offs. Hand-offs separate knowledge from responsibility, action, and feedback. "A hand-off is a disaster because it

**BOX 4.7   HOW TO REMOVE WASTE OF UNNECESSARY
MOVEMENT OF INFORMATION**

Definition: Unnecessary movement of information between people, organizations, or geographical locations.

Ease of waste identification: Easy.

Is the removal of this waste controversial? Removal is usually not controversial.

Is the removal of this waste difficult? The waste is easy to remove simply by instructing the stakeholders to move the information based on the following principles:

- Move information along the most direct path, eliminating unnecessary intermediate stops and steps.
- Organize the information into well-defined and standardized packets, cases, files, forms, or spreadsheets to ensure that both the sender and the receiver have the same understanding of what is being moved and why.
- Move the information by the fastest possible means.
- These instructions are critical if a bank has branches in many geographical locations, involving several languages, time zones, and cultures. The probability of significant information loss during each hand-off is very high in that situation unless superb standardization levels are achieved.

results in decisions being made by people who do not have enough knowledge to make them well or the opportunity to implement them" [Ward, 2007].

Hand-offs cause a loss of information (the originating person understands the context of the matter; the person to whom the information is handed off does not). They also induce miscommunication and misinterpretation. To avoid hand-offs, Toyota workers are trained to communicate directly with the person who has the needed information without having to go through managers or other parties. Employees are also trained to ask questions in such a way that only one of the two answers is possible: yes or no. This minimizes the chances of misinterpretation during a hand-off.

Compare the following two questions. (1) "How are you planning to arrange that shipment from X to Y?" (2) "When arranging the shipment from X to Y, are you planning to send a personal courier?" The first question is open ended; it invites a verbose answer and opens the door to potential misinterpretation and miscommunication. The second question can only be answered by a yes or no, with little chance of misunderstanding.

4.2.6 Waste of Overprocessing of Information

This waste occurs when an employee tries to increase output to a level higher than needed by internal customers. Box 4.8 provides details on eliminating this waste type.

Example 1: Waste of risk analysis beyond practical levels— Risk analysis is the kernel of bank operations, and proper assessment of risk probability and consequence is critical to bank success. Sometimes, however, overeager employees in the risk department demand excessive amounts of information about a client—more information than needed to make a rational risk determination.* Some of the excess demand for information is caused by personal risk aversion on the part of a bank employee ("I want to protect myself").

Prescribing proper risk levels is beyond the scope of this book. Bank policy, national and international regulations, and experiences of risk managers are all factors that play a role in decision making. From the view of waste, it is important to remember that risk reduction involves a point of diminishing returns, beyond which bureaucracy and waste take over, causing losses of customers and bank competitiveness. Only competent and experienced employees should make risk decisions.

Example 2: Waste from lack of standardization—Many employees unfamiliar with Lean see their work as unique and special—and not conducive to any standardization. They do not realize that only the data flowing through the processes is unique and most banking work can and should be cast into standard optimized processes and skill sets that best execute the process. Standardization is discussed at length in Section 5.5, but it is

---

* It is interesting that bank client companies listed on the stock market in many countries are not allowed to provide banks with information beyond what is available in their annual reports for fear of inside-information fraud. In contrast, private clients and non-public companies have no such protection and banks are permitted to ask very intrusive questions.

BOX 4.8 HOW TO REMOVE WASTE OF OVERPROCESSING OF INFORMATION

Definition: Work of excessive refinement that produces a higher level of output or fidelity than the customer needs.

Ease of waste identification: Finding this waste may be difficult and requires experience.

Is the removal of this waste controversial? Yes, usually. The person responsible for the waste is usually trying to refine or perfect the work without realizing that each element has a level of "good enough" for value creation.

Is the removal of this waste difficult? Removal is easy but requires a good understanding of Lean. Why blame the worker for his or her eagerness to make a task as perfect as possible? Deciding whether the level achieved is good enough must be made by a highly experienced person. A refinement that creates noticeably higher level of value (lower cost, better quality, quicker service) probably makes sense. The "good enough" level is achieved when the process becomes consistent, predictable, error-free, and effective, particularly if the improved process will be used repeatedly and is important for making the bank more competitive.

Eventually, additional improvements tend to bring diminishing returns, and an experienced bank manager should determine when to halt the improvement work.

Possibly the most difficult decisions concern software testing. The work of eliminating all software bugs is almost always justified because bugs yield uncounted wastes over the long term. The best approach is to consult a software engineering expert.

Removal of the waste is easy after it is identified. If a waste is a one-time occurrence, a simple instruction to the employee to cease the excessive refinement is enough. If the waste recurs, a standard procedure or checklist should be developed and stakeholders trained to use it.

useful to mention here that good standards and checklists free employees from remembering mundane steps. This allows them to perform more creative and intelligent work while also promoting predictability of operations. Standardization avoids uncontrollable variability that causes the wastes of mistakes, defects, rework, and delays.

Example 3: Waste from using excessively complex software— While banks must use common software tools across all branches, common databases, and common formats for external transactions (e.g., regulatory reporting), a number of smaller local operations may be performed using the most convenient tool available: a spreadsheet. Many banks ideologically insist on using complex software tools on principle, even though the data processed stays in one office. Large complex programs require expenditures for purchasing, maintenance, training, and infrastructure. They are prone to errors and tend to yield wastes of waiting, rework, overprocessing, and excess inventory. It is good practice to ask how the information will be created, used, and stored, and select software that will minimize waste over the long term.

4.2.7 Waste of Inventory of Information

This waste results from retaining and storing more information or supplies than needed. Information should be created in the right amount and only when needed. Creating information too late causes the next person in the value chain to create waiting waste. Creating needed information too early risks the waste of rework because the information may become obsolete if conditions change before it is used. Creating too much information causes the wastes of inventory, overproduction, and waiting. Box 4.9 contains guidance on identifying and removing this type of waste. The waste of inventory may cause a domino effect by leading to other types of wastes as described in Example 1 below.

To prevent this waste, information and supplies must be stored to ensure easy access on a moment's notice, subject to good security and safety rules. This requires effective record keeping and efficient configuration management, databases, and general orderliness in all office and computer spaces. Section 5.1 describes the 6S method that addresses these bank operations.

Example 1: Messy inventory causes a domino effect of other wastes—During the recent economic crisis, most of the management of a bank left, making the bank somewhat dysfunctional. The remaining employees

BOX 4.9 HOW TO REMOVE WASTES OF INVENTORIES OF INFORMATION OR SUPPLIES

Definition: Keeping or storing more information or supplies than needed.

Ease of waste identification: Excessive inventories of paper documents and supplies are obvious. Excessive inventories of electronic information are difficult to find.

Is the removal of this waste controversial? The removal may be controversial. Employees may remember being chastised for running out of needed supplies: so now they want to play it safe. Compliance is achieved with good Lean training.

Is the removal of this waste difficult? As all banks migrate toward paperless operations, it is critical to separate electronic inventories from paper documents and supplies. The rules for avoiding the two inventory waste types are different. Electronic documents require a combination of security, safety, privacy, and ease of access when needed. A bank needs safe and secure databases that permit information to be saved, stored, catalogued, and retrieved immediately and efficiently. Information storage must balance the need for security, safety, and privacy of bank data with the need for immediate (and legitimate) retrieval and use. This trade-off is one of the biggest challenges of modern bank back office data handling. The databases have to be searchable by history, document type, or customer identification. It is desirable to install fool-proof computer features that prevent both honest errors and unauthorized access to electronic documents.

A different set of rules applies to paper documents. Inventory waste is avoided by directing that only documents needed for current task may be in plain sight and all others must be returned to storage. A somewhat more draconian but effective rule is that all desktops must be cleared at the end of each work day. Some companies mandate housekeeping staff to dispose of all items left on desktops as trash to be shredded. Any item an employee wants to keep must be kept inside the desk or stored in a designated area before he or she leaves the office.

> Section 5.1 describes the 6S rules for maintaining order and allowing efficient retrieval of information without wasting time.
>
> The inventory of office supplies should be designed to last until the next resupply plus a small extra quantity in case the vendor fails to deliver.

and the new ones hired in a rush had great difficulty locating all the information they needed to run the new operation smoothly. Information was collected and retained in disorganized manner and feelings of hopelessness soon spread. Employees wasted significant time looking for information and the information they found was frequently incorrect or incomplete. Completed transactions had to be redone. The extraordinary steps required to keep the bank functioning created lots of waste and overproduction.

Example 2: Excessive office supply inventories—An eager bank employee responsible for buying supplies kept storage areas overflowing with computer paper, writing pads, coffee filters, printer cartridges, pens, pencils, file folders, and more. One manager estimated that two years' worth of office supplies were on hand. A significant part of the inventory became waste. Computer paper collected humidity and could not be used. Printer cartridges and coffeemaker filters became obsolete when the bank replaced the printers and coffeemakers.

The best reordering policy is Just-in-Time. In practice, it means keeping just enough inventory to last until the next resupply period, plus a small extra amount in case the supplier fails to deliver on time.

4.2.8 Wastes of Talent and Enthusiasm

We all can remember when we first started working in a professional paying job. We wanted to make genuine impacts by demonstrating our best abilities and showcasing our creativity, eagerness, enthusiasm, teamwork, and manners. We were also excited to put our technical skills to use.

Within a few years after joining a poorly run bank, enthusiastic employees can turn into minimalists, doing only what is required and keeping low profiles. What happened in those few short years is tragic. Instead of shaping a workforce into creative problem solvers who contribute improvements in productivity, quality, and cost cutting that over time put a bank in a superior competitive position, an inefficient bank transforms new employees into mindless

---

**BOX 4.10 HOW TO REMOVE THE WASTE
OF TALENT AND ENTHUSIASM**

Definition: Waste of human talent, creativity, eagerness, and enthusiasm.

Ease of waste identification: This waste is obvious to Lean practitioners and employees and invisible to traditional managers.

Is the removal of this waste controversial? Yes, but only before Lean training. After Lean training, employees are eager to change the culture.

Is the removal of this waste difficult? This waste is probably the most difficult and takes the longest to remove because it requires a significant change in bank culture, management, and leadership style. It must be addressed throughout the entire operation. We offer detailed specific advice for removing this waste in Chapter 6 covering Lean implementation.

---

robots who think only about grievances, bad bosses, and low pay. These wastes of talent and enthusiasm represent the most serious wastes of all.

When the employees become totally demoralized, managers call them "deadwood." As Scholtes [1997] points out, we hire "live wood" and "kill" it through our management style. Toyota showed the world the extraordinary benefits of empowering ordinary workers. Any bank that treats employees as assets rather than commodities will win over the traditional banks that manage by fear, blame, and shame.

Box 4.10 contains guidance on how to identify and remove this waste type.

* * *

The various types waste examples listed in Sections 4.2.1 through 4.2.8 are intended only to "whet the appetite" of the reader. Any experienced bank employee should have no trouble expanding this list from personal experience.

4.2.9 *Muda, Mura, Muri, and Hejinka*

The eight types of waste described in Section 4.2 are collectively called *Muda* (waste in Japanese) and the word and principles it covers have been adopted in many western industries. Two other Japanese terms are useful in Lean Thinking: *Mura* (uneven workload) and *Muri* (overwork).

One barrier to good workflow is the unevenness of workloads over time. Known as *Mura,* this waste arises when a manager allocates all work assignments at one time (e.g., during weekly staff meetings). Allocation of work to all employees at the same time without prioritization triggers an immediate and steep increase in workload. Managers and employees are unable to handle all the assignments at once and grow frustrated by backlogs, delays, and competition for resources and react by saying, "We do not have enough people and need to hire more." Banks often hire more employees but the unevenness of work is not resolved because all the wastes in the system stifle progress. In contrast, when the work is planned better and distributed evenly, fewer resources can serve more needs.

> "Lean is not about pushing people to work faster or to be in two places at the same time. Employees, when first hearing about Lean, joke about the need for roller skates so they could zip around faster. Lean thinkers, instead, ask why employees have to travel such long distances and search for ways to eliminate the need for moving faster."
>
> **Mark Graban, 2009**

Muri means overburdening a person with work, making it impossible to deliver quality work on time. Just imagine three bank employees performing their tasks in sequence; the second person is overloaded, working frantically, while the first and the third ones just wait. This process creates little value. In Lean, it is important to observe the flow, identify the overloaded workstations, eliminate bottlenecks of capacity, and balance the work among all employees. Ideally, when all employees working in sequence are loaded identically, they can synchronize the work and flow it in single pieces in a common rhythm as if the work moved along an assembly line. It is possible to achieve a moving line even in banking applications!

White-collar, not to say professional employees (and many employees working in bank back offices have at least some college education) work at the speed at which their education, training, experience, and brain capacity allow them to work. The pathological cases of intentionally slowing down the work to aggravate managers or sabotage the operation are extremely rare and must not define the office discipline. Forcing a worker to work faster is counterproductive; it leads to mistakes and resentment. The Lean concept is "Work smarter, not faster" to eliminate wastes from the processes and allow value-added work to be executed at its natural speed.

This does not mean that bank management should not seek process improvements that would cut work time and improve quality—normal activities required for continuous improvement to maintain progress and remain competitive. Such improvements should not be confused with arbitrary pressures on employees to deliver faster what they can barely handle now. Box 4.11 and Figure 4.3 illustrate this point.

BOX 4.11   CASE STUDY OF TIME MANAGEMENT

Consider the following common office waste scenario. A supervisor shows John, a competent bank employee in IT, some task specifications and asks how long John needs to revise a table. John reviews the specifications and says, "This is simple; just needs entering the numbers and some testing; it should not take me more than two hours." The supervisor directs John to proceed but the job is not finished for days. The frustrated supervisor calls John and says, "You promised me the output in two hours; almost a week has passed; you need to learn to work faster."

Let us analyze this situation. See Figure 4.3a. John could not start working on the task because the same supervisor told him to finish a prior urgent task and did not tell John that the new task had a higher priority. Eighteen work hours elapsed (NVA) before John was ready to start on the new task. However, when he opened the case file, he saw that some data was incorrect, some was missing, and some was unclear. He sent e-mails to colleagues in an effort to obtain the correct, absent, and clear data he needed to perform the task. That consumed one hour NNVA activity.

John then waited 13 hours for the data (NVA). Finally, at hour 32, correct complete data arrived and John finished the task in two hours as he promised (VA) and delivered the results to the supervisor's in-box for approval as he is trained to do. The supervisor is away for 13 hours (NVA) and forgot to tell John to e-mail the results rather than place them in the in-box.

When the supervisor returns, he does not get to John's task because of other urgent chores waiting for his attention. Finally he finds John's output, signs off (VA), and the task is truly finished. However, the entire cycle took almost 48 hours rather than the two estimated and the frustrated supervisor urges John to work faster.

Figure 4.3b groups the task times by type (NVA, NNVA, and VA). We can see how nonsensical was the instruction to John to work faster. John worked as fast as his brain allowed him to work (generally work speed is based on education, training, and experience). Forcing John to work faster (cutting the VA in Figure 4.3c) is counterproductive: John is likely to feel stress and make mistakes, may need to extend the delivery time, and certainly will feel frustration with the supervisor.

Trying to cut VA time by forcing employees to work faster will not improve the overall cycle time. Even if we could speed up VA time by a dramatic 50%, the overall effect would be minimal, accompanied by dramatic risks of mistakes. Smart managers understand this, and focus not on speeding VA work but rather on cutting NVA and NNVA activities (Figure 4.3d). Since NVA typically exceeds VA, NVA presents real opportunities for improvement. How? By identifying and reducing the eight wastes. John's case involved waiting (eliminated by better coordination and planning), and defects and rework (eliminated by training, improved procedures, and use of checklists). He should have had access to the correct data as soon as he needed it.

How much waste exists in a bank? Section 4.3 describes formal processes for identifying and removing waste using value stream mapping. But a quick approximation is readily available right away. Consider a typical banking process conducted in the back office and involving several people. Based on your experience, estimate the total amount of time the process now requires including all normal wastes for waiting and rework. Call the estimated amount the lead time. Next, imagine yourself traveling with the information involved in the process from desk to desk and from computer to computer. Ignore all the times of waiting for the next process, for approvals, for meetings, access to databases, and time spent looking for data and searching files. Also ignore all cases where one step is performed multiple times; consider only one execution.

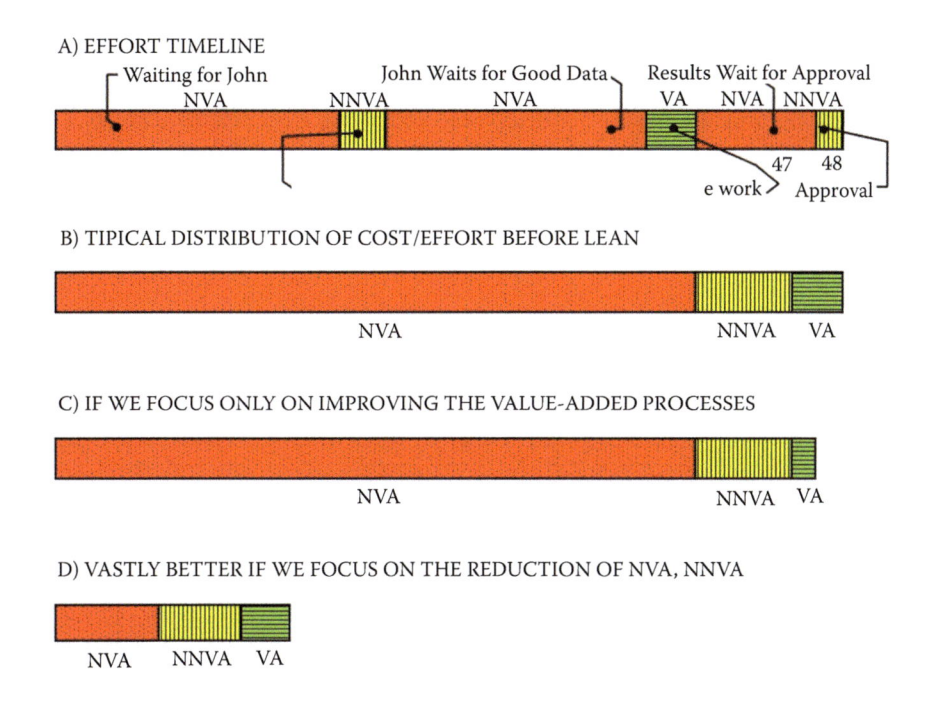

Figure 4.3 Time spent on a task.

For each step, consider only the value-adding times of bank employees doing useful work such as making a decision, analyzing a risk, or entering data. The sum of the value-adding activities is called the touch time. If your bank is like most others, the total touch time is only a small fraction (typically 10% to 30%) of the lead time due to all the wastes in the system. The remaining 70% to 90% of employee time roughly represents the bank's productivity reserve.

* * *

Final remarks on waste—Experience indicates that training employees on value and waste elimination before implementing Lean in actual activities is a critical factor. Without adequate training, workers will be naturally suspicious of the activity and may confuse the attempts to eliminate waste with attempts to eliminate their jobs. A panic about imminent layoffs may spread rapidly. With good training and management assurance that no layoffs will follow, workers will readily join the efforts to identify and eliminate waste.

4.3 Lean Principles

The amazing general Lean process used to create value without waste has been captured into six Lean Principles. They appear simple but the reader is cautioned against interpreting them as "simplistic." In fact, they are concise descriptions of the most profound work organization system developed to date in human civilization, and it took the genius of Womack and Jones [1996] to frame such complex concepts into simple words.

The six Lean Principles are abbreviated as Value, Value Stream, Flow, Pull, Perfection, and Respect for People. The first five were formulated in the seminal book by Womack and Jones [1996]. The sixth principle, often called "the second pillar of Lean" [Sugimori et al., 1977] was added later, to emphasize the profound importance of good human relations at work [Oppenheim, 2011]. It plays a critical role in Lean success. This is not to say that the original formulation by Womack disregarded human relations. They were considered profoundly important and embedded into the other five principles. The latest trend is to make Respect for People an explicit principle to ensure its maximum visibility. The principles and their definitions are described in detail below.

4.3.1 Principle 1: Value

Definition: Capture the value proposition defined by the customer— Customer may be external or internal. As noted earlier, the external customer pays for bank services. An internal customer is typically an employee who receives the output of an activity and usually does not pay for it. In both situations, the customer defines what constitutes value. Employees should make every effort to ensure that every customer is satisfied on the first attempt to deliver value.

We cannot overemphasize the importance of capturing a task, process, or project value with precision, clarity, and completeness *before* the work begins to prevent unnecessary rework and delays. Most rework and waiting waste occur because the value specifications were incomplete, mutually conflicted, unclear, or ambiguous when the work started or because the creator did not understand the value perfectly.

Waiting and rework wastes in a bank can consume half of the entire work time of back office personnel. The wastes represent a huge productivity reserve that can be tapped by understanding and capturing value specifications correctly. Experience indicates that it is always better (and cheaper and faster) to invest time before starting work than correcting or redoing defective work.

Experienced managers know that written specifications tend to be imperfect ways to define value and often require additional verbal clarifications.

Any text written in a natural language—including specifications and requirements—is always somewhat ambiguous, if only because many words have multiple meanings. Furthermore, many employees and managers lack effective writing skills and are too rushed and impatient to write perfect specifications.

The lack of writing skill may be attributed to the lower standards of general education, the encroachment of computer technology, and the Internet culture. This book is not the place to diagnose or discuss this social phenomenon. However, the reality of poor writing skills must be noted as a factor that can impact bank operations.

Another problem with written specifications is that the writer's brain holds the entire context of the need for the given aspect of value, but the person reading the specification has no access to that context. The difference in understanding between writer and reader means that reliance on written specifications often results in misunderstandings, defects, rework, delays, and frustrations. How can we prevent these problems? First, create clarification channels between the specification originator and the person doing the work. Each involved employee should study the specifications for a specific task, make every attempt to understand their intent, and begin the work only after he or she has an absolutely clear understanding of the value to be created.

If a question arises about the meaning of the value before or during execution, a clarifying conversation should take place immediately. To facilitate such contacts, each written specification should include its author's name, e-mail, and phone number. Time is the most treasured commodity in Lean, so we should pursue all means to eliminate delays.

4.3.2 Principle 2: Mapping Value Stream

Definition: Plan and streamline an entire workflow or process while eliminating waste—The generic definition of planning has two components: (1) corporate-level planning and preparation of resources and (2) process or project planning.

Corporate level bank managers should prepare all needed resources (people, processes, and tools) that will serve subsequent projects and all routine work. Resources should include an infrastructure for the security and safety of data and physical spaces; continued employee education and training; creation of one or more communities of practice; a central database containing lessons learned and all procedures and data intended for reuse;

optimization and standardization of processes; preparation of physical and electronic infrastructure; rotation of key people; and strategic decisions for reuse of previous solutions in future projects. These activities will serve all subsequent bank processes and should be handled at the corporate level to enhance the long-term competitiveness of the bank. In contrast, process or project planning encompasses all the planning efforts for a specific bank project or process. This section will focus on this type of planning.

A key concept to grasp in the transition from a manufacturing environment to banking domain is that manufacturing involves transforming and moving material; while banking processes create, transform, move, and store information (data).*

At this point the hierarchy of terms (task, process, project, and value stream) should be defined.

A **task** is a self-contained work element or action that adds value and is performed by an individual employee or small team of cooperating employees. We define a task as a work element that is clearly specified and capable of transforming provided inputs into needed outputs without additional information except possibly for some clarifying information from an internal customer or supervisor (Figure 4.4). We assume that the employee performing a given task has appropriate levels of education, training, and experience (see vignette below). For a task to add value, a customer must need its outputs. If an activity has no customer, it is by definition a waste and should be eliminated.

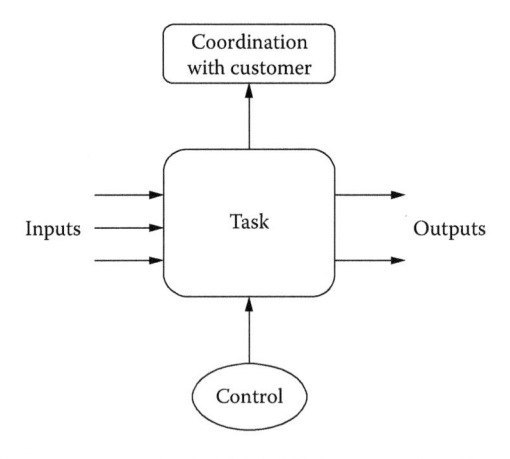

Figure 4.4   Task with inputs, outputs, control, and coordination with customer.

---

* Interestingly, in healthcare, the patient moves and his or her health is transformed.

Task Execution: Fundamental Rules for "Right the First Time"

- The employee knows what to do and has sufficient education, training, and needed tools.
- The employee has adequate time to complete the task well.
- The employee knows the internal customer by name and coordinates the task proactively with the customer (even when the customer provided prior written specifications). Both parties have achieved the same understanding of task scope and needed outputs. (This point can be waived for routine tasks that are unlikely to involve misinterpretations.)
- The employee knows what data to use in inputs, what constitutes good data, and where the sources of the data are.
- The employee knows his or her control person and mentor.
- The employee knows how to execute the task without the wastes of overproduction, overprocessing, defects, and excess inventories, waiting, transportation, and movement.
- The employee knows to pass the task results on to the customer immediately upon completion.

A **process** is a defined chain of tasks executed sequentially and/or concurrently, designed to create value for an internal or external customer. Each task in a process creates an element of value (Figure 4.5). The outputs of a task serve as inputs to other tasks. The final task delivers the expected value to the process customer. Some processes can be executed entirely within one department. Other processes such as loan approvals extend over several departments (sales, risk analysis, account service, IT, funds release, and possibly others). See vignette below.

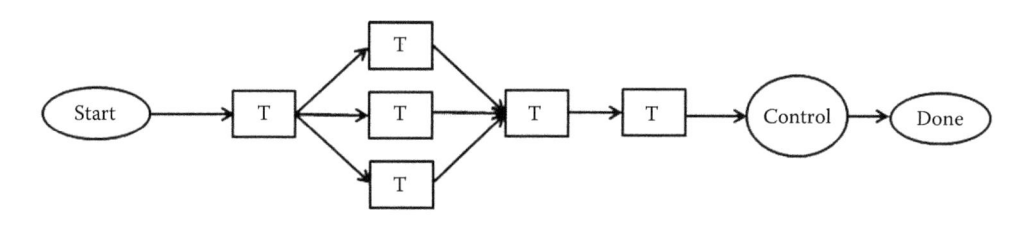

Figure 4.5   A process is a chain of sequential and concurrent tasks (T) that create value, with a control point.

Multi-Task Process Execution: Fundamental Rules for "Right the First Time"

- Each task is executed as listed in the Task Execution box above; tasks may be executed by a number of people or by a single multi-skilled individual.
- Each process has an "owner" who acts as the contact point for the process. The owner is responsible, accountable, and has authority (RAA) for the process success, and knows the work status at all times.
- Before a process is started, the value proposition it is to create has been captured completely, clearly, and without ambiguity.
- In the event questions arise or coordination is needed before or during process execution, the person originating the question must immediately seek the answer from the relevant party (customer, owner, mentor, supervisor).
- The process must be in a state of flow from the beginning to the end of the value creation. Waiting between tasks should be eliminated.

A **project** is a collaborative enterprise, typically involving in-depth analysis or design of a new bank product, service, transaction, or tool. A dedicated manager with adequate project management skills should lead a project team to create a desired value or benefit. Typically, each project consists of a number of processes. In bank environments, a typical project involves approximately 5 to 30 dedicated people for a period from several days to several months. Chapter 8 describes a super-efficient technique called Lean Product Development Flow (LPDF), which is highly applicable to most bank projects.

In most banks, the work of employees performed in back offices can be grouped into three categories: (1) one-time tasks or processes, (2) routine operations, and (3) special projects. Normally, only a minority of employees are assigned to dedicated projects. Another minority performs single custom-ordered tasks such as extracting or creating non-routine information needed only one time. Most employees work in routine bank operations and execute processes, such as in a tightly predefined sequence of activities.

For example, after a credit line or loan application has been filed, it follows a series of processes, such as approval decline of application; set up and activate account; make it operational for the user; assign employees to service the account; enter details into appropriate bank records; and perhaps dispense funds.

From the view of an individual employee, each process may appear as a single independent component he or she performs on a computer without even talking to other people. However, all bank processes must be well integrated, planned, prepared, executed, and monitored to enable the bank to function properly. This requires close cooperation of a number of employees and is the area where Lean provides dramatic benefits by helping organize and connect the work of many individuals into perfectly synchronized, integrated, streamlined, fast, and effective value streams.

This definition of a **value stream** has been adapted for banking applications from Womack and Jones [1996]. A value stream is a process required to create a specific bank product or service value. Normally, three critical management tasks are involved in a value stream: design and planning of the product or service, queue information flow, and value realization. Before a customer walks into a bank to request a loan, credit, or other service, the bank must have processes in place to be able to satisfy the customer; then address the information flow; inform employees what they are expected to do and when; and finally conduct the product or service realization, that is, actually perform the work that creates the value that the customer needs.

4.3.2.1 Mapping Current State Value Stream

The value stream is a widely accepted tool to help bank managers and employees observe the entire operation across the borders between departments. Value stream maps (VSMs) involve similar logic to the traditional process maps used with other improvement tools. However, they also include important vital information about time, wastes, and frustrations.

While no manuals focus on value stream mapping in bank operations, we recommend one that details value stream mapping in projects and product development programs [McManus, 2004]. The reader will also find useful handbooks on value stream mapping in the library of the Lean Enterprise Institute (LEI). The handbooks are slanted to manufacturing but the logical processes they describe can be adapted easily to bank operations.

All processes in all organizations including banks are of four forms:

1. What top management believes a process is
2. What the process really is (current state)
3. What the ideal process could be (ideal state)
4. What the process will be after streamlining (future state)

A critical first step is to visualize the existing process, capturing all its tasks, decision points and workflows, as well as all process wastes, problems, and frustrations by developing a current state map (CSM). We capture the information visually using simple index cards displayed on a wall to indicate all the tasks performed and the sequence in which they are performed. If the workflow splits into several paths depending on a decision, all such paths and decision points must be included. In fact, capturing paths and decision points is usually the key to Lean improvement because most bank waste hides in such convoluted decision points and paths.

If the entire process is contained within a single bank department, only employees from that department are needed to map it simply because people understand the work of their own departments. When the flow extends over multiple departments—most bank processes fall into this category—mapping becomes more complex because departments are specialized and most employees have only superficial knowledge of activities in other departments. High-level managers are normally not helpful in mapping because they are not familiar with the work details of specific departments.

Many wastes occur at the boundaries between departments. Typically, one department rejects data provided by another department on the basis that it is incorrect, incomplete, unclear, or not formatted correctly. The results are wastes of rework, waiting, and overproduction. Some data waits in long queues when crossing departmental boundaries; some bounces back and forth between departments like a ping-pong ball, halting progress and frustrating employees.

What is the solution? Value stream mapping by a team that includes a competent person from each department involved, led by a leader experienced in Lean. Before proceeding, the team must identify the customer, understand what value is being created, and establish a clear starting point for the process. The team should not try to devise a CSM sitting in a remote room, because they will risk mapping the process how they believe it is rather than how it actually is.

The best way to create CSM is to walk through the process work area, from person to person and from task to task to visualize the components of the map to be created, all the time being mentally "attached" to the information being created. Team members should talk to each person along the way, observing and measuring task durations, asking pointed questions, and recording the answers on index cards (one per task or decision point). Suggested questions are:

- What happens next in this process?
- Which task should be done next?
- Who is the internal customer for this task?
- What outputs does the customer collect?
- What frequent frustrations do you face in executing your task? Examples are waiting, quality problems, rejections and rework, training issues, tool downtime, unclear instructions, procedures or checklists, and excessive variability of outcomes.

We continue the questioning for each task until we reach the point at which value is delivered.

Each task is categorized and posted on a card in the appropriate color (green for value adding; yellow for necessary non-value adding; and red for pure waste). The colored cards or notes are displayed on a wall as soon as they are completed for each task or decision point.

Do not count on mapping the entire workflow in one pass through a task area. More often, the answer to "What happens next" is "It depends." This answer may represent a decision fork (an "if" statement in computer programmer language) where a worker must decide which of several possible paths is to be followed and when and why. The decision points should be shown on pink or purple cards placed on the wall at 45° angles to the floor, with different paths illustrated at the corners. Unfortunately, "It depends" usually indicates that an employee does not know what happens next, that decisions are made ad hoc, and the workers do not follow a planned process.

These points of a flow usually reveal waste. Lean practitioners look at them as "gold" because they represent opportunities to improve a process, eliminate the wastes, and streamline the flow. In this case we keep asking (and asking, and asking …) until we define all the tasks, their paths and sequences, inputs and outputs, and all wastes and frustrations. This process should not be carried out by impatient people. It requires patience and tact and cooperation with team colleagues to analyze workflow and distill the steps on cards for display.

In mapping, there is no good substitute for observing the actual work. Unfortunately, observation often intimidates employees and makes them nervous and suspicious. It is important that leaders inform the involved employees that they will be contacted and observed. They should be notified before mapping starts and understand that the sole purpose of the observation is to examine the overall workflow. Usually, a leader can boost confidence of his employees by asking them about their frustrations. A leader should never criticize; his or her goal is to find imperfections in the system.

The best people to involve in the mapping are those who are well trained in Lean and who understand the work details and frustrations. If only supervisors perform mapping, employees may fear negative judgments, particularly if a supervisor is not well liked. People working on mapping should keep in mind that it is always better to ask *why* than to ask *who*.

As we place the cards on the wall, we should draw the connecting lines between them to indicate the direction of workflow. The first CSM is usually a mess. It should be redrawn with clean, non-intersecting lines, standard symbols, and clearly aligned color cards. Figure 4.6 illustrates the standard symbols of value stream mapping.

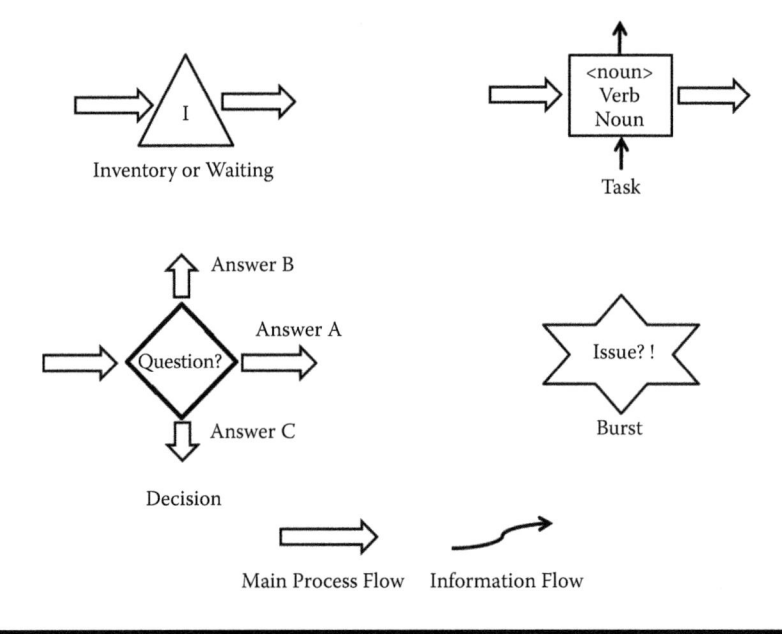

Figure 4.6 Standard symbols used in value stream mapping. (From Lean Academy, 2008. With permission.)

The current state map on the wall should show all tasks in actual sequence, all decision points and paths, and all wastes and frustrations of the present system. The CSM is a big milestone because it indicates a good understanding of how tasks are performed. Many employees are stunned when they see the extent of the existing wastes and they are ready "to convert" to Lean Thinking.

Performing VSM in an office where experienced people routinely execute bank operations often leads to amazing observations, for example, "We did not really understand the flow of work; everyone had only a myopic view of one's own operation." After a CSM is generated, the level of understanding of the whole picture rises dramatically. The completion is exciting because it is the first illustration of all the waste and it clearly shows numerous opportunities for improvement.

Development of a CSM takes one to a few days for a medium complexity banking process but the time is not wasted. The reward comes next when we map the future state map (FSM).

4.3.2.2 Mapping Future State Value Stream

During the FSM process, we eliminate all NVA activities revealed by the CSM, minimize all NNVA activities as much as possible in compliance with all regulations, simplify the flow, enable the remaining activities to flow without rework, backflow or stopping (see Principle 3), and improve quality. The same small team of competent people from each department should perform both CSM and FSM. They should already be familiar with Lean tools and the various categories of wastes. Helpful questions to ask during FSM are:

- Is this task really necessary?
- Does it contribute to value?
- Who is the internal customer for the task? If a task has no customer, it is likely a waste and should be eliminated.
- Can the task be simplified by requiring fewer data entries on a form?
- Can we reduce overproduction waste?
- Is this task in the right position along the time line? Should it be moved forward or back?
- Can the task be combined with another step to save time or to eliminate redundancy?
- Can the task be executed concurrently with one or more other tasks? (More tasks executed at the same time shorten overall process lead time.)

- Do we need this separate path? It is a bureaucratic path that contributes nothing to value?
- How can we eliminate every waste and frustration discovered in this task?
- Is this task a bottleneck? Would the flow accelerate if we increased the capacity of the task? By how much?
- How can we make this task more predictable, less variable, of higher quality?
- Is the task well defined? Is it accompanied by a clear procedure or checklist?
- How can we optimize the task to make it execute faster without anyone working faster but everyone working smarter?
- What components of this task cause stakeholder complaints? What can we do to eliminate the frustrations and improve communication and coordination?
- Does data move along efficiently in single-piece flow without delays from batching?
- Would it make sense to introduce tools of Lean (Chapter 5), such as *kanban*, visual controls, and mistake-proofing devices?

Typically, even a first-attempt FSM can indicate a dramatic reduction in the number of tasks, workflow paths, and decision points. Figure 4.7 illustrates a CSM and FSM for a large bank credit approval process. Figure 4.7a shows the CSM for a traditional stove-piped bank where department tribes matter more than bank clients.

Four departments are involved: Sales, which works with the client to collect data needed for credit application and prepares the application package, then Risk, Credit Committee, and even Management Board if large credit is sought. The package is sent to the Risk department, which first assesses the risk based on available pre-computed guidelines, and then sends the result to the Risk officer. The Risk officer often determines that the application package is incomplete and sends a request for the missing data to the Sales department. The Sales representative contacts the client, obtains the missing data, and resubmits the application, which follows the second path through the Risk department. The Risk officer may now reject, approve, or change the terms of the credit—in which case the package is sent back to the client for another iteration. The application process may still be sent to the Credit Committee for a decision, which again may be approval, rejection, or a change of terms in which case the package returns to the Sales department

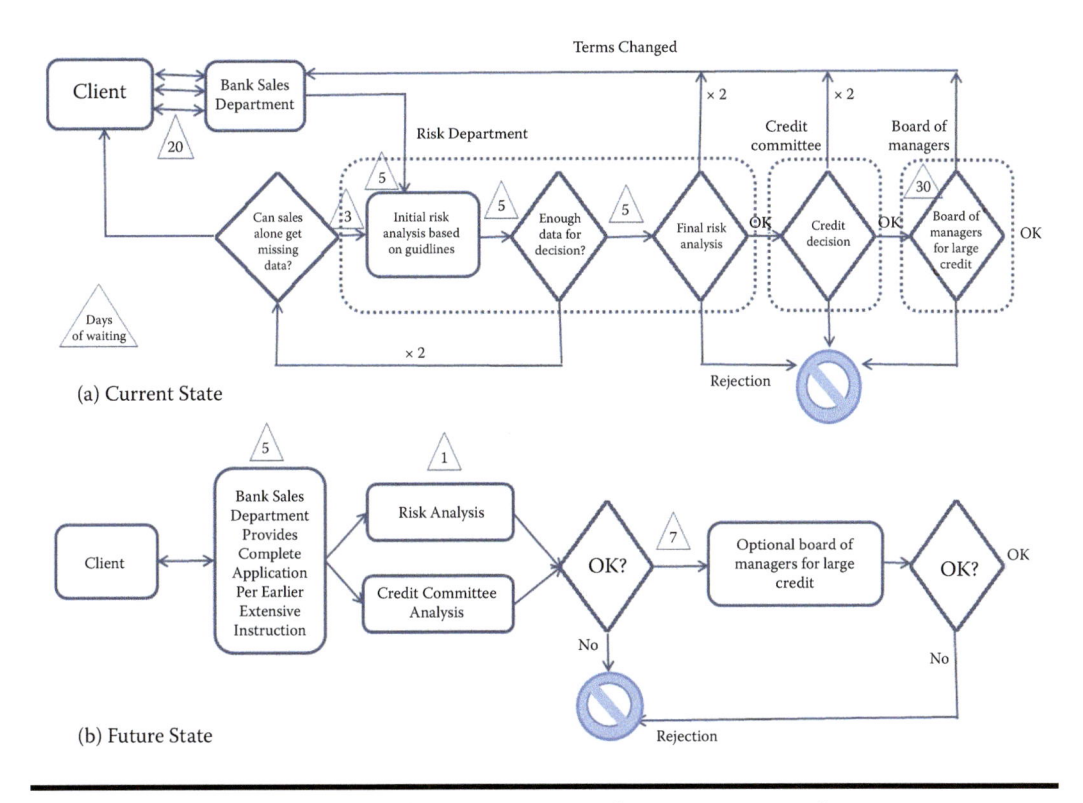

Figure 4.7   (a) Current state value stream map. (b) Future state value stream map.

for coordination with the client. If the Credit Committee approves the application and the credit is for a large amount, an approval by the Board of Managers may still be required. Since the Board meets only monthly, up to one month may elapse before the Board decision is announced, which again may be approval, rejection, or change of terms. If the Board changes the terms, the decision goes back to Sales and the client, and the process is restarted. Summing up the days of waiting, we obtain between 38 and 120 days for the entire approval process, depending on the number of iterations and the calendar of the Board. And we have counted only the waiting wastes. In reality, wastes of other types may be concealed in the process. Banks must understand that few clients are willing to wait a minimum of 38 days for a decision. In the highly competitive banking industry, some clients will give up and seek a more efficient bank.

Figure 4.7b illustrates a possible FSM for a Lean bank. All sales officers have rotated through the Risk and Credit departments to learn about their requirements or pursued in-depth training in preparation of complete application packages to ensure that all data required by all groups involved in processing the transaction is included. A bank should have no need to ask a client to reiterate an application if it works closely with its clients and follows efficient procedures, checklists, and guidelines. Sales staff should prepare a complete and error-free application package in five days or less with full explanations of all credit terms. The package should go immediately to Risk and Credit groups for prompt (maximum of one day) analyses and decision using parallel processing.

The bank would have no need to reiterate the package if it is well prepared at the start. If the Risk and Credit groups approve, the application is ready for account initiation; if the amount exceeds a predetermined level, the transaction is referred to the Board that should be set up to make its decision in seven days or less. Thus, the client receives a decision in six to twelve days. Clearly, a bank that completes the large credit application transaction in one or two weeks is far more competitive than a bank that needs twenty weeks.

Experience indicates that process time and cost reductions of 30% to 40% can be expected on the first attempt of moving from the CSM to FSM. With experience, this number may be significantly higher. Lean practitioners laugh when people speak of a cost or time reductions of a few percent. The power of Lean in uncovering productivity reserves is dramatically greater than a few percent.

The opportunities to streamline FSM never end. The more efficiency we discover, the more opportunities we see for improvements. Each FSM iteration creates new cost and time reductions and quality and customer satisfaction improvements. Employees become enthusiastic when they see significant improvements in a short time. Additionally, the mapping process fosters teamwork that improves cooperation among departments. Employees understand the importance of speed and quality of an entire process rather than focusing on activities of their own departments. Cooperation improves work quality and productivity; stove-piped operations become weaker.

4.3.3 Principle 3: Flow

Definition: Flow work through planned and streamlined value-adding steps and processes, without stopping, idling, unplanned rework, or backflow—Work must flow continuously. Managers who do not understand Lean may claim, "It is OK for a project to wait as long as people are busy on other projects and do not waste bank time." This rationale is completely wrong in Lean Thinking.

Processes create value. A process that becomes idle delays value creation and makes process customers wait. Internal processes exist ultimately to serve external customers. The faster we create value to external customers, the faster we can collect profits. A wise man said, "Our bank does not pay wages; the external customers pay our wages; our bank only moves the money." Keeping people busy for the sake of keeping them busy does not contribute to value creation, external customer satisfaction, or competitiveness. The key to making profits is to think in terms of workflow and processes that contribute to creation of value for customers.

We all work in corporate organizational structures that are divided into departments. Each employee has a department manager who allocates the work, sometimes receives the result and checks its correctness, plans and manages department resources (people, processes, tools, and budgets), and coordinates the work with other departments. In Lean banks, supervisors see their primary responsibility as enabling their people to enable the entire horizontal* flow of value through the process tasks, across their own department and on to the next department along the value stream. Good managers provide the best resources, procedures, training and mentoring, motivation, and coordination for their department to contribute to the horizontal flow of value creation with minimum waste.

In contrast, in many traditional banks, the entire mental focus seems vertical. The supervisor assigns a task to an employee who creates and returns the output back to the supervisor without knowing who created the inputs (typically not the supervisor) and who is ultimately the internal customer for the output after the supervisor sees it. All energy is directed to satisfying the supervisor because all employees in traditional departments know the supervisor evaluates and judges their work. This type of operation follows a stove-piped or vertical focus; it is the curse of traditional organizations.

The vertical focus places little importance on coordination and speeding the workflows across the departments. Traditional managers forget that their key role is that of a traffic cop who coordinates, directs, and enables processes in the most efficient way. In traditional banks, the boundaries between departments tend to be tribal, rigid, and territorially protected by their managers. The legitimate needs of security and safety exacerbate these problems. In Lean banks, work flows efficiently across all department

---

* The terms *horizontal* and *vertical* have meaning when we look at an organizational chart of the bank. Horizontal flows are across departments. Vertical flows are within departmental or divisional *stovepipes*, from supervisor to employee, and back, or to/from higher-level managers.

boundaries and remains fully compliant with all security and safety rules and regulations.

Lean banks focus on organizing all work into efficient horizontal value streams that ultimately serve external customers. Each value stream is optimized and standardized, and all resources—people, processes, tools, and budgets—are aligned toward value creation. Each value stream has an "owner" whose primary responsibilities are (1) to ensure the fastest and best quality creation of value for the internal or external customers (or groups of customers) engaged in the value stream, (2) follow the progress of the value stream, and (3) know the status of work at all times. It is critical to eliminate "orphan" processes for which no one feels responsible.

Because the horizontal flows are so important, it is logical to ask why a bank needs a departmental structure. The vertical organization is needed for several good reasons: maintaining security and safety of bank and client data; developing specialized and state-of-the-art skills, tools, processes, and resources; and developing skilled employees. The departmental (vertical) organization works well as long as the departmental managers and their employees keep in mind the need to serve their internal and external customers via horizontal workflows.

Some bank departments such as the risk group must have significant autonomy. A healthy bank risk department assesses the risks of proposed transactions without undue pressures from colleagues in other departments. Every effort should be made to serve the internal and external customers of the risk department as efficiently as possible.

The implementation of a future state map tends to be a highly satisfying task. Chapter 5 describes a number of flow-enabling tools. As a bank implements a future state map, employees and managers tend to see tangible improvements in productivity and quality almost from the onset. Before Lean, work flowed from manager to employee and back. In the future state, flow will be horizontal, like a river that flows as employees add value. Employees can see the entire flow and become more involved, engaged, and eager to contribute. They see a higher purpose in their work and understand how their work fits into the larger operations of the bank.

As waste is removed, the flow gains speed, not because employees work faster, but because the bank eliminated the causes of slow-downs that impede flow like rocks in a river. The flow becomes more visible and more predictable. Employees do not work faster; they are much more engaged and eager to perform better. They work smarter. This is the beginning of a seemingly endless process of continuous improvement. Suddenly, we see the imperfections, flow gaps, waiting, and quality problems that we never saw earlier or found too late—when a controlling manager detected a problem or a client complained. Now, we discover imperfections as we work. We are motivated to fix them to speed up the flow until we see the next imperfection, and so on. The operation becomes a positive feedback loop; the better we become, the better we want to become, and the improvement process never ends.

4.3.4 Principle 4: Pull

Definition: Let customers pull value. Do not push work onto the next task; let work be pulled by internal customers as needed.

In manufacturing, the pull principle is profoundly important. It led to the incredibly efficient system called Just-in-Time (JIT) in which parts and material arrive and are used exactly when needed, without having to maintain batches or inventories. In banking applications, work does not proceed exactly JIT, but the pull principle has three important aspects.

1. The inclusion of any task in a process must be "pulled" or justified by a specific need of an internal or external customer. Too many tasks are ordered by managers' whims, based only on a bureaucratic need to cover his or her butt or minimize the risk of criticism. In poorly managed organizations, as many as 30 to 50% of all tasks executed are not needed. Everyone in a bank should resist unnecessary tasks aggressively. Someone must need every task output. The need must be legitimate, necessary to create value for a customer, and not performed for bureaucratic reasons.

   Often in bank applications the "devil is in the details." Consider a complex form containing many boxes for data. Is it possible that some of the boxes were added ad hoc for a one-time special need? If so, why are they still there if they are no longer needed? Some forms have fields for data that is needed only in exceptional situations, but the average person completing the forms will not know that. If an internal customer can justify asking for such exotic data in special cases, make the relevant data entry optional (applicable only to special cases) and relieve the 99% or so of the customers completing the form from the task. Of course, the form instructions should describe the exceptions. Normally, this step alone will free significant productivity reserves.

2. A task should be completed when the customer needs the output; excessively early completion leads to "shelf life obsolescence," including possible human forgetfulness or changes of external situations, currency conversions, regulations, and other factors. Late completion leads to schedule slippage. In other words, tasks should be completed early enough to prevent waiting but not so early that they will become obsolete and need to be redone. To resolve this dichotomy, experienced managers must make rational decisions.

3. Banks waste significant amounts of time and human effort redoing what could have been done right the first time with better preparation. In some departments, as much as 30% of all work must be redone, even though it could have been done right the first time with better planning, training, mentoring, coordination, and communication. As noted above in the discussion of the Value Principle, employees often rely on imperfect verbal or written specifications and instructions, and do the work according to their understanding of what needs to be done, only to hear "this is not what I needed" from their internal customers. When that happens, emotions flare, managers become involved, mutual blaming and shaming follow, and the task needs to be redone, obviously wasting time and resources.

In our complex world, we should not rely exclusively on quick verbal or even written specifications for a task. Additional clarifications are needed for most non-routine work. Typically, such clarifications need not be extensive; often a five-minute direct conversation between the parties involved is sufficient. Thus, we introduce the following rule:

> To avoid the wastes of defects and rework for every non-routine task, identify your internal customer (the next person in the value chain and not necessarily your manager), and coordinate the task scope, outputs, formats, and whatever else needs to be coordinated with this individual before you begin working on the task. When both sides have a perfect identical understanding of the task, proceed to execution. If questions arise during execution, contact the internal customer again for clarification.

By routinely practicing this rule, banks can avoid rework and execute tasks right the first time. This can help boost productivity. For best results, one needs a Lean Thinking internal customer as well as a Lean Thinking information supplier. A customer who makes arbitrary demands prevents a Lean outcome. Uncontrolled pull tends to create chaos. In the cases of rare disagreements about task scope, the appropriate manager should be consulted [Oppenheim, 2011].

4.3.5 Principle 5: Perfection

Definition: Make all imperfections visible and use Continuous Improvement to pursue perfection.

Global competition is a brutal "race without a finish line" [Schmidt et al., 1992] that requires continuous improvements of processes, services, and products. Despite the brutality of the race, no bank can afford to spend resources improving every operation all the time. To clarify the issue of what to improve and when, we must distinguish between processes and process outputs.

Perfecting and refining the work output of a given task must be bounded by the overall value proposition (product or service success plus budget and schedule considerations) that defines when an output is good enough. Otherwise, waste from over-processing may result. Experienced bankers who are responsible for the overall flow of value should judge when an output is good enough. In contrast, banking processes and procedures must be improved continuously for never-ending competitive reasons. It is important for a bank to understand the distinction between perfecting a process and perfecting the process output, and provide resources accordingly.

Next, we must ask which processes to improve. No bank has enough resources to improve all its processes all the time. How should a bank prioritize its needs? Two features of Lean suggest the answer: (1) making all imperfections in the workplace visible to all and (2) prioritizing by eliminating the greatest impediments to flow (or largest rock slowing the river flow). Seeing problems as they appear in real time is conducive to better decisions about corrective actions and better prioritization of improvements. Remember that imperfections tend to grow into crises. When noticed early, imperfections are usually easier and less expensive to fix than subsequent crises that may require heroic actions. The visibility of imperfections motivates employees to apply continuous improvement in real time [Morgan and Liker, 2006].

A Lean bank should create an effective infrastructure for capturing knowledge, lessons learned, and continuous education to make each subsequent work effort better than the last. An office culture in which employees are not afraid to identify imperfections (mistakes, defects, rework, excessive effort) requires highly developed human relations based not on "being nice to each other," but more importantly on teamwork, honesty, openness, respect, leadership, job stability, and lack of fear. The blaming-and-shaming culture will effectively kill Lean initiatives and has no place in a Lean bank. Lean Principle 6 emphasizes this point.

4.3.6 *Principle 6: Respect for People*

Definition: Develop teamwork, highest levels of skills, honesty, openness, respect, leadership, job stability, and lack of fear.

Only about 50 years ago, corporate culture was based on harsh discipline, lack of job stability, fear, and lots of yelling, blaming, and shaming. Only managers knew best and line employees knew to "check their brains at the door" [Graban, 2009]. The present corporate culture tends to be superficially more pleasant; people tend to be polite to each other and avoid confrontations, but this culture is still a long way from the Lean ideal.

A Lean bank organization recognizes that its people are its most important resources and adopts high-performance work practices [e.g., Gittell, 2003]. In a Lean bank, instead of blaming each other, employees strive together to eliminate system problems. They are not afraid to identify problems and imperfections honestly and openly in real time, brainstorm to find root causes and corrective actions, and plan effective solutions together to prevent problems from recurring.

When issues arise, the system (not the messenger) is blamed. Employees are empowered to make decisions and resolve conflicts at the lowest possible level. Experienced and knowledgeable leaders lead, train, and mentor; they also empower line employees to solve problems immediately. Employees feel that they are a part of the same team and help each other. They do not compete among themselves; they compete ferociously with competition banks. Such an environment requires a culture of mutual respect and trust, open and honest communication, teamwork, and synergistic and cooperating relationships of stakeholders [Sugimori et al., 1977]. An effective corporate culture involves more than just "being nice."

Respect for people does not mean that managers give employees latitude to do their jobs however they please out of a sense of trust as long as the results are good. In a bank that uses Lean principles, managers and leaders frequently verify work details. This is done out of respect for the external customer to ensure proper outcomes and quality, and can be achieved in a way that shows respect for employees. The goal is not happy employees because that could be accomplished by several superficial (and costly) methods that might not improve customer service. Respect in a Lean context means challenging people and pushing them to perform better in a constructive way and developing employees and their careers.

Mark Graban, 2009

4.4 Lean Applies to One-Off Projects Equally Well as to Repetitive Work

A frequent concern of people unfamiliar with Lean is that Lean applies only to repeated production and is not applicable to unique work in a bank. Not so. The genius of Lean is that it captures the characteristics of all work types, from totally unique to repeated processes such as making deposits and assembling cars. Lean draws a critical distinction between a process and process content defined as the information flowing through the process. Lean helps us notice that processes involve common steps or tasks.

Process content (data moving through the process) is, of course, unique every time. The understanding that processes are common leads to important next steps: process optimization, streamlining, and standardization to ensure that any unique situation flowing through the process can be executed predictably, in the shortest time, with minimum cost and maximum quality, with no one working faster.

A common myth is that standardization is the enemy of creativity and that it removes intelligence from the process. In Section 5.5, we provide solid arguments showing why this myth is totally wrong. In fact, standardization aids creativity because it frees employees' intellectual capacities from having to reinvent the wheel every time and allows them to focus on better ways of doing the work. **Standardization is supposed to capture the current best way of doing work, and is subject to change when a better method is discovered.**

The myth that "Lean applies only to repeated production and not to my unique project" can be easily dismissed by a simple mental exercise of stepping through the six Lean Principles to confirm that every principle applies just as well to a unique one-off situation as it does to repeated work.

The Value Principle notes that we must properly capture the value of whatever task or process or value stream before we start the work. This is obvious and clear: we must understand what we need to create. If we do not understand what is to be done, how can we create it well? The chance that we will create something useful by accident is nil. This reasoning applies as much to one-off as to repeated work.

The Value Stream Principle: After we understand what needs to be created (the value), we must plan the work without waste using our best experience, knowledge, and comprehensive coordination among the stakeholders. Without planning, we are bound to waste our time and resources, repeat steps, wait for others, and bounce back and forth. This clearly applies to any quantity of work items, from unique one-off jobs to repeated work.

The Flow Principle: When we understand value (what needs to be done) and the value stream (streamlined plan showing how to do it), we are ready to do the work. Ideally we should flow the work as a continuous sequence of tasks performed with no waiting, backflow, or rework. The work status and progress must be fully visible. The work of a process must move. If the flow does not move, the value creation halts and the effort consumes only time and resources. The ideal continuous flow clearly applies equally well whether we perform a task once or repeat it many times.

The Pull Principle: Performing the work only if and when needed and connecting the individual tasks on the basis of need is the essence of efficient streamlined work. Again, this concept applies to one-off as much as it applies to repeated work.

The Perfection Principle: Creating a system in which all imperfections become immediately visible is conducive to continuous improvement and elimination of problems. This applies equally to one-off and repeated work.

The Respect for People Principle: By striving to develop the best possible human relations, all employees feel as if they belong on the same team, working together, respecting each other, and creating the best work quality possible. This principle applies to both one-off tasks and repeated work.

In conclusion, we see that all six Lean Principles apply to unique one-off work situations as much as to repeated or routine work. Womack and Jones

[1996] deserve our gratitude for capturing the essence of all Lean work into these six simple principles.

4.5 Symphony of Lean Principles

The six Lean Principles fit together like a symphony of orchestra players, in perfect alignment to create the best music (value) with minimum waste, and satisfying the audience (stakeholders). The Lean Academy [2008] illustrates the alignment in Figure 4.8.

All six Lean Principles are critical to success; none can be ignored; and no principle is more important than any of the others. However, the principles differ in their degrees of implementation difficulty. Experienced bank managers will agree readily that even highly technical challenges are easier to address than changing human relations and bank corporate culture. Let us review these challenges individually for each Lean Principle.

The <u>Value Principle</u> is easy to formulate for routine bank operations. However, for complex financial products and services, value formulation with sufficient clarity and completeness may be a challenge due to a complex regulatory environment. The initial understanding of a needed outcome is often vague and incomplete, but the outcome must be produced perfectly. Success requires a robust but efficient process of capturing value, cooperation of all stakeholders formulating the value proposition, and leadership.

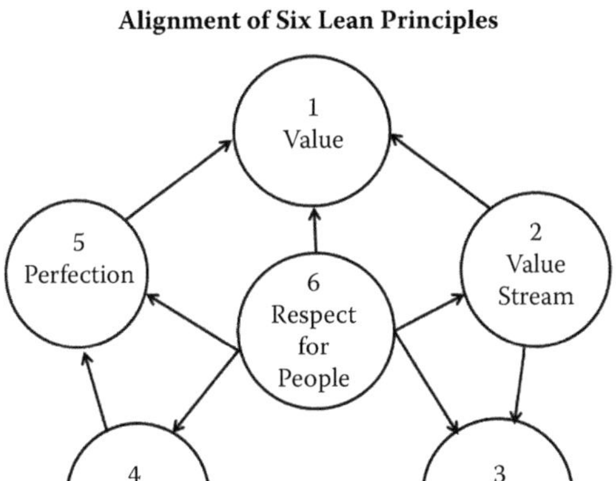

Alignment of Six Lean Principles

Figure 4.8 Alignment of the six Lean Principles. (From Lean Academy, 2008. With permission.)

Success also needs people with solid experience in bank operations, the ability to think in sufficiently large contexts, and creativity.

The Value Stream Mapping Principle requires a good understanding of three disciplines: banking laws and internal safety and security regulations, customer needs, and Lean practice. It also needs teamwork, a solid understanding of waste, patience, and the time to create the plan properly. Good value stream mapping can pay tremendous dividends in cost and schedule savings and value quality. Therefore, mapping must not be rushed. The initial effort may involve a steep learning curve, but each subsequent project becomes significantly easier as a bank practices value stream mapping.

The Flow Principle: The ease or difficulty implementing the flow principle depends on the clarity and stability of the value proposition and the degree of detail on the future state map. If both requirements are filled properly, it is much easier to achieve robust, predictable, and efficient flow. In a well-functioning Lean process, employees and managers know when flow progressing along a path stops without the need for exotic and expensive metrics.

Flow efficiency absolutely requires workers to treat each value stream "as the most important thing in the world," and the designation of one person ("owner") who is responsible and accountable and has the authority to pursue process success and always knows the status and progress of the process. The owner must have a vested interest in seeing the workflow continuously without stopping, backflow, or rework. He or she pushes the workflow across departmental boundaries and does not allow it to sit idly on desks or in computer memory.

The Pull Principle: In manufacturing, the Pull Principle and the closely related Single-Piece Flow production (Section 5.8) are the most challenging steps to implement because they require perfect and predictable production and delivery of parts and materials just-in-time. In contrast, in bank operations, JIT is not as crucial. Tasks must be completed *before* their outputs are needed (too-early completion may make the output obsolete; too-late completion causes waits and delays). The exact timing of outputs in a bank is not as strict. Instead, solid planning of task precedence and excellent coordination of tasks for a right-the-first-time execution are critical and fairly easy to implement. A bit more difficult aspect of the Pull Principle is tailoring tasks and eliminating unneeded tasks, as discussed in Section 4.3.4.

The Perfection Principle requires that imperfections be made visible along with motivation and infrastructure for continuous improvement of processes. To make imperfections visible, employee fear must be absent (this requires the Respect Principle to be in place). The Perfection Principle also needs an infrastructure for handling a knowledge and lessons learned database, training, mentoring, and education.

The <u>Respect for People Principle</u> may be the most difficult to implement if an enterprise starts from a traditional authoritarian, stove-piped, bureaucratic culture based on fear. The transformation requires solid knowledge of Lean, excellent leadership, corporate support, workforce training, mentoring, and lots of good examples.

Finally, and most importantly, effective Lean implementation requires strong support from top executives.

Chapter 5

Tools of Lean

This chapter describes a comprehensive set of powerful tools for implementing Lean Thinking in a bank. Most of the tools described originated at Toyota's manufacturing facilities* and some emanated from high-performance work practices [Gittell, 2003; Oppenheim, 2011]. Over the past two decades we have learned that many of the tools are extremely useful in office and service applications, so we have adopted them to banking. These tools are powerful enablers of the Lean process.

For didactical reasons, we describe the tools individually in this chapter. However, the tools represent an integrated system of Lean and every tool described here is important to success. All the tools discussed are conducive to waste elimination and better creation of value.

It is important not to limit Lean deployment to the tools; this will almost certainly guarantee failure. The Lean tools constitute just one element of the comprehensive integrated and balanced Lean organization of work.

In Section 5.1, we begin with the **6S method** intended to order the workplace, minimize the time and effort spent looking for documents and information, and decrease the risk of losing documents or using the wrong items. The 6S technique represents the six phases[†] of creating order in the workplace. Conceptually, the approach is as simple as the annual cleaning of a closet or garage. In the context of bank operations, however,

---

* The set of Toyota Production System tools developed for factories is larger than what we present in this book. We ignored tools that do not apply to bank operations, at least not in the early phases of Lean implementation.

† Their names start with a sound similar to the English *s* in Japanese; thus the unusual name.

computer data structures and bank and client data security, safety, and fraud prevention take the 6S standards to new levels of perfection.

Section 5.2 introduces **quality assurance**, a rich topic critically important to Lean success. As is well known, banking operations have very low tolerance for mistakes and work defects. While perfectly balancing all financial transactions is a matter of bank routine, mistakes, defects, and rework are common, and we describe the best known methods for avoiding them that are far more effective than top-down discipline.

Section 5.3 addresses another rich area critical for all banks: **continuous improvement (CI)** of processes. The banking industry is very competitive, forcing all banks to continually improve their products and processes, and we discuss the challenges of prioritizing various improvement needs and describe the most powerful improvement methods. Lean deployment cannot be separated from CI. As in the line that "love and marriage go together like a horse and carriage" from an old song,[*] Lean and quality should be seen as an inseparable pair of management paradigms. Lean focuses on ensuring the best flow of work through various predictable processes, with minimum waste, in the fastest possible time, at minimum cost, and with the highest quality. In practice, as the workflow accelerates, it inevitably encounters impediments in the forms of excessively variable or dysfunctional processes. This is when we use the CI tools to make processes predictable and efficient. Typically, as we improve a process, the overall flow of work accelerates until it meets the next biggest impediment, which we then fix using CI methods, and so on. This is a never-ending process of work improvement. The more we implement Lean, the more opportunities we discover for more levels of quality improvements.

Section 5.4 describes **benchmarking**, the process of comparing our bank to its competitors and learning from the comparison. This requires banks to know their competitors, assess their quality of work, and learn how these competitors do business legally and ethically.

Section 5.5 deals with other critical bank operations: **Standard Work**, **work procedures**, and **checklists**. From their observations in a wide array of industries, the authors conclude that procedures and checklists are common but not implemented effectively. These standards and procedures are ineffective for many reasons including lack of process optimization, lack

---

[*] The Frank Sinatra song begins with "Love and marriage, love and marriage, go together like a horse and carriage. This I tell ya, brother. You can't have one without the other." Copyright Cahn Music Co., 1955.

of clarity, failure to test, inadequate training and time to learn standards, absence of follow-up after the release of a procedure, bureaucracy, and poor corporate culture. Section 5.5 explains the ideal development and implementation of effective procedures and checklists and the significant benefits to be gained from effective standards.

Section 5.6 describes the Japanese ***Kanban*** system. It is a set of simple, user-friendly, powerful visual or electronic signals of readiness for the next element of work. When implemented properly, it can eliminate the need for most central planning of work sequences, reduce excessive inventories, and balance and synchronize work elements easily.

Section 5.7 presents **Visual Controls**—another amazingly simple but powerful tool of Lean used to display all important information about work status, quality, delays, imperfections, trends, and other non-confidential important data on large marker boards (or TV screens) visible to all employees in public spaces such as main walls and corridors. Visual Controls display all the information that employees need. Of course, it does not display confidential or financial information. It is used to show important trends such as the number of clients, transaction processing times, loan or credit application times, measures of customer satisfaction, and other factors. The boards and TV screens are used in Lean work to trigger an important psychological effect motivating employees toward effective teamwork focused on value creation with minimum waste. The controls help uncover problems early, avoid waste, and prevent crises.

Section 5.8 describes the so-called **Single-Piece Flow** of work and destroys the popular myth that work in batches is more efficient. Hopefully our arguments are powerful enough to completely eliminate batch processing of work cases.

Section 5.9 illustrates adoption of the **Production Work Cell** concept to bank processes to achieve dramatic improvements in processing time, quality, and morale. What normally takes a week now can be done in one day and no one has to work faster!

Section 5.10 provides motivation to design and use various mistake-proofing devices, automated alarms, and warnings that detect employee and client mistakes, and immediately prompt a user to make a correction. The devices are collectively known as ***Poka Yoke***. We all know such devices from our daily work and life; an example is an electric water kettle that automatically turns itself off when the water starts boiling. Because we all rely so heavily on computers for our work, it is relatively easy to implement these devices in software to enhance work efficiency and quality. Bank processes offer particularly fertile ground for using such devices.

Section 5.11 describes the managerial practice called *Gemba* by which managers frequently visit and become engaged in the workplaces of their employees and look for opportunities to improve systems. The managers do not visit work areas to check on, control, or intimidate employees. The aim is to assist employees with problems proactively to prevent more serious issues and delays from affecting bank operations.

Section 5.12 promotes the use of comprehensive and well-designed **Databases** of lessons learned and former risks and case studies. Banks that are capable of learning from their past experiences and mistakes tend not to repeat the mistakes. A bank that fails to learn or cannot find the time to fix problems repeats the same mistakes and ultimately destroys its own competitiveness.

Section 5.13 describes various **Communities of Practice** for sharing bank experiences at department and corporate levels and through professional societies at local, state, and national levels. These communities of practice tend to be voluntary, informal, friendly gatherings of people who perform similar work, learn from one another, exchange experiences, discuss case studies, and provide advice. Of course, these communities do not share bank secrets or sensitive information. They involve informal discussions of best practices and lessons learned.

Finally, Section 5.14 introduces a preformatted **A3** form for routine reporting and addressing problems. The A3 effectively and efficiently replaces wordy or unclear memoranda and time-consuming reports. It helps develop and efficiently presents proposed solutions to problems and provides a standardized format for sharing, sorting, cataloging, documenting, and archiving information.

Figure 5.1 illustrates the interconnectedness of the tools in the "Lean house" model. As noted earlier, several Japanese terms have become so well established in Lean practice in the Western world, that we use them in this book and in the figure. Most of the terms explained in this chapter are also listed in the glossary at the end of the book.

The overarching goal of a Lean bank is to achieve the highest possible customer satisfaction by providing the highest quality of services and products at the lowest cost and creating value in the shortest time. Only an

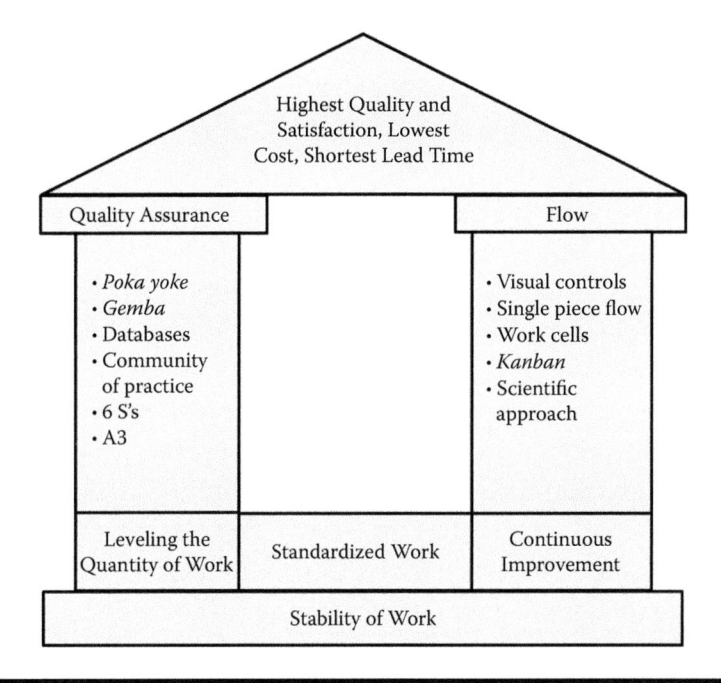

Figure 5.1   The "Lean House." (From Lean Academy, 2008. With permission.)

extraordinarily developed and motivated workforce can achieve these ambitious goals.

Stability of work is the foundation for such a workforce, illustrated in Figure 5.1 as the house foundation. Toyota is among the noble group of companies that hire employees "for life." The company selects candidates carefully, trains them for months, rotates them in various jobs, and develops them to become the best they can be. Managers are promoted from within. An employee's engagement in work increases when he knows he is hired until retirement age, and does not have to fear layoffs and firings.

Above the house foundation in Figure 5.1 we find three critical practices: standardized work, continuous improvement, and work leveling. These practices serve as the bases for the remaining tools. Next are the two pillars of workflow and quality assurance. Each pillar involves a set of specific tools enabling work quality and flow. The tools include a workplace organization method called 6S; *kaizen* (continuous improvement); *hejinka* (work leveling method discussed in Section 4.2.9); scientific problem solving; *poka yoke*, (mistake-proofing tactic); *gemba* (managers' presence throughout the work areas); effective databases and communities of practice;

single-piece flow; work cells; visual controls, and *kanban* (visual signaling system). We discuss each tool individually.

5.1 6S Method: Orderliness, Security, and Safety

One walk through a bank back office reveals a lot about the operation to a Lean expert. A bank should boast about and demonstrate its orderly, uncluttered, well-organized office spaces to customers, competition, and job candidates. The underlying principle is to get rid of all unneeded items and keep all needed items in perfect order and readily available.

Lean is about elimination of waste and creation of value. Obvious manifestations of the wastes of waiting, inventory, and overproduction are the effort and time required to look for documents, supplies, information, and other items that are needed for work and cannot be found.

Ask yourself the following questions:

- Do I have a perfect system for storing computer files, paper documents, and supplies and can I find everything I need in seconds?
- Are my archives of older cases well organized so that records are easy to find when needed?
- Is my desktop clean except for the items needed for the current task?
- If I am absent, can my supervisor or colleagues find what they need in my office without wasting too much time?
- Are office supplies well organized and replenished just-in-time without excessive inventories?
- Will a new hire find the workplace easy to navigate?
- Is the office free of old and obsolete items (files, forms, procedures, announcements) that no longer apply, occupy precious space, and confuse employees?

If you answered *yes* to *all* these questions, your bank is perfect and you can skip this section and move on to quality assurance. If any answer was *no*, your bank is among the vast majority that may benefit from the Lean advice given here.

This section deals with the organization of ordinary office, storage, and computer spaces.

The most critical aspects of organizing bank documents and storing information are the safety and security of client and bank operational data and physical security. All banks need stringent rules to protect the confidentiality of client data,* preventing inside information abuse,† fraud, unauthorized access (spying, hacking, eavesdropping), physical break-ins, and robberies.

Some of these rules are imposed by outside regulators, some arise from bank policies, but all banks must develop and use elaborate systems to meet regulations and protect clients. These systems are beyond the scope of this book. While we acknowledge the extraordinary importance of such systems for bank operations, we leave them to experts.

Most modern banks now offer comprehensive electronic banking services; some operate only online and have no front offices. Electronic banking has become so popular that customers expect full functionality all day every day, with global access, full safety and security, and fail-safe transactions. These Internet-based operations require sophisticated infrastructure, techniques, and background operations. Again we leave technical explanations to experts.

In this section, we deal with ordinary messes in bank spaces. In spite of all the sophisticated tools and methods available to banks, employees still waste significant amounts of our time frantically looking for documents, data, forms, supplies, and other items. Wasted time comprises 10% to 30% or more of total work time in some back offices. Figure 5.2 illustrates a not unordinary mess in a bank office.

One of the world's leading aircraft makers provides an interesting example of introducing orderliness. Its engineers were brilliant but not orderly. The following scenario occurred frequently. When a mechanic from a remote airfield called an engineer to seek advice about some aircraft repair,

---

* The confidentiality protection is implemented with "Chinese walls." A Wiki search yielded the following description: "In business, a Chinese wall is an information barrier implemented within a firm organization to prevent exchanges of information that could cause conflicts of interest. For example, a Chinese wall may be erected to separate and isolate persons who make investment decisions from persons who are privy to undisclosed material information, which may influence those decisions. In general, all firms are required to develop, implement, and enforce reasonable policies and procedures to safeguard insider information and to ensure that no improper trading occurs. Although specific procedures are not mandated, adopted practices must be formalized in writing and be appropriate and sufficient. Procedures should address the following areas: education of employees, containment of inside information, restriction of transactions, and trading surveillance." A bank may possess information from several clients who are competitors; release of such information could jeopardize a client business position. Therefore such clients are handled by different employees in different office spaces, and client names are kept separate from many bank activities.

† "Closed periods" are used to prevent inside trading abuse. During a closed period, a bank is prohibited from trading in securities of a company whose investments and business plans were supplied by a client, until the time when the plans become public knowledge.

Figure 5.2 Mess in a bank. (Photo courtesy of M. Felbur.)

the engineer would typically answer, "I need to look it up and will call you tomorrow." In the meantime, the aircraft waited on the tarmac for 24 hours and lost a lot of money for the airline.

When a company executive learned of the waste, he ordered a massive sorting and cleaning of all engineering work spaces, files, records, and equipment and mandated that every document the engineer ever created, regardless how many years ago, had to be found "within 30 seconds of the request." This became known as the 30-second rule. While this is a somewhat extreme example, a short time is undoubtedly conducive to increased productivity.

At the same aircraft company, a clean desk rule was imposed. At the end of a workday, security personnel checked all offices to make sure no confidential information was visible. If a confidential document was discovered, it was removed immediately for safekeeping and the office occupant was penalized. (Banks usually perform similar checks to ensure no confidential client data is left out in the open.) Furthermore, any other item left on a desktop was considered trash to be removed by janitors—a strong motivation to leave a clean desk!

This book was written during the Digital Age. Most critical documents dealing with bank operations and all client data are now maintained in digital form. However, paper documents are still received, produced, and stored: correspondence, regulatory communications, taxation information, reports, newspaper clippings, and older documents that have not yet been digitized, as well as daily working documents created and disseminated by bank employees.

The following guidelines for paper documents are recommended:

- Each document and group of documents has a distinct and well-organized name, type, ID number or descriptor, and date and time stamp.
- All documents and office items are stored in designated places indicated with visible signs and are easy to find.
- By the end of a workday, each employee returns all protected documents to the designated storage area or locks them securely in his or her office. Unprotected documents are placed into desks, cabinets, or designated departmental storage place.
- Each employee keeps only the documents he or she needs at the time in the work area.
- The rules for document labeling and storage are published in a booklet.
- All employees must be trained in handling of confidential materials so that they all follow the same rules without exception.
- A bank developing rules for document storage should consider ergonomics, convenience, and frequency of use.
- Each employee desk has bank space for official documents, manuals, and other records and private space for personal use such as displaying photos of loved ones.
- Management sets a good example by consistently following the guidelines.

Experienced bank employees are needed to develop such rules in detail. Of course, the rules must be published and all employees informed of them. All new hires should receive training in the new rules.

In Japan, a method originally named 5S has become popular because it promotes workplace organization and cleaning. The first five Ss were named for Japanese words that begin with the "s" sound; they are translated below. A sixth S was added to cover security and safety of people and information. The components of 6S are

Seiton   Planning for storage of documents and other items
Seiri   Sorting (organization)

Seiso   Sweeping and shining (cleanliness)
Seiketsu   Standardization
Shitsuke   Self-discipline for sustaining the first four Ss
Security   Maintaining safety and security of bank clients, employees, data, securities, and assets

Lean cannot be implemented in a messy environment. A bank that tolerates messes must deploy the 6S steps before deploying Lean. In other words, the 6S program is a prerequisite to Lean. We describe the six components in order.

5.1.1 Seiton (Plan Office and Computer Spaces)

The first step is developing a comprehensive plan for storing paper and electronic documents, office equipment, and supplies. We begin with the most important aspect: a complete, uniform, and error-proof system for labeling all documents.

Modern banks do not need to "reinvent the wheel." Many organization rules are already in place (e.g., electronic document naming and storage regulations) for maintaining client financial and identity data (identification number, wealth management data which is kept separately, authorizations to handle funds and securities, credit applications), reports for outside regulators, taxation, and export control bodies, and others. Typically, a system must be developed only for items not covered by bank rules or legal regulations—the items that clutter spaces and increase the mess level. A small team of experienced employees should be tasked with developing appropriate rules covering the issues described below. In general, each document and file, whether paper or electronic, should be labeled with

- Year, month, and day created (or initiated)
- Document or file type
- Unique identification number using system intelligently designed to include all possible document types
- Department responsible for storage

The next task is planning computer spaces. Ideally, all bank computers should have identical subdirectory tree and file-naming conventions. In addition to bank space, employees should be allocated some personal computer space available for private files, but no bank document may be filed in personal spaces. The separation of bank and private computer spaces must be clearly explained during training.

The following rules should be implemented to ensure efficient and safe security and storage:

Digitizing paper documents to electronic form—When to digitize after a document is created; how to store computer files (file names, subdirectory locations, security rules), and disposition of paper original.

Retention of paper documents in local storage and in archives— Active documents should be kept in a convenient file cabinet. File cabinets should be in convenient and logical locations. Documents that are not accessed frequently but may be needed within a year should be stored in "recent archives" cabinets. Finally, documents that are unlikely to be needed but must be retained for years by law or bank policy should be maintained in long-term archives, perhaps offsite in labeled storage boxes. All cabinets and boxes must be labeled clearly and systematically. Archiving rules should specify what to archive, when to archive, where to keep it, how to keep it (digitized or paper), and how to access it quickly when needed.

Digital safety and security and computer backup—Where are backup servers to be located? How many backup servers are required? Who is allowed access to servers? How often are backups performed? What levels of protection should be installed?

Returning documents, files, drawings, manuals, parts, tools, etc.—All these items should be returned to their proper storage places at the end of each workday. It is fundamental that every document has only one correct place. Duplicate locations for documents and other items are confusing and inefficient.

Storage of office supplies—Ink cartridges, computer and other types of papers, and smaller items like pens, staples, erasers, pencils, and clips should be organized on clearly labeled shelves or in drawers, bins, boxes, or other appropriate containers. Running inventories for all supplies should be maintained in storage areas. Office supplies represent a large budget item for a bank. Furthermore, messes hiding behind cabinet doors defeat the purpose of 6S.

Walls and floors—The most clearly visible wall areas should be kept empty so that they can be used to post critical information. Visual controls are discussed in detail in Section 5.7. Unoccupied floor space (e.g., hallways and areas between desks) should be kept clean and clear.

Desktops, standard office and cubicle arrangements, orderliness— At all times, desktops should contain only documents needed for current work. All other documents should be put into their designated storage facilities. Housekeeping people should be directed to remove all items found on desktops after employees leave. Such items should be treated as trash; all documents should be shredded. Private wall space should be designated in all offices and cubicles for display of employee photographs and other personal items. Shelf storage in cubicles and offices should be standardized. Standard spaces should be allotted for necessary reference materials such as standards, policies, manuals, and forms so that these materials can be found even if employees are absent. The massive digitization of bank documents should reduce the need for maintaining paper documents.

It is a good practice to leave the development of storage rules to local employees because they know best what they use and how often. If they devise their own rules, acceptance is likely to be easy.

5.1.2 Seiri (Sort)

Once the rules for storage have been developed, published, and the office employees familiarized with them, the next step is to sort all documents and office artifacts according to the new rules, as follows:

- Place clear standardized labels (barcodes, if applicable) on all locators, cabinets, doors, aisles, shelves, bins, hangars, etc. In both common storage areas and in employee offices.
- Digitize all applicable documents and dispose of the paper originals unless instructed otherwise.
- Rename computer subdirectories and files according to new rules and move the electronic files accordingly (it is good practice to copy the original disk in case a problem occurs!). Secure electronic files.
- Move paper documents to designated storage places.
- Place color-coded tags on all unneeded items to indicate they should be disposed of as trash, shredded, sold, scrapped, moved to archives, or filed in cabinets or drawers in office areas.

One weekend day may be needed to complete this sorting work. No one likes working on weekends, but a weekend all-together effort can be made into both a productive and fun exercise. The benefits of investing the time and effort into the sorting appear immediately; no more time is wasted searching for items or finding the wrong items!

5.1.3 Seiso (Sweep and Clean)

- Require total cleaning and dusting of all desktops and work tables at the end of each workday.
- Do not allow any paper to be placed or piled on floors.
- Introduce zoning for carts and other heavy office equipment.

5.1.4 Seiketsu (Standardize)

- Introduce innovative visible management so that abnormalities become visible. For example, draw a contour for a cart on the floor so that all employees will notice when the cart is parked out of its assigned place.
- Post standard guidelines in visible places and distribute them electronically to all employees.
- Use signs, color coding, locators, content lists, arrows, and other visual aids to help employees locate items with minimum effort.
- Use standard and easily understandable words and phrases; avoid slogans.
- Use signs to indicate who is responsible for keeping order in a given area; each sign should state the responsible individual's name, phone number, location, and e-mail address.

5.1.5 Shitsuke (Discipline)

This S deals with the discipline of all bank employees to follow the first four S's routinely every day. All areas and all employees should participate. Employees should be encouraged constantly and rewarded for suggesting better ways to organize office space. New employees should be trained in the 6S principles and awareness can be enhanced by the following practices:

- A friendly competition for "cleanest and best organized" bank space could be motivated with small rewards such as movie tickets. Peers rather than managers should evaluate the areas and make the determinations.
- Violations should yield minor penalties; start with admonishment, then reprimand for subsequent violations.
- Organize an all-together cleaning blitz every year and make it fun.
- Publish and distribute a 6S manual.
- Post maintenance and repair frequency signs and last-maintenance log signs on applicable office equipment.

5.1.6 Safety and Security

As noted above, this S deals with keeping bank employees, assets, and information safe and secure from all unintended, intentional, or illegal acts. It involves a complex and interrelated system of physical, electronic, and logical security and safety measures including:

- Protection of bank spaces, vaults, computers, equipment, and offices from break-in, robbery, terrorist attack, fire, radiation, flooding, explosion, earthquake, tornado, water, and chemical damage
- Electronic security and safety of all data
- Safe and secure transport of cash and other securities
- Safety and security of safe deposit boxes
- Security and redundancy of data backup systems
- Privacy of customer account, wealth information, and transaction data
- Also, regularly practice emergency drills, especially those dealing with fire, earthquake, terrorist attack, robbery, shooting, unauthorized access, and all other relevant security and safety emergencies.

All these systems must comply with applicable state, national, and international laws and regulations and internal bank rules.

The sixth S is the most critical. Any violation of security and safety rules can disrupt or halt bank operations. As stated, all these measures require specialized knowledge of experts. While we fully acknowledge the need for perfect safety and security, we must also keep in mind that some elements of safety and security may slow Lean implementation. In this trade-off, the overarching focus should be this: we must have perfect safety and security, but safety and security must not be used as an excuse to resist Lean implementation.

The 6S steps may appear overwhelming, but they are not. Employees may resist by claiming, "I used to be able to find everything in the old system, and now I can't find anything." This type of resistance indicates that employees have not yet been trained adequately to be comfortable with the new organization or perhaps the new rules are not clear enough. Examples in thousands of offices in all kinds of industries demonstrate that 6S greatly streamlines office work.

5.2 Quality Assurance

Banking is an industry that cannot tolerate mistakes and thus requires top-notch quality assurance in all operations. Obviously, all financial transactions must balance down to the last cent. All bank accounts, statements, and financial interactions with customers must be exact.

Bankers generally understand and practice this quality requirement very well, but certain areas of bank operations that suffer from imperfect operations can benefit from understanding and practicing quality assurance. This section describes various quality assurance methods and tools. Quality assurance is a huge subject and our coverage is limited to basics. First, let us define quality of work. In banking operations, quality is defined as the sum of the following attributes:

1. The work is free from defects.
2. The work is executed right the first time (after initial training and mentoring).
3. The work is consistent and involves predictable outcomes, costs, time, and effort.
4. The work is robust (outcomes are predictable regardless of natural factors such as bank branch, time of day, customers served, or employee performing work).
5. The work is resilient (the operation is able to avoid disruptions, is able to survive a disruption that cannot be avoided, and is able to recover from a disruption that has occurred). This principle is critical for electronic transactions.
6. The work is measurable and verifiable.
7. The work is efficiently executed (correctly, at minimum cost, without wasting time).
8. The work is "elegant."

The first seven attributes are measurable and verifiable. The final attribute is subjective, but often obvious to experienced practitioners. "Elegant" work involves well-designed processes and standards that are immediately accepted and even liked by employees; they appear to be executed almost effortlessly.

Quality is not the same as features. Quality combines the eight attributes above and indicates how well work is performed and how satisfied customers are. Features are like "bells and whistles." They constitute numerous options and choices intended to attract customers. A bank product or activity may have many features but be of poor quality, or conversely, may have few features and be of excellent quality. In this chapter we leave the selection of features to marketing experts whose role is to position a bank relative to its competition; we will focus only on the quality of bank work.

How do we establish quality? We can measure the first seven attributes objectively. Quality also has a relative meaning resulting from comparisons to expectations. Work quality that exceeds expectations tends to produce delight; work failing to reach the expected levels produces disappointment or even disgust from internal and external customers.

The most important quality assurance concept is customer satisfaction. Every transaction involves at least two people, one of whom is an internal or external customer. Lean work must be good enough to satisfy each customer on the first attempt.

Unconditional customer satisfaction is the constant, overwhelming, obsessive goal of a well-run organization in a global economy and banking is an integral component of the global economy. Customers will go to the bank that offers the best combination of quality, features, financial benefits, scheduled hours, and service. A customer who becomes unhappy with one bank moves to another. Digitization makes it as easy to change banks as it is to change shoes.

All customers in a global economy expect the best world-class combination of quality, price, delivery time, and level of service. Customers are spoiled. How a bank judges the quality of its work is irrelevant if its customers disagree with the assessments. The customers are always the final judges of quality. Some banks desperately try to draw customers by aggressive and costly advertisements, hoping to overcome bad reputations with great ads. This may work in the short term ("You can fool all of the people some of the time or some of the people all the time, but you cannot fool all of the people all of the time").

A dissatisfied customer does not hide dissatisfaction; instead, he or she will tell many colleagues, friends, and family members about "that lousy bank." Formal studies [e.g., Deming, 1982] confirmed that one dissatisfied customer may cause a strong negative multiplying effect, risking losses of business of many potential customers. Fortunately, the opposite is also true: a satisfied customer is the best advertising and it's free. It brings new customers and expands market share. Good banks understand this point well and train their employees to create "wow" reactions from all its customers.

Two quality attributes ("executed right the first time," and "consistent and predictable outcomes") are vital for a productive and competitive organization. Uncontrollable variation is the archenemy of quality because it indicates an inability to create work outputs predictably at expected quality levels within cost limits and on schedule using known amounts of resources. A process with uncontrollable quality indicates that no stable process really exists. A company that lacks stable process never knows what will happen.

A process that takes one day may require four hours the next day and two days thereafter. An organization that cannot promise accurate lead time, cost, or quality to an internal or external customer will overpromise or underdeliver or pad estimates. These practices are destructive to an organization's operations and its reputation.

In contrast, Lean strives to make processes consistently predictable. Within a small margin of error, a bank can predict the amount of effort, time, and cost needed to generate a product or service and rely on output quality. Bank management does not have to wonder who will execute a task because all people assigned to the task have been trained and qualified and can be trusted. The task is performed robustly (it is insensitive to normal environmental variations such as time of day, employee doing the work, branch, equipment, etc.). The task is resilient (will yield satisfactory outcomes even if disrupted). The outcomes are always predictable and correct. We can achieve this level of excellence by following the steps described below.

1. Understanding sources of variation in a process. In a bank back office, variations arise from inadequately trained personnel; absence of standards and treating each task as unique; changes and misunderstandings of regulations; modifications of software and other tools; and management changes.
2. Design work to be insensitive to sources of variation. This goal is achieved by implementing excellent standards (Section 5.5), and effective training and mentoring (Chapter 6), and using mistake-proof tools and alarms (sounds, messages, lights) to warn of deviations.
3. Implement tools for error proofing. Most bank operations are now computerized and computer systems provide ideal environments for mistake proofing. Software should be designed to act as a user-friendly quality assurance tool, raising an alarm whenever a mistake is about to be made. This mistake-proofing feature is known as *poka yoke* in Japan and is described in Section 5.10. Modern software provides amazing

mistake-proofing features. Without realizing it, we are surrounded by such devices. (To see some clever examples, perform an Internet search of *poka yoke.*) Lean banks promote mistake proofing in every step of every process.

4. Train and qualify employees to perform according to standard procedures. This should enable them to know whether work is correct and seek help if it is not. Finally, they should know whom to ask for help and feel confident that the person will respond immediately and not blame or shame.

5. Support employees in their efforts to improve work. In traditional banks, some supervisors repeatedly see employees make the same mistakes. This only frustrates both parties. A Lean thinker would know the solution if a manager knew how to do the work and his or her employees did not. The manager should change his role from inspector and supervisor to mentor and trainer. He or she should teach employees how to avoid mistakes and consistently create perfect work outcomes.

In Lean banks, every employee is trained to have "two jobs": (1) regular work and (2) inspection of his or her own work to ensure quality. All employees should be trained to know exactly what constitutes good quality in their work, how to identify mistakes and defects, and how to correct problems immediately. Supervisors should be called only when an employee cannot solve a problem independently. Defective task outputs must never be allowed to leave their workstations under any circumstances. When a defect is discovered, the process must be stopped and the defect eliminated. This is known as local quality assurance.

Of course, supervisors must monitor the quality of work of their employees. In a perfect bank, this check is a pleasant formality because perfect quality is consistent. Any imperfection detected must be treated as an opportunity to improve the system by conducting additional training or improving the process. After a level of certainty is reached that the process is perfect and employees do not make mistakes, the supervision can be relaxed to only occasional random spot checks.

Local quality assurance is far better than relying on final inspections to find mistakes and defects. Final inspection is rarely 100% reliable. There is never enough time to find all defects; some will inevitably pass to external customers (who tend to be perfect inspectors who find all defects quickly!). Final inspections are costly and constitute necessary non-value-added activities. In contrast, local quality assurance is far more reliable after thorough training of employees. Local quality assurance prevents the transfer of mistakes from employee to employee and then to external customers.

Lean terminology calls this type of mistake prevention "stopping the line." The concept was invented at Toyota where every assembly line worker was trained, empowered, and encouraged to stop an entire moving production line at any sign of imperfection to prevent defects from moving further along the line.

The cost of catching a mistake and fixing it as soon as it is created may be orders of magnitude smaller than the cost of not catching it at all. The cost of a mistake made in one task is usually only for rework. If five other tasks follow the mistake before it is discovered, all five tasks must be repeated and five reworks are obviously far more costly. If a mistake is passed to an external customer, the bank incurs the high cost of fixing it *and* it faces potential destructive consequences arising from the impacts on its reputation and market share. The idea that "an ounce of prevention equals a pound of cure" applies totally to Lean banking.

A bank that experiences a non-zero defect or error rate should implement graphical visualization of error trends over time. The number of daily or weekly errors and defects should be plotted as points on a large marker board (or TV screen) displayed on a wall and visible to all workers at all times. The plot should display the cumulative or average values for an entire department, not performances of individual employees. The plot should be used to monitor the system, not shame employees. It will reveal objectively whether quality does or does not improve over time or decreases. Experience indicates that the graphs should not be implemented as personal computer screens because employees cannot see the graphs when they are performing other computer tasks throughout their workdays. Displaying the information on a wall for all to see provides a strong motivation to improve.

Five levels of work quality ordered from worst to best are defined as follows:

- Passing defective work to external customers (if this continues, get ready to close the bank).
- Defective products are not delivered to customers but comprehensive (and costly) final inspections are required, making the bank uncompetitive.
- Defects are subject to immediate corrective actions and are not repeated; final inspections by managers provide useful feedback; inspectors become mentors.
- Defectives are not passed on to the downstream position. Employees are trained as their own quality inspectors.

■ Processes have been perfected so that they do not create defects. Mistake proofing is effectively applied, making mistakes practically impossible. We call this level "zero defects."

Is it possible to achieve zero defects? Of course it is. Consider the routine work in obstetrics hospitals. Doctors and nurses do not drop babies on the floor. Similarly, no accidental explosion of a nuclear weapon has ever occurred. (A few have dropped from airplanes but they never exploded.) A bank must strive for a similar goal. Tolerating even a small defect rate may have deadly consequences. Managers may boast about their excellent quality, with defect or error rates of only 1%. To show the absurdity of this statement, consider that a 1% defect rate can cause:

■ One hundred commercial aircraft catastrophes in the US every day
■ Forty-one thousand babies dropped on hospital floors every year
■ One hundred nuclear missiles launched by mistake
■ One hundred million errors in online transactions worldwide every day

Zero defects must constitute a standard in modern Lean banking. A bank can achieve zero defects by utilizing excellent standards, processes, information technology, security and safety, *poka yoke*, training and mentoring, excellent human relations, and continuous improvement.

A story popular among Lean practitioners describes a high-level executive from the Toyota corporate office who visited a new Toyota plant in North America. The plant was said to be extraordinarily successful in all areas: quality, safety, productivity, and team member and community satisfaction. The visitor praised the plant managers and then asked about their next challenges and problems. "None," they answered. The visitor tried again, and heard, "We have no problems." On the third try, he replied angrily that, "You are all fired; if there are no problems, no managers are needed." Whether true or not, the anecdote clearly illustrates the critical responsibility of managers to identify and solve problems. Problems always exist and Lean sees them as opportunities for improvement. Lean culture involves making all imperfections visible so that they can be addressed immediately.

5.3 Continuous Improvement

The histories of many companies including banks demonstrate that the traditional "don't fix it if it ain't broke" system is clearly a cause for failure. Having achieved big successes, many such companies relaxed, stopped striving to improve, and allowed the competition to overtake them.

Competitive offers from banks bombard customers daily. To survive, no bank can afford to remain self-satisfied and static. It must adopt the mindset of continuous improvement of all aspects of its business (products, services, practices, standards, processes, culture, training, management, and facility appearance) to keep up with and then overtake competitors.

In the present global economy, competition should be regarded as a brutal race without a finish line. This race is often illustrated as a wheel of quality that must be continuously pushed up an incline (Figure 5.3). Walter Shewhart, "the grandfather of Total Quality Management," described it as a "cycle of continuous improvement" that represented a revolution in thinking. The continuous improvement cycle known as PDSA (Plan–Do–Study–Act) consists of four phases:

PLAN—brainstorm problems, state the objectives, prioritize candidates for improvement, and plan the improvement steps

DO—deploy the improvement and measure the outcomes

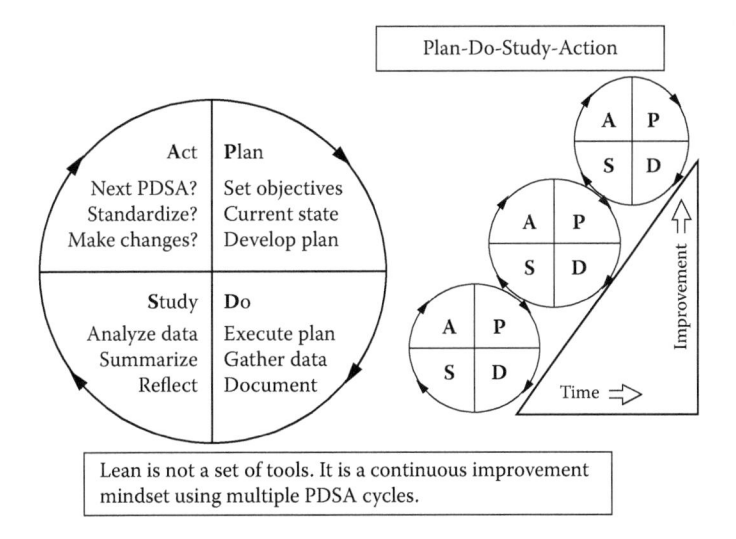

Figure 5.3 Plan–Do–Study–Act (PDSA) cycle. (From Lean Academy, 2008. With permission.)

STUDY—study the outcomes, ascertain that the improvement has indeed worked as intended

ACT—act on the results, implement success as a new work standard, re-think failures

After a cycle is completed, it is repeated with a plan for another improvement.

What should a bank improve? Every process can be performed better, and we only need to prioritize to determine what we should improve first. The candidates for improvement in a bank operation are obvious:

- Safety, security, and other types of risks
- Systemic causes of repeating delays, break-downs, frustrations, imperfections
- Other big risks
- Customer complaints
- Greatest impediments to workflow and sources of variability and quality problems
- Employee suggestions and ideas
- Standards, procedures, and checklists
- Training and mentoring
- 6S issues (sorting, neatness, cleanliness, standardization, discipline, safety and security)
- Conflicts and human relations issues (teamwork, mutual support, openness, abandonment of "blame and shame culture" and fear, increasing mutual loyalty levels between employees and the bank)
- Degree of robustness, predictability, and efficiency of processes
- Planning, communication, and coordination

The priorities of the listed items vary. Most managers will agree that the first four items deserve urgent attention and should be addressed without procrastination. If unattended, these problems will likely develop into crises. The remaining items are just as important, but they have longer time scales. All these improvement areas should receive steady ongoing attention and resource funding from bank managers.

In the past, various industries tried formal statistics-based Six Sigma processes to prioritize competing improvement candidates. The present authors hesitate to recommend such formal methods and are convinced that managers know which issues are most critical at any given time. When a new problem (error, defect, delay, complaint) occurs, we must ask two fundamental questions: (1) Why did the problem occur? and (2) What can we do to prevent recurrence?

We attack the first question with root-cause analysis, which is a simple logical process of seeking relevant answers to successive *why* questions; each question should dig deeper into problem causes. The Lean Home Building Website [2013] contains an excellent example of root-cause analysis.

Why *Five whys*? The number is based on experience but is not a hard rule. A root cause may be found after four *whys* or even more than five; it will seldom be found after only one. Wise managers understand that any answer to the single question before "Why did this problem occur?" may be incomplete, perfunctory, and superficial. Most problems require more than one *why* answer to uncover the root cause because modern civilization is too complex for mental shortcuts. All companies, including banks, are bombarded daily by economic, social, political, and technological turbulence that does not tolerate simplistic approaches.

Consider the example provided by Lean Academy [2008] for analyzing the root cause of surface deterioration of the Jefferson Memorial in Washington, DC. Asking *why* might yield a guess of "environmental pollution," suggesting replacement of the external surface of the monument with a more durable one at a cost of hundreds of millions of dollars. Now, let us approach the reasons for deterioration of the Jefferson Monument using the method of *Five whys*:

Why?	Because it is washed all the time.
Why?	It attracts bird droppings.
Why?	The birds enter the monument to feed on spiders.
Why?	The spiders are feeding on gnats.
Why?	The gnats are there because the lights are always on.

So, the root cause is leaving the lights on all the time. The lights attract gnats that attract spiders that attract birds whose droppings require frequent washings of surfaces that deteriorate the monument. By simply switching the lights off during the daytime, we reduce the deterioration rate by 40% to 60%, depending on the season, at practically no cost. As demonstrated in this example, once we find the true root cause of a problem, it is easy to find a remedy.

The method of *Five whys* requires more time than a single *why*, but provides a much higher likelihood of finding the true root cause. The answer to

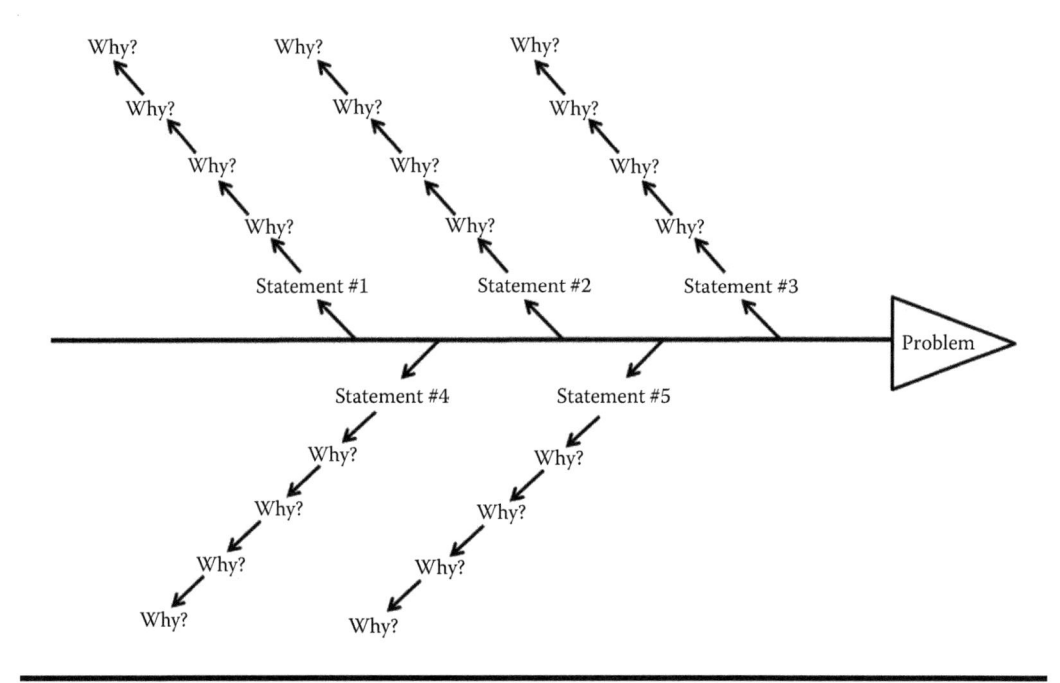

Figure 5.4 Ishikawa (fishbone) diagram.

the final *why* should yield a specific root cause that is clear and conducive to finding an actionable and effective remedy.

Ending the exercise by determining a large-scale root cause (e.g., incompetent management) is usually pointless (even if true) because the root cause is not actionable. It is unlikely that a bank will replace its management as a corrective action.

Often, after we ask the first *why*, more than one answer will appear plausible. It then is helpful to construct a simple diagram showing all the possible causes of the problem as branches on a horizontal tree, as shown in Figure 5.4. The branches denote different possible causes, and the problem addressed is shown at the tree end, on the right. Such illustrations are known as Ishikawa, fishbone, or cause-and-effect diagrams. We follow each major branch (possible cause) asking *Five whys* until we find root causes for all the branches. Analysis frequently reveals that multiple branches may yield the same root cause (e.g., lack of training), although this should not be taken as a hard rule.

Figure 5.5 illustrates the logic of *Five whys* with three branches. Each of the three branches is intended to identify a root cause to determine why the bank's B transactions are always completed late. The first *why* identifies three possible candidate statements: (1) clerks wait too long for customer forms to process transactions; (2) clerks are too busy to work on a

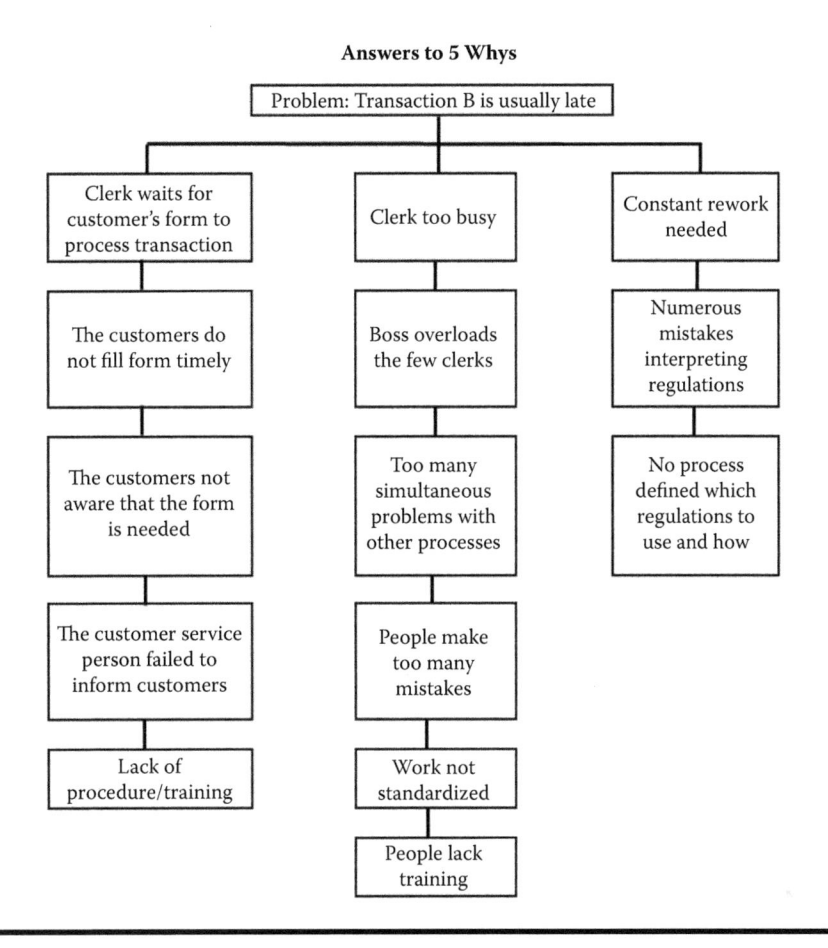

Answers to 5 Whys

Figure 5.5 Example of logic of the *Five whys*.

transaction; and (3) the constant rework required delays transaction delivery. These statements are summarized in the top boxes in Figure 5.5.

Next, the stakeholders performing the given transactions were asked *why* several times in sequence. Their abbreviated answers are also listed in the figure. Looking at the lowest boxes in each branch, we see that two related root causes for the lateness of transaction B have been found; (1) the lack of a standard procedure and (2) the lack of training of the employees doing the work. The identification of these root causes makes the corrective actions obvious: standardize the process and train employees to follow the standard.

Usually, an effective root cause analysis will unveil an obvious remedy. Occasionally, the *Five why* exercise may involve more than a verbal exchange (e.g., a diagnostic test).

Graban [2009] noted that Lean culture requires a number of conditions to ensure finding a root cause:

- An environment where employees are encouraged to stop and solve problems as soon as they appear
- Available time for root cause problem solving (best freed up by prior waste reduction)
- A blame-free environment where employees are not punished for identifying problems for root cause problem solving
- Cross-functional cooperation for working together on problems generated in an upstream department that create waste for a downstream department

We recommend several improvement methods, depending on the problem size: improvements suggested and executed by an individual employee or small local improvement team and large efforts for addressing complex bank-wide problems. They are described in the following sections.

5.3.1 Bottom-Up Improvements Suggested by Individual Employees

Suggestions made by individual employees represent the most powerful improvement methods. This method can transform an entire workforce into an army of creative problem solvers, each contributing a small improvement. Over a long period, improvements achieved by this method will establish a bank as a strong, superior competitor. Instead of focusing on grievances and poor management, employees think about ways to improve their work by making it simpler, faster, and better, needing less effort, at a lower cost. The employees who operate a process are the closest to their problems and frustrations so their ideas carry substantial weight. Toyota largely credits this approach to its extraordinary success; the remaining credit is attributed to the Respect for People principle.

Typically, the suggestion system works as follows: An employee brings his or her idea about an improvement possibility to the supervisor. The idea relates to the employee's work area; people improve their own work, not the work of others. All supervisors are trained to be disposed positively to suggestions and receive small incentive payments to reinforce this habit. The supervisor alone or with one or more experienced workers evaluates the idea. The employee who suggested the idea is given the resources (tools, materials, time, even overtime pay if it makes sense in the situation) needed to try the idea. After the idea is tested and verified as a better way of doing the task, it is implemented, the relevant work procedure is updated, released, and disseminated around other bank offices so that others can benefit from it and the employee receives a bonus that reflects the magnitude of the improvement.

The work on the improvement is achieved with minimum bureaucracy and only one or two simple objective metrics to determine whether the change makes sense. The typical metrics should relate to one or more of the following components of bank work: process time, cost, effort, quality, or service to customers. In addition, the supervisor should receive a small bonus (typically 5% of the employee bonus) to promote the good habit of welcoming suggestions.

Toyota has a special budget and infrastructure for implementing suggestions. In some Toyota plants, 90% of employees submit improvement suggestions, of which 60% are implemented on paid overtime. The experiences of many organizations indicate that over a long term the employee suggestion system yields the most power improvements. It promotes creativity, empowerment, even enthusiasm for work. It is very effective in reducing union militancy and is also a perfect tool for Lean deployment.

> "Give people the tools to become problem solvers and then create working conditions that applaud solving problems instead of sweeping them under the rug.... Without a continuous improvement environment, people become frustrated. They don't have the tools or the permission to fix problems."
>
> **Mark Graban, 2009**

Compare this wonderful system to a traditional bank in which managers "know everything about everything" and line employees are to "check their creative brains at the door." In this culture, managers are rarely aware of problems that plague the daily work. From their remote perspectives, they cannot see the problem details that are obvious to the employees who work with the problems. As a result, many opportunities for system improvement are missed and managers are often too busy with daily chores to think of improvements. Even if the managers wanted to work on improvements and had the time, there are far fewer managers than line employees. In contrast, converting an entire workforce into an army of problem solvers is a vastly more powerful approach.

5.3.2 Kaizen Blitz: Quick Improvements by a Small Team of Stakeholders

The direct translation of *kaizen* is *improvement*. In the West, *kaizen* has evolved into a number of different improvement practices. The most common meaning is the quick reaction of a small group of people closest to the problem (problem stakeholders) to find the root cause of the problem and eliminate it once and for all while optimizing the process for robustness and quality.

Blitz is often used to emphasize the urgent need for eliminating a problem. The size of the problem is typically bigger than what a single employee could resolve and the scope of the problem typically extends into more than one department. The typical effort involves two to five people working in a dedicated manner for a few hours or days. They should work with few formalities and focus on the problem at hand. The necessary conditions for success include selecting the suitable people, giving them time to address the problem, management support, free format, immediate feedback, and tangible recognition of success. Typical steps for a *kaizen* blitz are:

- Ensure manager's support and resources.
- State and clarify the problem to be eliminated.
- Identify and gather stakeholders of the problem (the most qualified individuals who are experienced in all important aspects of the problem).
- Analyze the present situation, especially the sources of uncontrollable variation in the process.
- Brainstorm (see below) the causes and draw an Ishikawa diagram (Figure 5.4).
- Brainstorm the root causes (*Five whys*).
- Brainstorm the best actionable and effective solution.
- Make a plan for deploying the solution listing steps, schedule and budget, and metrics of success.
- Deploy the plan and measure the metrics.
- Evaluate the new method. It is better? Neutral? Worse? If better, capture the new method into as procedure, train employees, and disseminate the new procedure.

The *kaizen* blitz team should report progress daily or more often to a supervising manager. A manager experienced in Lean Six Sigma may have to act as a team mentor. The team should focus on a practical, actionable, permanent, and stable solution rather than on a quick, unstable fix. *Kaizen* blitz failures are attributed often to the lack of needed resources, lack of management support, lack of steady dedicated commitments of team members, inadequate metrics of success, and inability to see "the big picture" of the problem: context, consequences, and system faults.

5.3.3 Six Sigma for Large Formal Projects

Six Sigma* is a disciplined, well-structured, company-wide effort intended to fix large, complex, multi-disciplinary problems that are larger than those that can be resolved by a *kaizen* blitz. Six Sigma teams often involve experts in several disciplines (security, safety, law, economics, IT, etc.). The approach originated in precision electronic manufacturing, but has since been extended to all corporate enterprises including banks. Numerous large companies claim success from implementing this method; examples are General Electric, Allied Signal, Polaroid, Texas Instruments, Motorola, Boeing, Lockheed Martin, Raytheon, Maytag, Canon, Bombardier, ABB-Indiana, and many others. In Chapter 3, we cited successful Six Sigma improvements in several banks.

The Six Sigma method focuses on improving processes using statistics. It relies on rigorous data gathering and statistical analysis to pinpoint sources of errors and ways of eliminating them, with heavy reliance on performance metrics. Selected volunteers are trained for weeks in improvement methods and earn various Six Sigma competence grades designated by *ju-jitsu* belt colors (yellow, black, etc.) They work full time or part time on dedicated Six Sigma projects. The typical project size is large, taking weeks or months and involving several stakeholders with various areas of expertise. Candidate projects are prioritized from the top down using formal statistics for maximum benefit.

This method can be made effective for large complex problems involving high-level managers but the risk is the expense of implementation. Some organizations create vast prioritizing bureaucracies that waste great amounts of company resources trying to measure what they think needs to be measured; let us keep in mind that the process of measuring waste can also be wasteful! Often the most urgent problems are obvious and no expensive formal prioritization is needed.

---

* The Six Sigma name originates from a statistical property of the normal distribution of production defects. The Six Sigma quality level creates, on average, no more than three defects per million actions or items created. For our purpose, Six Sigma should be treated only as the name of a method; this book does not cover statistics.

Another risk—and it is big—is that the Six Sigma bureaucracy kills the spontaneous suggestion and *kaizen* blitz initiatives and the spirit of quick improvement, with terrible results for a banking enterprise. Finally, the emphasis on rigorous, "objective" prioritization and evaluation promotes a false impression that "everything that exists can be and should be measured," which is nonsense. In fact, the most important aspects of human existence: loyalty, teamwork, love, marriage or partnership, raising children, and human relations at work are practically impossible to measure numerically even though they are self-evident to the people involved.

This is not to say that metrics should not be used. Process time, quality, cost, effort, and customer complaints can and should be measured objectively. However, if we place an excessive and fanatical ideological emphasis on metrics, we risk focusing improvements on the mechanical, less important aspects, and ignoring the biggest problems: human relations at work.

Harry and Schroeder [2000] define eight phases of the Six Sigma process. After employees have been trained in the methodology they should be able to:

- Recognize operational issues that link to really important aspects of business.
- Define the improvement candidates, Six Sigma projects, questions, and variables.
- Rigorously measure the performances of projects.
- Analyze results in relation to operational goals and prioritize problems.
- Improve the problems with the biggest impacts.
- Control inputs and monitor to ensure that problems do not recur.
- Standardize the best practices.
- Integrate the new standards into policies and procedures.

As mentioned earlier in this section, the Six Sigma program in a bank requires an infrastructure, formal training courses, and dedicated management. The implementation of this system is beyond the scope of this book. Readers interested in more knowledge about Six Sigma are advised to read Harry and Schroeder [2000].

5.3.4 Other Improvement Methods: Brief Review

Over the past few decades, several other improvement methods were popular. Detailed coverage is beyond the scope of this book, but we list them here for completeness.

Total Quality Management (TQM) was described in Chapter 3. It was a popular paradigm between 1980 and 2000. TQM must be credited for developing concepts and practices for improving processes, people, and tools such as continuous improvement, suggestion systems, *kaizen* blitz, standardization, variability reduction, training, and excellent human relations. Excellent leaders and managers are trained to align and use the entire workforce as creative problem solvers, employing root cause analysis of problems via the *Five whys* method, statistical process control, experimental design, and generation of practical diagrams such as Ishikawa and Pareto diagrams, histograms, and others. In short, TQM was an excellent and important step, but business practice has evolved further.

Strategic Planning is a popular top-down effort used by banks to (1) objectively identify its current strengths, weaknesses, opportunities, and threats; (2) formulate effective vision and mission statements; (3) plan strategies for success, and break down the strategy (including schedules and budgets) into specific concrete tactical steps, goals, and assignments.

Lean thinkers emphasize that while all free-market firms want to be profitable and grow, they should not focus their strategies directly on profits and market shares. Instead firms should zealously focus on satisfying and delighting their customers with great service, quality, low fees, and short lead times. Banks should also strive to attain the best work from dedicated and motivated employees. Profits and growth will come naturally as by-products of this strategy. The mission statement of the uniquely successful Toyota NUMMI factory is enlightening:

"Through teamwork, safely build the highest quality vehicles at the lowest possible cost to benefit our customers, team members [employees], community and shareholders."

NUMMI Mission, Fremont, California

The order of words in a mission statement indicates an organization's priorities. Notice how the words in Toyota's statement reveal its priorities. Teamwork is the most important part of the mission, safety is next, followed by product quality and cost. The parties who should benefit are also named in priority: first, external customers, then employees, followed by the community (schools, city residents, local businesses), and finally shareholders who collect the profits. Note that shareholder profits are last in line. These priorities are not yet popular among traditional banks even though hard evidence indicates that they represent the best way to run any business over the long term.

Re-engineering is for making radical changes. Processes or products that are "beyond repair" are abandoned and replaced with totally new ones in one radical step. We already know that all businesses need to eliminate non-performing processes and products. However, the re-engineering method became somewhat discredited due to the brutal firings that often accompanied the radical changes driven by overzealous consultants.

Theory of Constraints is both a method and the name of a popular book by Eliyahu Goldratt. In brief, the method recommends focusing on the greatest current impediment (bottleneck) to a workflow—eliminate the impediment which automatically speeds the entire flow—then focus on the next biggest impediment, and so on. The theory recommends visualizing the impediments as big rocks in a river that impede its flow. The book contains numerous examples and fascinating details. The only criticism we have is that the book could transmit its message in one tenth of the text.

Clearly, Lean banking requires quality people, processes, and tools. Quality people (educated, trained, motivated, empowered, aligned) are needed to invent and execute quality (effective, efficient, predictable, secure, safe, robust, competitive, defect-free) products and processes. Quality leaders and managers are needed to lead and manage quality people. Quality processes require quality (effective, efficient, robust, reliable, resilient) tools designed by quality people. Indeed, this quality spiral permeates every activity we perform in our bank.

The body of knowledge of continuous process improvement is significant, covered in hundreds of books and taught in university-level courses, and is beyond the scope of this entry-level book. We hope the present text is sufficient to enable the readers to work on initial Lean deployment projects, and whet their appetites for continuous improvement, particularly via bottom-up suggestion practices and participation in *kaizen* blitz teams. Two excellent easy-to-read and comprehensive books by Summers [2011] and Ozeki and Asaka [1988] are recommended for readers who seek more information about process improvement.

5.4 Benchmarking

Benchmarking is simply a process of comparing our products, services, and practices against the best in the business [Bogan, 1994]. Benchmarking involves learning:

- Who are our competitors?
- What new products and services do our competitors offer?
- How do we stack up against our competitors on items of importance to our clients?

As stated earlier, competition among banks in a global economy is like a race without a finish line. The best banks in a global economy are the world's best! This means that banks must constantly compete with the best of the best. All banks try to develop new products and compete via best service, quality, lowest fees, and shortest lead times for special services. The competition is dynamic, and the situation changes sometimes daily, even hourly. New banks, branches, and banking products and services are created and improved all the time. The recent economic crisis demonstrated that formerly great banks may suffer difficulties and formerly bad banks may suddenly explode with great ideas for products and services.

Figure 5.6 illustrates an instantaneous image of the relative competitive positions of a sample of banks labeled A through D on some critical scale. If we know the trends of various competitors, it is a good practice to indicate them with horizontal arrows: a left arrow means that a bank is regressing on the scale, and a right arrow indicates improvement. The arrow length should be proportional to the acceleration or deceleration. Of course, we rarely have enough data to grow such a graph completely, but whatever data we have should be displayed for all to see as a motivation to do better.

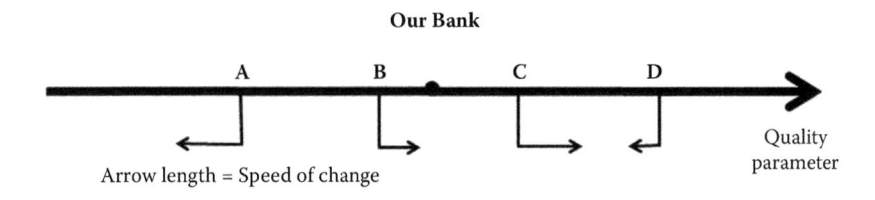

Figure 5.6 Benchmarking scale.

We have to observe the competition through an open lens because many global enterprises perform banking services without calling themselves banks (e.g., credit unions, private loan sources, savings and loan institutions, and others). At the time of this writing, large US corporations are awash with cash savings (over a trillion dollars) and many are creative in parking their money, possibly placing themselves in competition with traditional banks.

In some countries, central banks and private banking organizations publish extensive data about all banks, thus facilitating benchmarking efforts. Besides that data, benchmarking can be performed by other means (listed in the approximate order of decreasing effectiveness):

- Performing a formal study of Internet sites of the banks we wish to benchmark, focusing on their advertised products and services.
- Attending professional banking conferences and networking in the banking community.
- Attending continuous education courses on new banking knowledge.
- Having employees bank with competitor banks and report all big and small good ideas they observe.
- Hiring former employees of the competition even though their knowledge of the competition becomes obsolete at the moment of hire; beware of legal implications!
- Performing formal, professional mutual benchmarking visits with a bank that is willing to partner for purposes of benchmarking.

Note: This is not about spying! Spying must be regarded as a criminal activity and not a benchmarking exercise. Any bank caught spying on another can destroy its reputation and legal standing permanently.

Major banks compete on the accuracy of their macroeconomic forecasts that are disseminated in media. Long-term tracking of the quality of forecasts by various banks is a form of benchmarking.

We must not lose sight of the most important aim in Lean: to become as good we can be, free of waste and perfect in quality, creating the best possible customer satisfaction. This entails more than just matching our competitors. Toyota offers an interesting perspective on benchmarking. Believing it is the best, Toyota invites visitors to its manufacturing facilities as an effective advertising technique.

5.5 Work Standardization, Procedures and Checklists

Many employees in the banking industry and elsewhere detest standardized work and procedures, claiming that they kill intelligence, make work boring, implement bureaucracy, and stifle progress. Employees are often concerned about being turned into mindless robots. Experienced, highly skilled employees feel insulted when required to follow standards.

Having witnessed thousands of bad procedures across many industries, the authors fully sympathize with these emotions. However, good procedures describing standard work are extraordinarily powerful tools to combat all categories of waste. Standard procedures are supposed to represent "the current best way to complete an activity with the proper outcome and the highest quality, using the fewest possible resources.... More consistent practices lead to more consistent outcomes" [Graban, 2009].

> "Standard procedures represent the current best way to complete an activity."
>
> **Mark Graban, 2009**

Without work standards, good ideas tend to have short life spans; someone has a good idea, it works for a while, and, weeks later, when the employee has moved to another responsibility, it is forgotten, as shown in Figure 5.7.

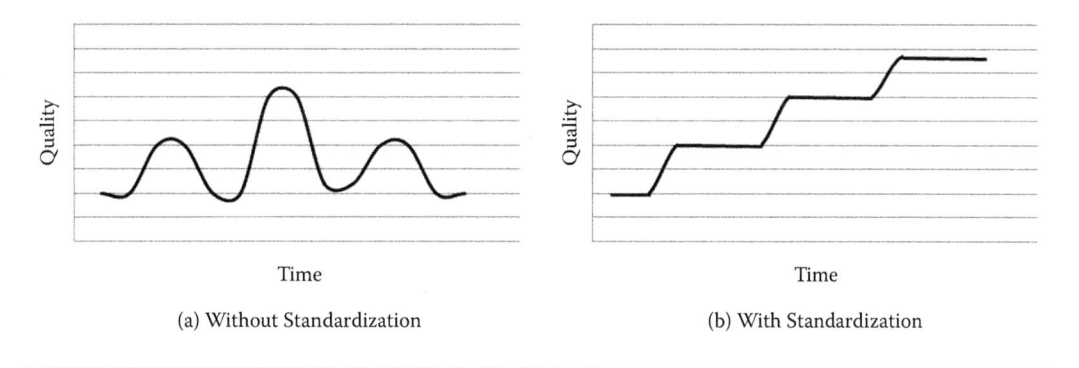

(a) Without Standardization (b) With Standardization

Figure 5.7 (a) Failure of improvements without standardization. (b) Improvements with standardization.

The overall quality of work oscillates up and down around a mediocre average as good ideas occur and expire. In contrast, in organizations with standards in place, employees think of better ways to do the work. These ideas are implemented as they follow current procedures, and the quality of work continues to increase over time, as shown in the figure.

Continuously capturing good ideas into a procedure ensures that bank competitiveness keeps improving. Standardizing does not mean keeping intelligence out of the process! Checklists and procedures serve the same purpose: capturing the best way to perform work. Checklists are simpler to create but require training of employees to ensure they understand the steps. Procedures are more verbose and less ambiguous. Management should decide which to use. In the text below, the term *procedures* includes both procedures and checklists.

Effective standard procedures must satisfy four conditions:

■ A procedure must help employees maintain consistent high-level productivity, quality, safety, and security.
■ Procedures must capture good new ideas efficiently and quickly with minimum bureaucracy.
■ A procedure must make sense; even the least experienced employee performing the work must be able to follow the procedure. The employees who are to follow the procedure must trust the system and management that the procedure is not intended to serve non-meritocratic purposes (boost manager's careers, fuel power struggles among stove-piped departments, etc.).
■ Procedures must improve quality, effort, time, and cost by making work outcomes more predictable, robust, and resilient.

This predictability is conducive to the reliable planning of work. It also enables an organization to make credible and reliable promises to customers, thus increasing customers' trust and the bank's competitiveness. Without procedures, no company can know how long any task will take, how much effort and cost will be expended, and what the outcome will be. Each time an employee attempts to perform work without a procedure, he or she suffers the anxiety of uncertainty. When asked to submit estimates, it is common to pad them with big margins to be "on the safe side," and the results are unrealistic estimates.

Many employees believe that their work is totally unique, unsuited for a standard procedure. This may be true for a physicist performing fundamental research for a flight to Mars, but few banking operations fall into the totally unique category. We should not confuse a process with process content. Processes can and should be optimized and standardized; when implemented properly, they should be general enough to serve a large variety of specific cases, customers, and transactions but be specific enough to ensure predictability. A good procedure will include all necessary repetitive steps, but may also have an open-ended provision such as "consult the manager when executing this step." Easy access to the right manager should then be ensured.

How does a bank create and implement a good procedure? The following recommendations for developing and implementing work procedure have been proven in hundreds of organizations worldwide.

1. The best employees who do the work should create a new procedure. Of course, their manager must mentor and support their efforts. Experts should be consulted. Keep in mind that standardized work should not constitute a command-and-control approach dictated to employees by managers. Employees are more likely to accept and follow a standardized procedure when they understand the reasons behind it.

   It is best to give a challenge to one or a small group (two or three) of the most experienced employees in a department to optimize all aspects of work that are to be captured by a procedure. Of course, procedures that deal with high-risk items or those that require special legal or financial expertise must be developed by experts.

   The procedure creators should begin by understanding current operations and all sources of variation, and then optimize the steps, eliminating the variations and making the outcomes predictable. The optimization may involve brainstorming sessions, interviews with stakeholders, and trials and errors. Within reason, people generating a procedure should be allowed to try and fail while experimenting because that is the nature of testing. The manager should only mentor and oversee the effort. Employees involved in standardizing work should plan to use the fewest possible resources (time, effort, supplies, space, other expenses).

2. After perfecting the process, the procedure should be drafted step by step. The manager may have to assist with drafting and writing the procedure to ensure that it is easy to follow. The least experienced employee in the department should be asked to try to follow the procedure. If this person can follow the steps without errors, the procedure is ready for finishing. If this person cannot follow the steps without errors, the procedure must be redrafted and clarified.

3. The draft should be finalized with graphics, examples, photographs, and any other feature that will help it be better understood. Within reason, procedures should be short and to the point and include explanations (see vignette).

> The formulation of a statement in a procedure can make a big difference in the level of employee acceptance. Consider an example. A bank manager posted a "DO NOT USE CREDIT INCREASE APPLICATION FORM" sign. The employees understood the sign as a lack of trust on the part of the manager because it limited their area of competence. They started talking about possible reasons for the sign, raising the level of suspicion. When the manager realized what happened, he changed the sign: "For the next 24 hours please do not use the Credit Increase Application Form because it is being reformatted and the software will reject the current form."
>
> **Adapted from Mark Graban, 2009**

4. The new procedure should be released efficiently (limit the number of approvals to the few truly needed; eliminate all bureaucratic approvals). Obtain the required signatures quickly, in hours or a few days. The procedure is a tool for doing our business better, so why wait?
5. Finally, as soon as practical, train all applicable employees in the new procedure. The training should be brief but effective, informing all relevant stakeholders that a new procedure has been developed to deal with a specific process, problem, or relevant stakeholders. Employees should be informed of the reason for the procedure, the highlights, critical steps, and do's and don'ts, and any employee questions about the procedure should be answered.
6. If a procedure deals with high-risk items, the training may have to be more extensive, covering every step in detail and followed by a simple test of comprehension involving the following questions:
   - Tell or demonstrate how you are supposed to do this work.
   - How can you tell whether the work result is correct?
   - How can you tell that a work result is not correct?
   - If the work is not correct, how can you correct the problem?
   - Whom do you call for help if you cannot eliminate the problem on your own (with full trust that you will receive help rather than criticism and shaming)?

Any employee who fails the test may present a risk for future problems, defects, and rework. Failing employees should be retrained or re-assigned.

7. While every reasonable effort should be made for the employees to buy in to a new procedure, managers must oversee standard work. As Graban [2009] noted, "As leaders, if you expect that employees will follow the standard work, you have to take time and to go and see, to verify that the standard work is actually being followed. If you tolerate people not following the standard work, you deserve the outcomes that result from the standardized work not being followed."

Traditional management looks at a set of procedures and thinks, "We invested a lot of effort into these processes so they must be good," without realizing that the procedures are not followed for logical reasons. It is not unusual to find that different employees do the same work differently, even with good standards in place. The reason may be that the procedure dissemination was ineffective or the training failed. If a manager notices that employees frequently deviate from the standard, he should first ask why rather than accusing employees and ordering them to follow the procedure before he understands why they do not. An example of a legitimate reason is a software malfunction. Employees who do not follow the standard for software use may be demonstrating heroic behavior by completing the work via others means.

Managers must be particularly sensitive to all instances in which an ineffective system (frequent computer crashes, lack of access to needed data, or an error or unclear formulation in a procedure) prevents employees from following a standard. Any problem with the execution of standardized work should be treated as an immediate call for help, requiring an improvement of the standard or system or additional training.

When creating effective procedures, we must find a balance between generality and specificity. Long or complex procedures that try to cover all possible cases and risks tend to be confusing and ineffective and may be more effective if divided into several shorter procedures. Do we really need to cover all those rare special cases and risks and prevent all possible "crimes and misdeeds" that may occur only 1% of the time or less? Would it not be better to replace numerous alternatives with a single step—consult your supervisor. The supervisor should have a special checklist explaining how to handle such unusual situations.

Examples are critical parts of a procedure. If a procedure involves completing a form, a completed example form should be included. Also, the amount of data to be entered on a given form should be balanced against excessive bureaucracy. Many forms ask for data that is exceptionally difficult to obtain or create and may be used only 1% of the time. Do we want to slow 99% of routine transactions dramatically to accommodate 1% of our applications? Such bureaucratic requirements severely inhibit productivity. Again, it may be better to cover 99% of the cases efficiently with a simple procedure and to handle rare cases with instructions to consult a manager.

Good standards cannot be separated from continuous improvement. Both managers and employees should observe the process to discover new opportunities for continuous improvement. All verified good ideas about improving work should be captured efficiently into standards. Standardized work without continuous improvement will create a stagnant workplace that will never improve. Continuous improvement without standardized work procedures as stepping stones would yield chaos because employees would try random steps that would not necessarily lead to improvements.

A final thought: Standards should describe daily routines for bank employees to make work predictable and consistent. They should never be created just to elevate speed over quality or increase the level of control over the employees.

5.6 *Kanban*: Simple "I Need" Signal

Kanban is another amazingly simple yet powerful invention of Toyota that replaces complex scheduling and planning algorithms. It is a simple visual queue (or signal) indicating that a worker needs or is ready for the next work element. We see examples of *kanban* in a supermarket where empty spaces on a shelf where boxes of a particular cereal are kept send a visual message that resupply is needed. Without knowing we are using *kanban*, we use the system daily in our work. For example, in tracking office supplies, a low level of a computer paper stack is a signal to an office assistant to refill the stack. An empty space where writing pads are kept is a signal that more pads are needed.

Kanban signals that indicate the minimum and maximum levels of an item are wonderful tools for preventing wastes of supply inventory and promoting just-in-time restocking. The level approaching the minimum is an alarm signal to resupply immediately. The maximum level signals resupplying to stop. Thus, the supplying and consuming processes become perfectly synchronized with a simple visual queue, without need for complex systems, commands, or software.

Besides controlling supplies, banks offer numerous opportunities to use *kanban* to promote process efficiency. One example is synchronizing a series of tasks in a flow as if they worked as an assembly line. As soon as each task is completed and sent downstream, a signal is sent to the preceding task to indicate readiness for the next case.

Another example is a computer file displaying a top-level screen with the status of all documents required to process a case (e.g., loan application). Missing documents are shown in red; documents that are incomplete or need rework are shown in yellow; correct and complete documents are listed in green. Other colors may denote approval status. Thus, a simple visual screen provides complete information about application status in an easy, visual format. Each red or yellow signal in *kanban* indicates, "More work is needed here."

5.7 Visual Controls

Galsworth [2005] stated that the purpose of visual controls is to reduce "information deficit." Indeed, what do we see when we enter a typical back office in a bank? We see people sitting at their computers, typing away or looking at screens. It is difficult to see what employees are working on, determine the status and quality of their work, and know whether their assignments are delayed or on time.

Unless we monitor all work using computer tools or ask the employees about their work, we cannot gauge progress. Even when monitoring computers, it is hard to determine the quality of the work, whether it is improving, and why it is delayed or does not conform. In addition, the knowledge that managers are constantly monitoring computer work tends to be intimidating and nerve-wracking for employees.

Visual controls are simple but powerful systems that display on marker boards (or on large TV screens suspended high on a wall) all important information that an entire team should see. Most important, employees can monitor and update the data to be displayed without the intimidation factor. Such boards tend to increase teamwork, motivation, and communication. They should be located in the most visible place to ensure that all department employees and guests can read the information.

Of course, much data handled in banks deals with clients' confidential data, which must be fully protected, safe, and secure. Visual boards must never display private data, but banks still maintain large amounts of information and quality trend data that can and should be shared among the employees. It is best if each department individually decides what information to display; typical examples are offered below.

5.7.1 Tracking Quality, Process Time, and Other Numerical Trends

Hopefully, the quality of each process should improve over time with experience, training, and good standards, procedures, and checklists. The quality metrics (number of errors, customer satisfaction index, and number of customer complaints) and process time should be displayed as a departmental (not personal) trend versus time. It is helpful to show goal lines. Figure 5.8 illustrates a typical trend curve. The trends should be updated often.

Along with process quality and execution times, a department can display and monitor network downtimes, number of transactions per unit time, transaction volumes, number of cases in queue, number of customer calls, number of customer complaints, and other data. In general, all information deemed important to a department should be displayed and displays can be programmed to alternate screens to show different information.

5.7.2 Task or Process Status Board

In Lean offices in which employees perform multiple, timely tasks, it is helpful to implement personal status boards. A marker board hangs on the outside wall or cubicle of each employee and is visible from a hall or

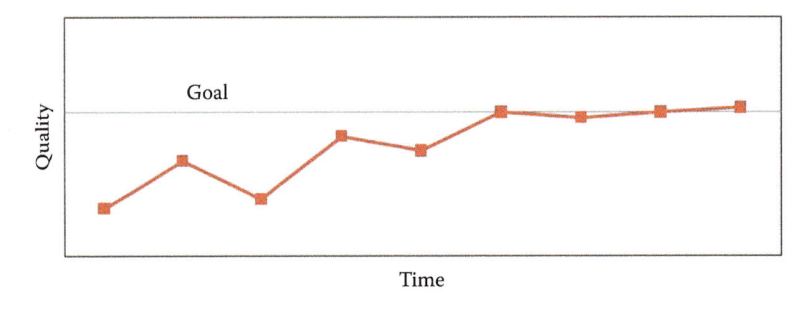

Figure 5.8 Visual control: monitoring quality trend.

passageway. The board displays the status of various tasks. Each row on the board contains information about a single task: name, deadline, status, and comment. Again, the task identity may have to be "sanitized" to protect all confidential data. Task status is shown in colors:

Green: I will meet the deadline, no problems.
Yellow: Problems, but I expect to meet the deadline without outside help.
Red: I encountered a big problem and need help from my supervisor.

The comment box contains a very short description of the problem and required action.

Figure 5.9 illustrates a typical task monitoring board. The red states can also be signaled to a supervisor by e-mail. After the supervisor reads the e-mail, she or he should contact (or approach) the employee and ask, "How I can help you?" Typically, the employee may answer, "That other department has not given me the data I need. I tried several times. I also talked to the manager. They say I have to wait, but we cannot wait or we will lose this client. Can you intervene?"

The supervisor who answers, "I will be glad to do this," will be respected highly by employees. Supervisors should not be afraid that their employees will abuse the system and try to make supervisors do the work. Such situations are very rare and if one occurs, a short private conversation with the employee tends to fix the problem.

Besides reducing delays and improving respect, the system tends to improve teamwork. When neighboring employees see problems on a

Employee: John Smith			
Task	Deadline	Status	Comment
Credit application X25234/2-13	01/07/2014	🟢	
New account for X38524-13	01/04/2014	🟢	
Beneficiery verif. X20542-13	01/03/2014	🟢	
Digitizing X18344-13-13	01/05/2014	🟡	digitizer down
Verif. assett value X25234/2-13	01/03/2014	🔴	client non-resp.

Figure 5.9   Visual control: employee task monitoring board.

colleague's board, they frequently offer help. We advise against implementation of the boards on personal computers because they do not offer the needed visibility and that defeats the purpose of displaying task status to all.

5.7.3 Skill Set Monitoring Board

All employees must complete certifications in bank security operations. For an employee to become a manager, a certificate in banking services and procedures is required. Employees in many departments are expected to complete various training courses and obtain appropriate certifications before they are allowed to perform certain operations. For example, risk department employees are certified in a number of financial modeling, risk assessment, compliance, and accounting practices. In such work environments, it is useful to install a board or large TV screen that displays the status of training and certifications of various employees in a department.

Figure 5.10 shows an example. You, the reader, should replace the skill set numbers shown here with the actual skill or certification names that apply to your department. The names of employees comprise the rows and the training modules, standard skill sets, and certifications are listed in columns. The board indicates which employees are authorized to perform certain tasks. A board or screen provides several benefits: (1) it motivates employees to complete more training modules (annual bonuses can be tied to training); it shows who is capable of performing certain tasks; this information is useful if an employee is absent; (3) it denotes department "experts" who can provide help to junior employees without need for a supervisor; and (4) it also promotes teamwork. Again, the display boards or TV screens should be installed in highly visible spaces in all departments whose employees differ in skill and certification levels.

Employee	Skill Set				
	1	2	3	4	5
John C.		√		√	
Barbara G.					√
Bohdan P.	√		√	√	√
Mike F.		√	√		
Eva G.	√				√
Azade B.		√			

Figure 5.10 Visual control: employee skill set monitoring board.

Visual controls are wonderful tools when used properly because they make work status visible for all stakeholders. They can be organized to signal imperfections in near real time, so that corrective actions can be undertaken without delay. They are conducive to teamwork by reducing unhealthy suspicions and favoritism. Visual controls aid employee efforts to achieve higher skill levels and create better quality of work. However, it is easy to abuse the information displayed, so we offer a few words of caution.

- The data displayed must never be used to blame and shame individual employees. The proper use allows a department team to objectively monitor service quality, costs, task execution times, and other measures, but the data displayed should never reveal or assess the performances of individual employees. Comparing the departmental average to one's own results should motivate him or her to improve (this must be done privately).
- The data displayed should not be used to cause rivalries among employees. If a department promotes teamwork, the stronger employees will help the weaker ones and overall performance of the team will improve. If we promote rivalry the few best employees will get ahead, leaving the weaker ones "in the dust." The department performance will stagnate and unhealthy emotions will permeate the group.
- The data displayed should not be used for advertising and promotional purposes. It is a tool to monitor work, not to advertise.
- Just ordering the employees to make fewer mistakes and work faster is counterproductive; they will rush and make even more mistakes. Without excellent training, mentoring, procedures, standards, and checklists, it is not fair or effective to demand improvement in the quality or quantity of work. Remember that the quality of work is a function of employee experience, training, mentoring, and also good procedures, standards and checklists. Quality usually worsens in an environment of fear, intimidation, and haste.

In general, visual control boards and screens have important psychological effects. They share information about vital work among the employees, engage them, and provide objective monitoring of work status in near real time. They also expose problems and imperfections without pointing at individuals. Most important, they motivate employees to use their best efforts in value creation and stimulate teamwork. Keep in mind that employees will embrace the status boards only if they foster an atmosphere of teamwork rather than an environment of rivalry, blaming, and shaming. The organizations that adopt the right culture and implement visual controls achieve significant productivity improvements.

5.8 Single-Piece Flow

Imagine a process that takes several days or even weeks to complete and involves several people, some of them doing work and one or more just approving. What would you say to the proposition that the total process time involving the same people can be shortened to a day or less, without anyone having to work harder? This is both possible and quite realistic. When we consider the time of the actual value-adding work by everyone involved, it is often measured in minutes per case. Typically, the work involves completing one or more forms, activating an account, verifying information against a database or regulations or a short computer analysis, and one or more approvals. Rarely does each step take more than several minutes or a few hours assuming, of course, that all the needed data is at hand, the tools are ready, and the worker knows the job. If several employees work in series and each one needs minutes or hours to contribute value to the process, why does the entire process take weeks or months?

Figure 4.3 demonstrated why a single task supposed to take two hours can take a week. Aligning several such tasks in a series can easily extend a process time from hours or days to weeks and months. In this section, we consider another source of delays: batching of cases.

One of the greatest myths of work is that processing work in batches is very efficient. Consider a group of employees involved in a process in sequence, each contributing information, analysis, or approval. On any business day, the first employee receives a stack of cases into his or her in-box. He or she processes one case at a time and places it in the out-box if it is completed or in a "hold" pile if the case is incomplete because the data provided is incomplete or incorrect. Having completed the first case, the worker then works on the next case, and so on. At the end of the day the worker moves all completed cases from the out-box to the next worker for additional processing or to a supervisor for approval. All defective cases are returned for rework.

The second person works in the same manner, processing the cases from the in-box to the out-box or designating it for rework. In Lean we call this method of working *Batch & Queue* (B&Q). It appears that all involved employees work on the entire batch of the cases simultaneously, but actually each person works on only one case at a time while the other cases wait idly in his input queue to be processed or in the output queue to be handed to the next person.

In an organization that employs the B&Q principle, cases can often accumulate very long wait times. They often spend 90% of processing time waiting in queues. This means they are processed actively only 10% of the time. As a result, a process involving several workers and one or two approvals that should be completed in only a few hours per case may take weeks or even months because it travels at the same speed as other cases in the batch. And this is assuming there is no backflow of cases due to wrong or incomplete data.

Any rework and other wastes add to the process time. Another strong disadvantage of the B&Q method is that when a worker makes a mistake, it is often repeated in all the cases in hand and discovered only when the entire batch then moves to the next process or to the approving person; the entire batch needs to be corrected.

A greatly superior system is called *Single-Piece Flow* (SPF). It originated in manufacturing but applies very well to bank operations. When a worker completes the work on a case, he or she passes it on to the next person immediately, so that that next person can start working on it right away. After the hand-off, the first person starts work on the second case, and the process continues. No single case sits idle at any step in the process. If all the employees work each case in series, the entire process of working one case could be completed in hours. Subsequent cases follow immediately and are processed in the same amount of time. SPF is analogous to a moving assembly line. Another advantage of working with SPF is that any error can be discovered on the first case, fixed, and will not affect subsequent cases.

Figure 5.11 compares *Batch & Queue* processing with *Single-Piece Flow*. For simplicity, imagine that each work case requires three tasks (A, B, and C) to be performed by three separate bank workers followed by approval (D). For simplicity, assume that each process takes one hour to complete one case. Figure 5.11a illustrates the B&Q method for a batch of five cases. Figure 5.11b illustrates SPF. Using the B&Q method, it takes five hours to process all cases in task A, another five hours in B, five hours in C, and five hours in D. The first case is completed after 16 hours (two work days);

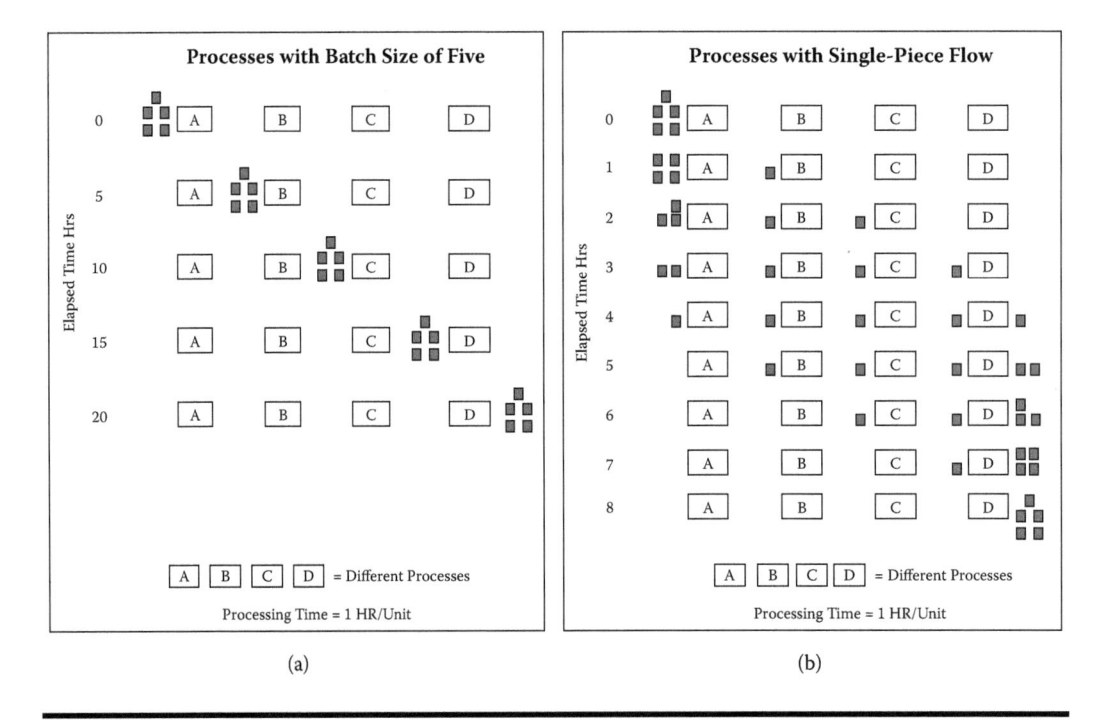

Figure 5.11 *Batch & Queue* processing (a) versus *Single-Piece Flow* (b). (From V. Brooks. With permission.)

all the cases are completed in 20 hours (2.5 work days). In practice, adding all the normal office wastes and the time of moving the pieces between workers, this time may expand easily to a week. In contrast, in SPF, the first case spends one hour in each process and is completed after only four hours. Subsequent cases follow at one-hour intervals, so all cases are completed in eight hours or a single workday and no one had to work faster!

If a batch size exceeds five cases and involves more than four workers, the difference between the B&Q and SPF methods will be even more dramatic. This simple illustration should convince every banking employee to work in SPF mode only. SPF is very easy to implement. It simply requires instructing each employee in a sequence to pass each completed case on to the next person in the value chain immediately after it is finished. No cases should sit idly in employee in-boxes or out-boxes.

5.9 Work Cells and Working to Common *Takt* Time

Imagine that all employees involved in a process are asked to work for a day in a conference room, all sitting comfortably around a large conference table, with all the items they need for work, computer, forms, etc. We organize the work beginning with the first person. He or she works on the first case, passes it to the next person as soon as it is completed, and starts working on the second case. At the same time the second person works on the first case and passes it on to the next employee and so on. Suddenly, the workflow reminds us of an assembly line. Whenever any person has a question or doubt, he or she asks colleagues and receives an immediate answer so delay is minimal.

Teamwork moves the line along and the most experienced person helps the less experienced. If a mistake is made, it is typically discovered within minutes by the next person in the sequence and corrected immediately. What used to take weeks and months now can be accomplished in hours or days and no one must work harder. Of course, the line or cell must be planned in conformity with normal bank rules of security, safety, Chinese walls, and other data confidentiality requirements.

A team-based work organization is vastly more pleasant than one where employees are separated by rigid walls. They have enough time to crack jokes or take coffee breaks together. This system works best when the tasks are designed to take approximately equal amounts of time. In production environments, the time units are known as *takt* times (*Takt* in German means rhythm). If one task takes much longer than the others (e.g., twice as long), the answer may be to assign two workers to the task, with each person working on every second case. This staggers the flow to ensure it moves smoothly. A task that takes three times as long may need three people to balance the workload and so on. Since different tasks rarely require the same amounts of time, some workers may be idle for a few minutes and may be able to help others. Again, this promotes teamwork.

A bank can achieve a dramatic improvement from using the work cell organization if several employees can be trained to perform multiple tasks. If the workload is small, one person can execute the first task, then the second task, and so on, until the cell process is completed. When the amount of work increases, we add a second worker and the two individuals divide the work. However, SPF must be followed and no batch processing is allowed. As workload increases, more workers may be added until the work cell has one person per task. If even more work needs processing, the options are authorizing overtime or starting a second work cell.

The wide flexibility in the number of workers assigned to a process greatly facilitates process management. The bank gains the ability to manage variable workloads with ease. Employees who are not needed can work on other projects, train to learn new tasks, or perform some 6S chores. The banks that learn to allocate employees where they are needed and organize processes into work cells can achieve dramatic improvements in productivity.

5.10 *Poka Yoke* and Error Proofing

In modern life, we are surrounded by various devices that help prevent mistakes. For example, a fuel cap on a modern car chassis is attached by a wire that prevents its loss; the prongs of an electrical plug allow it to be inserted into a wall outlet in only one correct way; a car beeps when safety belts are not latched; a computer emits a sound when a wrong key is pressed.

Based on Toyota practices, such error-proofing systems are known as *poka yoke* devices. (Readers may wish to Google *poka yoke* to access a menu of creative ideas for preventing mistakes.) Toyota is famous for preventing errors at the source. Most bank work is executed by computers so a bank represents an ideal environment for implementing computerized error-proofing devices.

All banks should take advantage of the creativity of their employees to find new ideas for *poka yoke* devices. Such ideas should be passed on to the IT team for implementation, and the author of the idea should be rewarded. Such ideas tend to produce strong productivity benefits over the long term by preventing countless losses, delays, and frustrations.

Errors should be hard to make, and obvious and visible when made. A bank should utilize systems that allow efficient and undamaged recovery from errors. (Error proofing should not be called "idiot proofing"; the term tends to offend employees.) As Graban [2009] points out, along with error proofing, organizations often need to "error proof the error proofing" to prevent easy ways to circumvent the error-proofing devices. When designing *poka yoke* elements, particularly those that increase the amount of work or make work more difficult, we should anticipate what employees may attempt to do to take short cuts or go around the error proofing.

The idea behind *poka yoke* is profound; investing only a few hours to implement a software or hardware device will make errors difficult or impossible to make, thus preventing countless future delays and frustrations to yield serious savings in the long term. Proactive prevention is always better than reactive correction that produces repeated delays, increased costs, and frustration. Employees like to see their *poka yoke* ideas implemented, and the bank may wish to name a new error-proofing device after its inventor.

5.11 *Gemba*: Walking to See Work

The traditional arrangement of a bank back office is a combination of offices and cubicles, with managers' offices often in remote locations. In extreme cases, managers' offices may be on a different floor or even in another building. This arrangement makes it impractical for a manager to walk to employee workstations regularly. Instead, managers monitor workers from their computers. When called to report to a manager, an employee knows the summons is for an unhappy reason.

The Japanese practice known as *gemba* is the opposite approach. *Gemba* translates as "go and see and help." At its simplest, supervisors and managers in a *gemba* culture walk to the place where work is actually done in order to help employees with problems or look for opportunities for improvements. In a bank environment, this means walking over to an employee, looking at his or her screen or documents, quickly diagnosing the problem or offering advice, perhaps calling someone to help, then moving on. In Lean systems, work efficiency is paramount. If an employee signals a problem (typically about data entry, interpretation of an unusual software message, process details, or customer inquiries), the supervisor should go to the employee's workstation and help immediately. The purpose is not control; the intent is to help the employee to enable the uninterrupted creation of value.

Gemba is vastly more effective for creating value than managing from a remote office. The benefits from *gemba* are numerous. Employee work (providing customer service) continues without delay. Employees feel grateful to their supervisors for help and learn from the interactions. A supervisor quickly learns which processes need to be improved, which checklists or procedures should be updated, and which area of training should be augmented. To facilitate such frequent *gemba* interactions, supervisors' desks should be located in close proximity to employee work areas.

When an employee requests assistance from a supervisor, the assistance must be provided in a friendly tone. Employees appreciate friendliness from supervisors. The supervisor should not presume that the employee wants him or her to do the work. Such abuses are very rare and easy to deal with in short private conversations. In most cases, a situation makes an employee feel lost and in need of help. First, the employee should ask a nearby colleague for help.

A Lean bank culture should strongly promote teamwork and mutual support (again, subject to legitimate restrictions on unauthorized access to certain data). If colleagues cannot help, the employee must be able to count on the supervisor. Consider that the issue or delay will not go away if no help is provided. The issue or delay will likely move downstream and grow, possibly to crisis proportions. In Lean, every effort should be made to identify imperfections, mistakes, and problems when they occur in real time, fix them immediately, and allow the process to resume and add value for customers.

When dealing with a problem, a supervisor should ask, "Why did it happen?" instead of "Whose fault is it?" Before blaming the employee, the supervisor should ask himself or herself several questions. Did the system of work fail to prevent the problem? Did I or someone else give the employee confusing instructions? Was the system not set up well enough to prevent the mistake? Did some unusual circumstance (e.g., a software glitch or cascading error from another location) make it difficult or impossible to do the work correctly? Was the training in this activity inadequate? Did it cover this problem? Does the employee need more training and mentoring? Did I assign the work to the wrong employee? Remember, there is no place in *gemba* for blaming and shaming.

When dealing with an error in the system, a supervisor should look at the severity of the error, the likelihood of occurrence, and the ease of detecting it. Every effort should be made to fix the problem right away. If a problem is too complex to be fixed immediately, a dedicated employee or small *kaizen* blitz team should be assigned to fix it as soon as possible. A root cause analysis should be performed, the remedy applied, and the applicable work procedure updated.

In general, we want to create a culture that does not tolerate mistakes and errors. However, mistakes happen, and when they do, we should blame the system rather than individual employees. When we discover an error, we must stop the work and fix the problem.

Employees should be rewarded for discovering system imperfections and not blamed for them. Of course, there are exceptions to this rule when we deal with what Deming called rare pathological cases: use of drugs, alcohol, unbecoming or criminal behavior, and other serious workplace behaviors. Pathological cases represent less than 1% of problem employees. It is not practical to design a system to police and frustrate the 99% to prevent bad behavior from the remaining 1%. Pathological cases are easy to handle with disciplinary or investigative actions.

5.12 Database of Lessons Learned and Risks

A bank that never has time to learn from its own mistakes is bound to repeat them many times. Smart banks understand that remaining competitive requires them to learn new tricks of the trade continuously as they learn from their own mistakes. Any mistake should produce two immediate corrective actions: one to correct the immediate problem, and the other to update the lessons learned database. To be effective, a database must be well organized and searchable historically by event date, topic, department, and customer account. Similarly, risks can be categorized and stored in the database by type, date, situation, mitigation solution, perhaps client type or even client name. Periodic training in lessons learned and risk avoidance should be offered to relevant employees.

A special type of lessons-learned database should catalog all safety, security, and fraud violations experienced by our bank and other banks to help our bank prevent and prepare for such violations and abuses in the future. The approach is similar to the anti-virus software we install in our computers. As new viruses are discovered, they are added to the existing lists along with anti-virus actions to prevent their toxicity in the future.

5.13 Communities of Practice

The high level of complexity of modern banking and the fast changes of banking knowledge require that individual bank employees have easy opportunities to share their knowledge, experience, and wisdom with their peers. The most effective platform for informal sharing is a broadly understood community of practice. It can be organized at a number of levels: within a department among employees of the same specialty; within a bank branch; within the entire bank corporation; within a local chapter of a professional society; and within national or even international professional societies.

Bankers participating in such communities of practice tend to stay *au courant* on the latest developments in their profession, department, or enterprise; learn faster; and overall become better bankers. Numerous organizations including banks have organized effective communities of practice at various levels, listed below.

- **Department Level**—The employees of a bank department meet periodically (perhaps monthly) to share their experiences, good and failed ideas, solutions to problems, and various do's and don'ts. It is a good practice to revolve the speakers and involve line employees (not managers) to discuss their experiences. The overarching team spirit should be, "We are all in it together; let us share our experiences so that we all become a better bank." These meetings should be informal, pleasant, and free of work hierarchy, while focused on honest sharing of knowledge and experiences.

  Snacks and meals help draw a larger number of people and are always welcome. If the bank cannot supply food, employees should be invited to bring their lunches and make the meeting a collegial working lunch. Better case studies should be written and made available in a lessons learned database to benefit all bank employees. Occasionally, a speaker from another branch, bank, or regulatory body may be invited.
- **Bank Level**—These meetings operate similarly to department meetings, but they include all employees of a certain specialty from all bank divisions. Normally, this community of practice requires more formality than a department level community (e-mailing list, regular meeting times [perhaps quarterly], a convenient or alternating location or an online meeting, advertised agenda). Speakers may be invited.
- **Local Chapters of Professional Banker Societies**—Professional societies have a long and rich tradition of organizing local chapters for sharing knowledge. These chapters organize periodic meetings to encourage friendly networking and sharing knowledge via seminars, lectures, tutorials, and workshops. These events tend to focus more on generic knowledge applicable to an entire industry rather than company-specific issues.
- **National and International Professional Banker Societies**— Professional societies* operating at national or international levels offer numerous benefits for a community of practice: conferences, tutorials, workshops, short courses, journals, books and newsletters, peer

---

* For example, American Bankers Association (ABA), or Association for Financial Professionals (AFP).

reviews, lobbying services, and even financial services such as credit union memberships and insurance.

■ **Web Pages with Case Studies**—Attractive web pages can be organized on an intranet for internal use by bank employees or on the Internet for public use. Interesting papers, presentations, accomplishments, lectures, seminars, tutorials, and information of interest to the community can be posted. If made public, the information helps the banking profession and aids a bank's promotion and marketing efforts. It is important to keep the content free of advertising.

5.14 A3 Form

Toyota invented an amazingly effective and efficient tool for written communication and problem solving known as the A3 form (Figure 5.12). The form plays two important roles. It replaces wordy and time-consuming memorandum and report writing and provides an effective and easy-to-use standardized template for reporting, solving, and managing problems.

Modern bank work continues to become increasingly more complex and thus requires far more communication and coordination among stakeholders. However, it is widely recognized that writing and communication skills are decreasing in many countries, particularly the US. The growing pervasiveness of personal electronics, computers, and social networks and less reading of books make any improvements in literacy skills doubtful.

Therefore, the A3 form is extremely important. It permits employees to enter information about the nature of a problem and proposed solutions in simple bullet form or with a few sentences instead of time-consuming memos and reports that consume inordinate amounts of employee time. The form is a template that contains fields for entering the problem identification number (ID), problem stakeholders, background of the problem reported, problem statement, root cause analysis, proposed countermeasure and solution options with cost indications, and issue resolution. The form should clearly and briefly describe the issue and show the name of the author, his or her title, office location, office and cell phone numbers, e-mail address, project or task identification, and mentor name if applicable. The form should also have a field to enter keywords that can be used for subsequent computer searches.

Problem IDs should be standardized across the entire bank as part of the 6S effort (Section 5.1) to allow consistent computer filing, archiving,

Author: name, title, office location, office and phones, email	Mentor:	
Problem ID:	Keywords:	
Stakeholders:	Root Cause Analysis	Plan
Background	Countermeasures/Solutions & Cost	Do
Problem statement and original goals	Study/Measure	Study
	Resolution	Act

Figure 5.12   A3 form (actual size is 11 × 17 [double letter] or A3 format).

and searching for the forms. Based on the overwhelming globalization trends in modern banking and the needs for massive interbank and bank–government–customer transactions, it is conceivable that an industry-wide standard for the A3 will be agreed upon and mandated for all banks. To prepare for that day, smart bank executives should implement A3 forms early. We hope that this text will aid in the process.

All employees who will use the form (most bank employees at all levels) should attend a short training course (typically two hours) demonstrating the use of A3, with instructions for how and when to use it to replace traditional memorandum and report communications. The original A3 forms were on paper. Now, of course, electronic versions of A3 allow easy e-mailing, storing, cataloging, and record keeping.

Note that the form reports a problem or issue and also asks for a root cause analysis and solution including cost data. The form is conducive to changing a bank workforce from whining passive complainers to active problem solvers—a hugely important cultural transformation in Lean. The standard A3 offers six other significant benefits listed below.

Simplicity—After some initial training and experimentation, employees will enjoy seeing their creative efforts directed toward problem solving and steered away from mundane, boring, and rarely effective tasks such as writing reports and drafting memos. The bank will witness continuous improvements as employees become more familiar with the form.

Organizing agendas—The standard A3 is an ideal tool for grouping meeting agendas by topics cited on the forms. With preliminary work completed as shown on the A3 forms, meetings can devote more time to delving deeper into problems and crafting more effective solutions.

Efficiency in perception—Because the forms are based on a standard template, the amount of time needed to read, understand, and comment on the form content is minimized.

Recordkeeping—The A3 forms are perfect for maintaining well-organized records. They can be computerized easily (and digitized if originally on paper), stored in databases, recovered easily, and reused, thus avoiding reinvention of the wheel.

Lessons learned—The A3 forms constitute a very efficient library of lessons learned. If stored electronically, the database can be easily searched by problem type, key word, or other parameter.

Use in LPDF Integrative Events—Chapter 8 described a super-efficient method for planning and executing bank projects known as Lean Product Development Flow (LPDF). Project employees report problems weekly or more often to a project leader using standard A3 forms. The leader then conducts a weekly comprehensive meeting called an integrative event to discuss issues cited on A3 forms. The A3 forms serve to organize the meeting agenda systematically, covering all problems, issues, trade-offs, and other items that surfaced during the previous week. This method of managing projects efficiently addresses all issues in real time and does not "kick the trouble" downstream for later resolution.

Chapter 6

Deploying Lean

Lead the organization as if you had no power. In other words, shape the organization not through the power of will or dictate, but rather through example, through coaching and through understanding and helping others to achieve their goals.

Kan Higashi, President of Toyota NUMMI

This chapter provides various recommendations for proceeding with Lean implementation, but the reader should appreciate the fact that there is no standard "best" way to implement Lean. Every bank is different and has its own set of challenges, priorities, culture, and expertise mix. Graban [2009] offers this advice: "Keep learning, keep reading, and keep thinking."

6.1 Beginning Implementation with 6S

The effort of implementing orderliness in computer spaces; designing directory trees, file and document naming conventions, and databases; and ensuring controlled, safe, and secure access to bank and client data is a huge undertaking subject to external laws and regulations. If your bank is already operating, it is likely that much of this work is already in place. If not, you should consult experts in bank practice because these activities are beyond the scope of this book.

Messy office spaces are not conducive to Lean deployment. If a bank (or a branch) suffers from poor 6S performance (see Section 5.1), with employees wasting significant time searching for paper or electronic documents (and perhaps not finding them), the Lean implementation should begin with intensive deployment of the 6S components. Only when office spaces are organized properly and employees are well trained and orderly, will a bank be ready for serious Lean deployment.

The implementation of most 6S practices in office spaces and storage areas, such as file cabinets, storage rooms, and desks, and removing clutter is an easy exercise and may be handled as a bottom-up initiative in each department. It should be pursued after initial 6S training. Managers should only encourage and mentor. The 6Ss planning, cleaning, and sorting effort can be organized into group activities.

6.2 Initial Lean Training

It is impossible for any organization including a bank to implement Lean via a top-down directive. Top management must make the strategic decision to introduce Lean and provide empowerment and support, but the implementation must be driven by the employees' desire to make an imperfect system a better one. Do not attempt to change the entire bank at one time. Instead, organize effective Lean training for as many employees as possible as quickly as possible and let them incorporate Lean into their work with help of an expert. Components for organizing comprehensive Lean training are described below.

6.2.1 Elimination of Destructive Myths

Inept, lip service implementations of Lean in a number of companies unjustifiably led to several inaccurate and unfair myths: Lean is mean; Lean leads to layoffs; I need roller skates to move faster in Lean. Hopefully, this book will destroy these mythical ideas before they reach your employees. It is critical to provide enough Lean training to defuse these myths before Lean work starts.

6.2.2 Team Effort

Lean involves good sense, but it has not yet become common sense. Lean thinkers represent only a small minority in society and a tiny minority in the banking industry. In contrast to traditional bank practices, some Lean ideas may appear radical to the uninitiated. Because Lean is a team effort often involving cross-functional teams, all members of a given team must be exposed to the same Lean training. If this is not done, the members who are not trained will not appreciate the changes, will be unable to participate effectively in team activities, and may grow to resent and oppose them.

6.2.3 Training

Banks tend to offer easy training logistics. Even in the largest banks, the initial Lean activities will involve relatively small groups of stakeholders. Typically, the groups will be small enough to attend a Lean training together. This ensures that their training is consistent and optimizes training costs.

The training must provide a solid understanding of what Lean offers, explain why it is worth the effort, and detail its specific elements: Lean culture, fundamentals (value, customer, waste, six principles), and tools. A weekend retreat (two full days) is normally sufficient to convince all trainees that Lean offers extraordinary opportunities and should be pursued as a long-term bank strategy. A retreat will instruct them in the basics of Lean (if attention is focused on the training and not on bank work or family matters). The weekend training will not make the participants experts in Lean, but should be enough to make them enthusiastic participants in Lean deployment.

Good training should include a significant number (about 50%) of participatory exercises to emphasize the power of Lean. Murman et al. [2014] describe a very effective introductory three-day training program called Lean Academy™ (available free of charge on the Internet) that has been perfected by delivery to thousands of individuals in diverse industries. Although the course cites some examples from manufacturing, 90% of the concepts apply to all environments including banking. The course can be tailored easily to two days because it includes topics that are likely to be known to many bank participants.

6.2.4 Culture Change and Management Support

By now, readers understand that Lean represents a significant cultural change from traditional banking. Lean, like all major organizational transformations, must be led by an expert. Expertise in banking is not required, but the leader should be familiar with typical bank operations and departments.

The authors are not aware of any successful transformations to Lean without wholehearted support from top management. Therefore, Lean training must include all top executives and high-level managers. The two-day retreat described above is recommended. Such training should make the executives enthusiastic Lean supporters, interested observers, and active participants in various Lean activities. Ideally, a common session for bank executives, managers, and employees would create desirable commonality of purpose and openness to changes. However, many executives and high-level managers prefer separate sessions and that preference should be respected.

After initial training, executives normally send an enthusiastic signal to middle management that Lean has been chosen as the strategy for the future, and immediately invite other managers and line employees to pursue Lean training. The groups invited to training should include both managers and line employees from the departments that work closely and cooperate with one another. Banks are fortunate in that the number of people involved in individual processes is small and they constitute ideal size for a Lean team. Several teams can be trained together to achieve efficiency and economy.

The total number of trainees per course should not exceed 20 to 25, because training involves simulations, interactions, and team exercises, and these are difficult to conduct in large groups. If the entire group of employees and managers serving in a bank back office is fewer than 25 or 30, as if often the case, a single training session should be organized for all of them. The common training teaches the fundamentals (value, customer, waste, principles, tools) and also develops consciousness of the most important cultural aspect of Lean, namely teamwork—the sense that "we are all in it together" and that former stove-piped tribal thinking no longer makes sense.

6.2.5 Determining Values and Identifying Customers

An excellent exercise to conduct near the end of the training session is the identification of each internal customer and the value to each customer. Each cross-functional team should select one typical and rather simple process involving specific tasks including approvals. It is best to select a process that is notoriously frustrating.

The tasks of the process should be listed in the sequence of operations along with the names of the people who perform the task. Next, each team member should identify by name his internal customer for the task (the recipient of the output—not his or her boss who acts as a traffic cop and mentor rather than a customer) and invite the customer to define the value expected from the task. The team then defines the ultimate external customer for the process and the value expected by that customer. An expert Lean leader should guide the effort.

This exercise leads participants to understand that it is pointless to see each task in isolation, and to blame each other, individuals, and departments for an imperfect system. They will recognize that they all need to join forces to make their system better for their customers. At this point, the training participants usually feel energized and ready to begin the new exciting Lean journey.

6.3 Lean Deployment

After training, each team should be ready to start work on Lean deployment. A good practice is to select a process known for problems: waiting and delays, defects and rework, and excessive movements of people and information, then generate a current state map (CSM) and redesign the process as a future state map (FSM). The selected process should be somewhat larger than the one used in the training exercise above, but not excessively difficult. A balance is needed; the initial attempt should not be too large or complex or it may exceed the knowledge and energy of the team. Conversely, it should not be too small or the changes may not yield enough impact. The Lean expert leader should provide advice on the project size.

Each team should be given sufficient wall space for the mapping (see Section 4.3.2). Of course, several teams may share the same room. Each team should begin with a list of facts: the process name, the internal or external end customer of the process, and the value of the process to the customer. It is best to include in the team the ultimate internal customer of the process. The team should create a formal but concise problem statement explaining why this process was selected and why it prevents the bank from achieving success. They should also determine the top-level goals to eliminate the problem and the metrics for evaluating improvements. Typically, the metrics relate more or less directly to the costs, work time, quality, service, and satisfaction of the process customer. The starting values of the metrics should be honestly recorded based on the end customer's needs so that subsequent improvements can be judged objectively.

One full day should be sufficient to map the current state of a small process, assuming that a Lean expert is available to guide and mentor a team that includes all key stakeholders of the process. The entire team should contribute. The leader should guide team members' emotions gently and foster a creative, enthusiastic environment free of fear.

During the mapping, the team must physically walk along all the steps of the process and identify all tasks, decision points, paths, and task categories (green for value-added, yellow for required non-value-added, and red for non-value-added), as explained in Section 4.3.2. The decision points are usually displayed in purple or pink.

The exercise during the training was only a rough approximation. The team is now ready to do the work in detail. The tasks, decisions, and paths should be captured and displayed on a wall so that all participants can see them. The mapping is, of course, a big brainstorming and trial-and-error process. The leader has a dual role: to guide participants in the technical aspects of mapping and prevent frustration of the group. When the team reaches the consensus that indeed the CSM represents a good representation of current reality, the CSM should be redrawn cleanly to be readable and later aid the creation of the FSM.

Normally, the team at this point has entered what Toussaint et al. [2010] describe as the initiation stage that involves interest but not yet commitment. Participants seek more information and want to become involved in Lean. They want to know more but are not yet ready to consider how the changes will affect them personally. This initial energy about change should not be mistaken for commitment; this will come later.

Next, the team should brainstorm the future state—discussing what must be done to eliminate the wastes and improve quality at every step. Section 4.2 contains specific advice on waste elimination. The focus should be on eliminating non-value-added wastes, reducing necessary non-value-added wastes, and simplifying convoluted process paths and backflows. The team should not yet attempt to distribute responsibilities (who will do what, when, and how). Again, the best outcome during the FSM effort is reaching a team consensus on what needs to change. When that milestone is reached, the team will likely exhibit a high level of enthusiasm from eliminating so much waste so quickly (at least on paper) as they increase teamwork.

After the team agrees on the FSM, detailed planning should cover who will do what, how, and when. Often, this requires changes in daily routines. As Toussaint [2010] notes, at this stage, employees are learning and testing the limits of the system, asking whether the promised benefits are real, searching for unknown downsides, and questioning whether the changes will help or hurt them. Many people achieve tangible successes from the changes and feel validated. A minority may not succeed because they are skeptical or resistant, and may find reasons why the changes cannot work. Some failed attempts will validate their opposition.

Strong positive reinforcement from the team leader is critical at this phase. He or she should remind employees that they did not become good drivers with a snap of a finger. While many converts embrace the change, a few will see that the change will require a real effort on their part. While the change will yield a less frustrating system when it is in place, it will take employees out of their comfort zones and require extra effort during implementation.

Some will ask whether they must "do this and my job at the same time?" The Lean leader should respond with, "Only for a short time, and you will get lots of help. Later you will find big productivity reserves that will lower the frantic pace of your work that was the norm until now." Some employees may actively or passively refrain from cooperating and conduct meetings in corridors to explain why the change will not work. It is important in this phase not to ignore emotional responses. The best way to convince people of the desirability of change is to organize a *kaizen* blitz team session to discuss some small but tangible aspect of the change while re-focusing on what is wrong with the current state and where we want to go in a reasonably short time. The objectives are to build consensus on the steps of getting from here to there, agree on the metrics, and distribute the assignments.

During the initial Lean attempts, management and executives should visit the teams and offer thanks for hard work, encouragement, hopes for big improvements, and congratulations on achieving milestones (such as the CSM, FSM, etc.). After achieving a tangible success with one process, employees should be empowered to continue improving it and also focus on the next process of Lean deployment. It is important to keep increasing the wave of Lean deployment by continuing to incorporate more teams and processes.

Over time, typically weeks (or a few months for a complex process), employees begin to be persuaded by solid facts that the new is better than the old and they can see clearly how the change benefits them personally. They notice that their focus has changed from dealing with crises to thinking of improvements. More importantly, they begin to notice new imperfections and treat them as further improvement opportunities, thus unleashing more energy and enthusiasm to implement the improvements. Employees begin to align with the changes and are to pursue more. The stakeholders of the change will tell others in the bank that "you should definitely try this Lean stuff." New behaviors become habits; data trends move in positive directions; and trust in Lean grows.

Over the long term, Lean will definitely yield tangible productivity improvements in a bank. Sharing some of the savings with the employees is always a good policy because it reinforces teamwork and fairness. Small tangible rewards (tickets to movies or sports events and gift cards) are always appreciated. If serious savings are demonstrated, formal (and identical) bonuses should be awarded to all team members.

6.4 *Hoshin Kanri* for Sustaining Lean Energy

During a long Lean transformation, it is not unusual to observe a decrease in the original enthusiasm for Lean when daily chores are allowed to overtake the Lean deployment attempts. This occurs most often in dysfunctional organizations that are trying frantically to meet current work deadlines and have no time left for improvements even though Lean will surely free up the needed time. An approach called *hoshin kanri* (strategy deployment) was developed in Japan to re-focus employees on Lean deployment. Three questions should be asked when the enthusiasm seems to deflate:

- What are the most critical current problems and opportunities for our bank?
- What initiatives do we need to undertake to address the problems and opportunities?
- How should we measure the success of our initiatives?

The answers to these questions will provide a new Lean focus. The selected problem or problems should be prioritized and captured on A3 forms. Depending on problem size, a simple *kaizen* blitz team of stakeholders for a small problem or a formal Six Sigma improvement process for a large problem should be organized. Because *hoshin kanri* tends to identify serious problems, each team will need to involve experienced bank employees along with a Lean expert to mentor and guide each team in the most effective Lean deployment. Progress should be measured by selected metrics. When any team achieves significant success, the team members will appreciate appropriate recognition from a high-level manager. The recognition will promote Lean as an effective paradigm for change.

Six Sigma practitioners may notice that the initial phases of *hoshin kanri* are very similar: identify problem candidates, prioritize them using disciplined measurements, and attack them using Lean Thinking. Toussaint [2010] observed that *hoshin kanri* offers good opportunities for aspiring Lean leaders to display their leadership abilities, effectiveness, and mentoring skills during frequent *gemba* walks, without "bossing" people around. Toussaint developed a list of desired leadership traits:

- Patience
- Inquisitiveness
- Keen interest in problem solving
- Good communication skill
- Desire to see people succeed
- Wish to work in the middle of the action instead of being stuck behind a desk

As with the initial Lean deployment efforts, it is highly desirable to have a Lean expert available for team guidance and mentoring. Toussaint [2010] notes, "In the literature of modern business management, there is great reverence for change agents, nimble companies capable of change, and just about every other kind of change. Change is good. Except, along with change, people require constancy of direction. Organizational systems and methods require consistency and steady direction as well." Sustained *hoshin kanri* practice is effective in "keeping the Lean fire lit."

6.5 Learning from Experiences of Others

Toussaint [2010] describes a Lean deployment that he led in a very difficult environment: a large health organization (ThedaCare in Wisconsin) employing doctors and nurses who had strong preconceived medical notions that were almost directly opposite Lean principles. After working in this environment for years and achieving notable success, Toussaint captured his Lean deployment experiences into 11 pages of wisdom. This text is regarded as a highly important asset for all new Lean deployment efforts, and we summarize it briefly below. All quotes in this section come from Toussaint's book. [Square brackets denote small changes in text made to facilitate reading by the banking community.] We use the original spelling of *hoshin kanry*. These summaries are intended to whet the appetite of the reader for more in-depth study of the original text.

1. **Identify Crisis**—"When the platform on which you stand starts to burn, action is the only choice." Indeed, observations of Lean deployment in many industries indicate that companies in crisis tend to adopt Lean more readily, seeing it as the last life raft available [Womack et al., 1996; McCormack, 2002]. For this reason, dysfunctional banks (see Chapter 2) may demonstrate stronger desires to implement Lean than successful banks.

2. **Create Lean Promotion Office**—"A Lean promotion office is critical for planning and managing change to ensure that employees are educated and involved in Lean. A high-level executive should be tapped to lead this office full time, reporting to the CEO."

   "An organization committed to Lean should aspire to have 3% of the work force assigned as full-time Lean facilitators. The goal should be that all managers have at least two years' full-time experience in continuous improvement. We also believe it is imperative to hire deeply knowledgeable teachers or consultants to work with the Lean promotion office. In the beginning, we didn't know what we didn't know. So, we also needed to visit other companies, participate on their teams, and learn from other executives experienced in Lean.… Next, move all quality functions in your organization into the Lean promotion office.… Finally, do not allow Lean and quality to become divided in the minds of your employees. If this happens, Lean will earn a reputation as being about cost cutting alone. Quality and efficiency are inextricably linked in a truly Lean organization."

3. **Find Change Agents**—"There are agents of change throughout your organization, just waiting to be unveiled. These supervisors and senior managers and front-line [workers] probably do not know yet that they have the capacity to lead major change.… Here is how you will recognize them: They will be complainers and local agitators who hear about Lean and seize upon it to make the changes they want. [Upon] discovering that Lean principles help them solve seemingly intractable problems, agitators become champions and early adopters. These are your change agents. Give them tools and air cover and they will help Lean take root in your organization.… Finally, find change agents on your board of directors. At least one of them will likely be implementing Lean in his or her company. Give all board members a chance to champion the changes. Keep them informed of Lean's progress and the barriers you find. Put them on *kaizen* teams. Without the support and

assistance of … board of trustees, our Lean journey would have completely derailed after three years."

4. **Map Value Streams**—"These maps have been an epiphany [for both
managers and line employees] who see just how difficult a [process]
path can be. This discovery usually drives them into action to use Lean
tools to create easier […] journeys."

5. **Engage Senior Leaders Early in Strategy Deployment**—"Another
common mistake of Lean initiatives involves outsourcing improvements. There are plenty of consultants who will launch Lean with a
campaign of *kaizen* events, explaining that everyone will learn by
doing. This leaves senior managers free to (probably) work at cross
purposes to Lean. Also, consultants who are not working closely with
senior management will not have a plan as to how the improvements
all fit together to improve [the customer] experience, reduce costs, and
serve the organization's long-term goals. Instead, senior managers must
be intimately involved in Lean through strategy deployment, or *hoshin
kanry*. As described earlier, *hoshin kanry* is a standardized process to
help an organization select and focus on the few key priorities…. We
spent six years asking the question, 'What is most important?' until we
all agreed on four things: [customer satisfaction], safety, quality, people,
and financial stewardship."

6. **Acquire and Disperse Knowledge Broadly**—"Strict learn-by-doing
meant putting 5,500 people through a week-long rapid improvement
event and the logistics soon became insurmountable. Therefore, large
organizations with even a low turnover rate need to combine *kaizen*-
type team weeks with something like hands-on, single day seminars
and internships. ThedaCare's seminars use simulations to present the
theory of Lean and group discussion on the reasons to pursue Lean.
It was not intended to be a comprehensive Lean training, but by using
seminars with simulations, all employees could receive some introduction to Lean within three months. Separate training for managers is …
necessary because they need to understand and use value stream maps,
PDSA, visual tracking … and many other tools. ThedaCare managers
struggled with Lean ideas for months until leaders realized that a Lean
training course specifically for managers was needed."

7. **Teach a Man to Fish (or Become a Mentor)**—"There are two basic
types of leadership: modern (Sloan) and Lean (Toyota). The Sloan
style is top-down and autocratic, while Lean leaders are teachers and

facilitators. Medical and business schools are not churning out Toyota-style leaders, so you will need to create the leaders you want…. Chief executive officers must lead the way to this change by modeling the behavior they want from subordinates. This means being out on the floor where the work takes place, at *gemba*, with top executives in tow, teaching, listening, and finding barriers to remove for front line staff. In this way, directors and vice presidents gain first-hand knowledge of Lean, see what the new expectations are, and learn to focus their energies on the place where value is created…. CEOs will need to see that bonus structures of top executives are rewritten to reflect Lean leadership goals. In the Lean world, saving the company money is not rewarded if [customer] care is undermined in the process…. In the perfect Lean world ThedaCare is always working toward, every employee is a problem solver and every executive and manager is a mentor, leading subordinates through a standardized process to solve problems so that they deeply understand what they are trying to accomplish for the organization."

8. **Involve Suppliers in Lean Efforts**—"Invite suppliers to join Lean improvement projects and then set new expectations for how those suppliers interact with your company…. The key in this work was partnership instead of competition."

9. **Restructure Organization into Product Families**—"This is a straightforward task in manufacturing where the design and manufacture of different models, for example, cars or snow blowers, can be clearly separated into product-family value streams." In banking, "it means co-locating steps in a process whenever possible to tightly coordinate all the steps."

10. **Do Not Let Anything Stop You**—"Once an organization becomes convinced that measurement is necessary, how and what to measure can become the topic of nagging disagreements and epic turf wars. Do not let that stop the work. This is perhaps the most important piece of advice we can offer from seven years of experience at ThedaCare: trust the improvement process…. Learn everything you can about Lean thinking, get all of your top executives on board through *hoshin kanry*, create an intelligent path, and the infrastructure to support that path. And then keep pushing the work forward."

6.6 Lean Metrics

Banks must monitor their operations accurately and in real time. All banks use a large number of financial metrics, and most of the measurements are automated, extracted from transactions. To summarize, each bank must monitor all its financial transactions including client accounts and activities, currency operations, security trades, general ledger operations, interbank and international transactions, transactions with the central bank, copious measurements required by regulatory bodies, and numerous statistics covering transactions. Banks are not short on metrics used for monitoring their financial activities, and we leave them alone.

This section focuses instead on the Lean metrics that monitor bank operations factors such as productivity and quality, process efficiency and effectiveness, and related human activities. The key to the right metrics is to measure the right things right. Recently a new body of knowledge called Lean Accounting evolved focused on measuring the right things right. We recommend two important books [Cunningham et al., 2003; Maskell et al., 2011]. The following material is based on these two sources. Cunningham recommends the following characteristics for metrics to be used in enterprises (we adapted them slightly for bank operations).

1. **Support Bank Strategy**—Each bank follows a certain strategic path. The metrics should measure the variables along the path that describe how well the bank advances toward its strategic goals. For example, if a strategic goal is to increase the number of branches, metrics should measure the number of branches currently operating and the number in various phases of development.

2. **Minimize Numbers and Use**—At best, metrics represent NNVA activities, and their use should be minimized to what is truly needed to monitor value creation or the future ability to create value. However, many enterprises drown in useless metrics. Some metrics were mandated for only a short time or for a single use. No one remembered to remove them, and they are still in place, wasting resources. Consider another example in which a manager ordered metrics for his own special assignments. The manager no longer works for the bank, but the metrics are still used. Every bank can supply a number of such nonsensical examples. The time spent collecting data for those metrics robs the bank from doing value-adding work and represents pure NVA. It is

important to sort all metrics used and discard those that make no sense or are obsolete.

3. **Be Mostly Nonfinancial**—Lean metrics should measure progress toward Lean goals rather than profits. Good metrics should focus on customer satisfaction and creation of value (decreasing lead time and costs while increasing quality and level of service). If a bank does a great job making external customers happy, profits will follow.

4. **Be Structured to Motivate Right Behavior**—Good metrics should monitor the right behavior (making the bank better and more competitive, increasing customer satisfaction, applying continuous improvement of processes, increasing quality of bank services and products, reducing customer wait times for loan and credit approvals, making processes predictable, and developing employees). Be very careful to avoid the unintended consequences that result from the wrong metrics that may foster undesirable behaviors such as rivalries between employees.

5. **Be Simple and Easy to Understand**—Good metrics provide information that is clear and does not require complex interpretations or algorithms.

6. **Measure Processes, Not People**—We should measure process performance and process improvements rather than people who are forced to operate in existing processes. In Lean, we must remember that people operate in a given system, executing given processes, and depend on others who execute upstream tasks. This comment is addressed to banks that practice management by objectives and use computerized management information systems to closely monitor each employee's work. The data collected from such a system may unfairly indicate poor performance of some employees using a faulty system that made good performance impossible or exceedingly difficult.

   For example, because of an inefficient system, an employee may have received incorrect, incomplete, or delayed data. In fact, the employee works heroically to correct the data and minimize delays, but the bottom line shows that he or she is regularly late. Penalizing this employee because a computer index revealed an isolated and misleading result is unfair and leads to a serious loss of respect for management.

7. **Measure Actual Results versus Goals**—Measure the levels actually achieved and compare them to the goals set. If the achievements fall short of the goals, the system must be adjusted (is more training needed?) or perhaps the goals are not realistic.

8. **Do Not Combine Dissimilar Measures into a Single Index**—Use metrics that measure single variables for simplicity of interpretation. Combining several variables into a single index tends to cloud the resulting image.

9. **Be Timely**—Good metrics monitor a variable in real time or after a slight tolerable delay.

10. **Show Trend Lines**—Few metrics are as valuable as trend line monitoring for analyzing critical variables such as quality, productivity, costs, lead times, customer satisfaction, and customer complaints. Trend curves inform us whether we are on a right path, improving or worsening; they steer us toward better management decisions. Figure 5.8 illustrates a quality trend over time.

11. **Be Visual**—The metrics that monitor bank operational variables that are important in Lean (quality, productivity, costs, lead times, customer satisfaction, and customer complaints) should not be kept secret. They should be displayed for all to see via visual controls such as boards or television screens. Any data displayed should show results for the entire bank, branches, or departments and never mention individual employees.

As a final thought, not every activity or result can be measured. While effective metrics are critical for effective decision making, many important aspects of the Lean culture are very difficult if not impossible to measure. Consider a family life example. It is not possible to invent valid metrics for a happy marriage or partnership or for raising good children. The most important aspects of family life such as love, empathy, devotion, emotional support, and commitment are not measurable but are obvious to the people involved.

The behavioral aspects that can be described by metrics are too superficial to be of any use. For example, imagine a gift-giving occasion such as Christmas or Hanukkah. A wife tells her husband, "You forgot to lower the toilet seat 17 times last year, so you do not get a present this year." He responds with, "You burned the soup 20 times so you do not get a present either." The exchange sounds absurd but it demonstrates how such superficial metrics never work. The most critical aspects of Lean are the culture of respect (teamwork, leadership, fairness, openness, and honesty) and lack of fear. These attributes are obvious to employees even though we have no good metrics to measure them. The authors emphatically disagree with business ideologues who claim that "everything can and should be measured, and if it cannot be measured it does not exist."

6.7 Teamwork

Recall the mission statement formulated by Toyota for its NUMMI plant: "Through teamwork, safely build the highest quality vehicles at the lowest possible cost to benefit our customers, team members, community and shareholders." *Teamwork* is the first noun and the most important word in the statement. The former president of NUMMI also said:

> "In my opinion, the key to the successful implementation of [Toyota Production System] at ... Toyota plants in North America has been the total commitment on the part of everyone to make it work. By that I mean all levels of the organization, from team members to the senior managers, have to be aware of the fundamentals of TPS and have to make their best efforts to practice and improve them day by day.... Team members appreciate management [...] on the floor only when they can see that we are out there to help them do their jobs, not as part of a command structure, bent on telling them what to do."
>
> **Gary Convis, 2013**

The masters of Lean view teamwork as the most important aspect of Lean operations. This lesson has been adapted in all environments where Lean has been used. It surely applies to banking as well.

No enterprise is free of problems. When a problem is discovered, the traditional response is to blame a worker. The Lean response is for a quick-reaction team to swarm the problem by identifying the root cause and eliminating it immediately. Some teams can be small: a bank worker and his colleague, or a worker and his supervisor, two managers from interfacing departments, or several stakeholders working together. Lean is all about the team spirit: we are all in it together, this is our bank; we must serve it well to ensure the bank has customers who will pay our salaries and bills; we have a shared conviction that every problem robs our bank of opportunities to serve our customers.

Lean relies on both formal and spontaneous teams. Formal teams of process stakeholders are needed to map value streams because no single employee or manager is capable of drawing this type of map across several departments. Teamwork should exist between each supplier and his or her internal customer in the value chain for every non-routine transaction. *Kaizen* blitz teams are needed to address every impediment to workflow that crosses two or more desks. Training involves a team of trainer and trainees. Lean Academy™ [2008] describes team dynamics as follows:

> "Strong teams usually can voice disagreements early, constructively, directly, and explicitly. Because they tackle these issues before they've built up, they can resolve them and keep moving. Contrast this with weaker teams in which team members bicker, argue, or hold grudges. Resolving disagreements is only part of the effective life of the team. Strong teams instinctively praise or appreciate the work of their teammates. Recognition of tasks well done doesn't have to be effusive, but some positive gesture often gives energy and life to a team."
>
> **Lean Academy™, 2008**

The same source lists characteristics of a good team. It:

- Promotes mutual respect for all people and jobs.
- Encourages contributions by all team members.
- Values different opinions.
- Fosters open and honest communications and seeks feedback.
- Pursues aligned goals.
- Works toward continuous improvement of individuals and team.
- Understands and uses synergy and cooperation.
- Recognizes that Lean deployment needs teamwork.

6.8 Training

Training of employees during Lean deployment is the most effective improvement tool available to banks. One good training session can transform employees with little practical knowledge into productive members of the bank team.

Training is the most effective way of implementing a new standard, procedure, or checklist. This type of training may be accomplished often in short sessions during staff meetings: here is a new procedure; here are the reasons why it was created; here are the stakeholders for the procedure; here are the do's and don't's; if you have questions, please ask the appropriate person. Even a short introduction to a new standard will increase buy-in. High-risk standards, of course, need more extensive training.

Training is the ideal solution to the frequent problem of a supervisor who often finds mistakes made by his or her employees. If the supervisor knows how to do the job and the workers do not, what could be more effective than a training session in which the supervisor shares his or her knowledge with employees?

Training offers the shortest payback period of any improvement method and is the least expensive of all options over the long term. The investment involves time of the trainer and trainees and the time required to prepare training materials (required only once since the materials will be reused many times). In practice, we invest a few hours or days of training in some aspect of work, and the investment returns a lifetime of better work by employees. If only the stock market could offer such returns on investments!

As noted earlier, in a bank environment care must be taken not to violate various Chinese walls and other rules intended to protect confidentiality, safety, and security of bank and client data. However, in departments in which several employees can perform similar work, it makes sense to introduce multi-skilled training of all people in the department. One benefit is that any employee can replace one who is sick or otherwise absent without loss of workflow. Another reason is that bringing all employees in the department to the same set of skills and credentials is conducive to teamwork and makes management easier. Employees should be motivated to acquire as many skills as practical, and annual merit evaluations should reflect the training and certifications completed.

6.9 Scientific Approach

Spear and Bower [2006] devote an article to an apparent paradox of the Toyota Production System. They write, "On the one hand, every activity, connection, and production flow in a Toyota factory is rigidly scripted. Yet at the same time, Toyota's operations are enormously flexible and responsive to customer demand. How can that be?" They explain that, "It's the very rigidity of Toyota operations that makes the flexibility possible," because Toyota operations can be seen as a continuous series of controlled experiments that have four rigid elements: hypothesis, test, evaluation, and standardization.

Every scientist recognizes these elements as the essence of scientific discovery. Applying these elements wherever there is an opportunity to improve a system makes operations flexible and responsive. The authors captured the approach into four work capabilities that we adopted to bank operations.

Capability 1: Work is designed as a series of ongoing experiments that immediately reveal problems—Every element of bank work must be planned, designed, and standardized in minute detail. Bank operations are too critical and carry too many serious risks to be tried ad hoc by employees, without standards. A bank must specify how work is to be done based on solid knowledge of all rules, regulations, laws, tools, and lessons learned. However, even the best planning does not guarantee that the process will perform as intended unless it is verified by experiment. Every operation must have effective built-in alarms to signal abnormal behaviors. The alarms can be automated in software like *poka yoke* or simple visual inspections of work steps.

Capability 2: Problems are addressed immediately through rapid experimentation—Bank operations cannot tolerate ongoing abnormalities. Whenever an abnormality or imperfection is discovered, the work must be stopped and the problem identified and eliminated immediately. Local stakeholders who best understand the problem should fix the problem. Interestingly, Lean culture does not insist that people succeed on the first attempt. Bank operations are complex and correction of a problem may require experimentation.

Often, a rapid experiment may be required to find an effective countermeasure using a PDSA cycle of small-step trials of improvements. Each cycle includes a hypothesis for the improvement idea, an experiment trying the idea, a study of the result, and rejection of the hypothesis if the result is negative or adoption and standardization if it succeeds. When we introduce changes to a process, it is important to keep an open mind about the outcome rather than insist that success will be certain because we are experts. If the result of an experiment is unsatisfactory, we abandon the hypothesis and try anew. All employees should be trained in this open-minded approach.

Capability 3: Solutions are disseminated adaptively though collaborative experimentation—Effective solutions achieved in one bank office (whether main office or branch) should be shared with all other offices to leverage the success and prevent other offices from expending the same efforts and costs. As soon as a new standard is created, it should be disseminated to all stakeholders in the entire bank to increase the overall quality of operations and enhance competitiveness. Lean replaces rivalries among bank branches with cooperation to allow the entire organization to compete ferociously with other banks.

Capability 4: People at all levels of the bank are taught to be experimentalists—Effective Lean training enables bank employees to locate wastes and problems they did not see earlier and notice new opportunities to improve the work system. The training energizes people to experiment with new ideas, but changes must be introduced carefully because of the high risks and zero tolerance for defects inherent in bank operations. Bank operations are too critical to allow spontaneous changes throughout the operation.

All proposed experiments should be discussed first with supervisors and their execution mentored by Lean experts. It is very important for supervisors to be open to suggestions for changes, appreciate the possibilities for improving operations, and allow employees to try new ways in a controlled way. However, every attempt must be formulated as an experiment involving a hypothesis, its verification, a study of the results, and an open mind as to possible success or failure. Clearly, experiments must be conducted carefully and safely without risking interruptions of bank operations. With that in mind, supervisors and managers must allow some experimentation or the Lean deployment will dissolve into resentful passivity.

6.10 Lean Deployment: Closing Thoughts

We wish to close this chapter with two quotes from known experts. The first is from the former president of Toyota's NUMMI plant.

> "What have I learned from my experience with the Toyota Production System [called Lean in this book] that I can pass along to you? First, I have learned that the human dimension is the single most important element for success. Management has no more critical role than motivating and engaging large numbers of

people to work together toward a common goal. Defining and explaining what that goal is, sharing a path to achieving it, motivating people to take the journey with you, and assisting them by removing obstacles—these are management's reason for being.... In other words, shape the organization not through the power of will or dictate, but rather through example, through coaching, and through understanding and helping others to achieve their goals. This, I truly believe, is the role of management in a healthy, thriving work environment."

Gary Convis, 2013

The second quote is from the medical field. Replacing *hospital* with *bank* will allow these profound thoughts to apply to banking environments.

"The questions that are sure to follow are: How do I get there? What will I look like when I'm done? First off, there is no *done* or *there* … with Lean improvement. There is always a problem to solve and waste to eliminate. After more than 50 years of developing and using Lean methods, Toyota still has waste and problems to solve. They are, however, significantly better than their competitors in many ways, and they continue to improve. There is no perfectly Lean company, so the term *Lean hospital* might really be shorthand for a *hospital that is using Lean methods to manage and improve.*"

Mark Graban, 2009

Chapter 7

Lean Enablers for Banks

This chapter presents important best practices developed for large engineering programs and adapted for banking work. From 2006 through 2009, one of the authors (Oppenheim) co-led a large project tasked with developing best practices based on Lean Thinking for complex engineering programs conducted under the auspices of the International Council on Systems Engineering (INCOSE). The project involved 14 experts and 150 practitioners from academia, large engineering (typically defense) companies, and US, UK, and Israeli governments. The intent was to create Lean-inspired best practices (Lean Enablers) that would guide program managers and their teams.

7.1 Success of Lean Enablers Project

The Lean Enablers were supposed to inject Lean Thinking into traditional engineering practices, not remove them. The outcome was the development of 146 Lean Enablers organized into the six Lean Principles. The Enablers were eventually published as a book, *Lean for Systems Engineering with Lean Enablers for Systems Engineering* [Oppenheim, 2011]. The team developing the Lean Enablers received several prestigious honors including the Shingo Award (highest award for operational excellence), the 2010 INCOSE Best Product Award, and several smaller recognitions. The book author was honored with the 2011 Fulbright Award. Subsequent worldwide interest in the Lean Enablers resulted in more than 50 lectures, seminars, tutorials, and meetings in 20 countries in the Americas, Asia, and Europe.

The success of the Enablers led to a follow-up project jointly sponsored by the Project Management Institute (PMI), INCOSE, and the Massachusetts Institute of Technology. Again, 15 experts and 180 practitioners cooperated in the development of best practices for integrated program management and systems engineering. The key people from the first project participated as experts in the second one, but most of the team members were new.

The initial INCOSE Lean Enablers were incorporated and about 170 new ones developed, for a total set of 329 best practices for managing engineering programs. *The Guide to Lean Enablers for Managing Engineering Programs* [Oehmen (Ed.), 2012] describes the project and results. The book received the 2012 Shingo Award, an INCOSE Award, and praises from the presidents of INCOSE and PMI. A large global dissemination effort continues.

7.2 Applicability to Banking Operations

What do the engineering practices have to do with banking? When writing this book, we realized that many of the Lean Enablers developed for engineering also applied directly to banking. We included 130 of the Enablers in this chapter after minor modifications to make them suitable for the banking community. They fall into 10 categories of bank management activities: leadership, culture, communications and coordination, general management, project management, process management, continuous improvement, hiring, planning, and suppliers. Of course, the categories overlap somewhat; a Lean Enabler may apply to more than one category. Many of the topics addressed by the Lean Enablers have been discussed in the previous chapters of this book.

These Enablers should be treated as Lean-inspired advice intended to improve and complement normal banking practices. They do not replace normal bank processes. Each Enabler promotes some aspect of value and/or reduces some waste. Many of the enablers deal with human factors that are often ignored in technical books on banking.

No bank should embark on implementing all of the enablers; that would be unrealistic. We recommend that each reader read all the Enablers (they cover only a few pages) and select for implementation those that offer the greatest benefit to his or her organization. *Lean for Systems Engineering with Lean Enablers for Systems Engineering* contains comprehensive, detailed information for implementing each Enabler, the value promoted, waste prevented, in-depth explanation, lag factors that slow implementation, recommended reading lists, and examples of practice.

7.3 Lean Enablers Designed for Banks

1. Leadership

1.1. Pursue Lean for the long term.
1.2. Give leaders at all levels in-depth Lean training.
1.3. Create a shared vision that draws out and inspires the best in people.
1.4. When staffing leadership positions, choose team players and collaboratively minded individuals over perfect-looking credentials on paper.
1.5. Leadership must mentor and provide a model for desired team behavior in the areas of trust, respect, honesty, empowerment, teamwork, stability, motivation, and drive for excellence.
1.6. Ensure clear responsibility, accountability, and authority (RAA) throughout the bank.
1.7. Invest heavily in skills and intellectual capital; engage people with deep knowledge of the product and technology.

2. Culture

2.1. Build a culture based on respect for people.
2.2. Understand that activities fail or succeed primarily based on people, not processes. Treat people as valued assets.
2.3. Build a culture of mutual trust and support (there is no shame in asking for help).
2.4. When resolving issues, attack the problem, not the people.
2.5. Proactively resolve potential conflicting stakeholder values and expectations, and seek consensus.
2.6. Eliminate fear from the work environment. Promote conflict resolution at the lowest level.
2.7. Ensure that each employee can see how his or her contributions contribute to the success of the vision.
2.8. Promote the ability to learn rapidly and improve continuously.
2.9. Allow a certain amount of failure in a controlled environment at lower levels so people can take risks and grow by experience.
2.10. Provide easy access to knowledge experts as resources and for mentoring; institute friendly peer reviews.

3. Communication and Coordination

3.1. Strive for perfect communication, coordination, and collaboration across people and processes.

3.2. Promote direct and face-to-face communication.

3.3. Promote direct human communications to build personal relationships.

3.4. Develop a general guideline outlining expectations for communication, coordination, and collaboration.

3.5. Develop and execute a clear communications plan that covers the entire bank and its stakeholders.

3.6. Publish instructions for e-mail distributions (specifically when and to whom to send carbon copies), instant messaging, and electronic communications.

3.7. Use frequent, timely, open, and honest communications.

3.8. Promote a flat organization* to simplify and speed communication.

3.9. Match the communication competencies of people with their roles when assigning roles.

3.10. Minimize hand-offs. Promote small batch sizes of information, low information inventory, low number of concurrent tasks per employee, small task times, wide communication bandwidth, standardization, work cells, and training.

3.11. Plan to use visual methods where possible to communicate schedules, workloads, changes to customer requirements, and other vital information.

3.12. For virtually co-located teams, invest time and money up front to build personal relationships in face-to-face settings.

3.13. Encourage personal networks and interactions.

3.14. Use concise one-page electronic forms (e.g., A3) for efficient, real-time reporting of cross-functional and cross-organizational issues and prompt resolution. Avoid verbose unstructured memos. Keep underlying data as backup material in case a receiver requests it.

3.15. Promote effective, real-time direct communication between each giver and receiver in the value flow based on mutual trust and respect, and ensure both understand their mutual needs and expectations.

3.16. For non-routine tasks, avoid rework by proactively coordinating task requirements with internal customers and stay connected to internal customers during task execution.

---

* A flat organization is one with few layers of management.

3.17. Support the development of informal and social networks within the bank.

3.18. Maintain counterparts with active working relationships throughout the bank and with suppliers to facilitate efficient communication and coordination among various parties.

3.19. Engage and sustain extensive stakeholder interactions.

3.20. Listen to stakeholders' comments and concerns patiently and value their views and inputs.

3.21. Publish a team directory and organizational chart and train new hires to locate needed nodes of knowledge.

4. General Management

4.1. Everyone in the bank must have a customer-first spirit.

4.2. Ensure tailored Lean training for all employees.

4.3. Set up a Lean training infrastructure; mid-level and executive managers must train and motivate their teams.

4.4. Start small by selecting the most beneficial Lean Enablers for your program.

4.5. Promote excellence under normal circumstances and reward proactive management of risks, instead of rewarding "hero" behavior in crisis situations.

4.6. Practice "walk-around management." Do not manage from a cubicle; go to the work and observe activities.

4.7. Expect and support people as they strive for professional excellence and promote their careers.

4.8. Invest in workforce development.

4.9. Promote and honor professional meritocracy.

4.10. Perpetuate professional excellence through mentoring, friendly peer reviews, training, continuing education, and other means.

4.11. Promote and reward continuous learning through education and experience.

4.12. Actively minimize the bureaucratic, regulatory, and compliance burdens on bank work.

4.13. Align incentives across the bank enterprise.

4.14. Top-level bank management teams and decision makers must exhibit high levels of teamwork, understanding, and appreciation of the realities in their various domains.

4.15. Maintain a consistent, disciplined approach to management, including agreement on goals, outcomes, processes, and communication and standardizing best practices.

4.16. Capture and share tacit knowledge to maintain work stability when team members change.

4.17. Never delay a decision because you are unwilling to take the responsibility or are afraid to discuss the underlying issues.

4.18. Take the time necessary to reach good decisions. Always explore a number of alternatives.

4.19. If you cannot make a decision, keep a record of it. Periodically review unmade decisions.

4.20. Proactively manage trade-offs and resolve conflicts of interest among stakeholders. Do not minimize or ignore them.

4.21. Anticipate and plan to resolve as many downstream issues and risks as early as possible to prevent problems.

4.22. Implement the basics of quality. Do not create, pass on, or accept defects.

4.23. Require only reports that are clearly necessary and align reporting requirements to reduce redundant reporting.

4.24. Ensure all review and approval steps are truly needed and add value.

4.25. Establish and support communities of practice.

4.26. Support all critical decisions with risk management results.

4.27. In management, regularly monitor and review risks, risk mitigation actions, and the risk management system.

4.28. Keep management decisions crystal clear while also empowering and rewarding the bottom-up culture of continuous improvement, human creativity, and entrepreneurship.

4.29. Ensure clear, bank-wide understanding of agreed-upon technologies and technology standards.

4.30. Publish instructions for artifact content and data storage, central capture versus local storage, and paper versus electronic retention, balancing bureaucracy with the need for traceability.

4.31. Adapt information technology tools to fit people and processes.

4.32. Minimize the number of non-critical software revision updates and centrally control the update releases to prevent information churning.

4.33. Ensure timely and efficient access to centralized data.

5. Project Management

5.1. For every project, appoint a project manager to lead and integrate the project from start to finish.

5.2. The project manager must have responsibility, accountability, and authority (RAA) over the project.

5.3. Ensure that the competency, technical knowledge, and other relevant banking expertise of the project manager and other key members of the team are on par with the technical complexity of the project.

5.4. Ensure that the project manager has an appropriate background in business, general management, and banking; he or she should also have leadership and people skills and experience working on complex projects.

5.5. Groom an exceptional project manager with advanced skills to lead the development, the people, and ensure program success.

5.6. Use lessons learned to make the next project better than the last.

5.7. Hold people responsible for their contributions throughout the project life cycle. Upstream activities must be held responsible for issues they cause in downstream activities.

5.8. Plan to utilize cross-functional teams consisting of the most experienced and compatible people at the start of a project to look at a broad range of solution sets.

5.9. Create a plan to integrate and align project management and other high-level planning and coordination functions appropriately.

5.10. Use formal frequent comprehensive integrative events. Resolve all frequent integrative events issues as they occur. Always ask *why*. Discuss trade-offs and options.

6. Process Management

6.1. Use Lean Thinking to promote smooth process flow.

6.2. Develop a robust process to capture, develop, and disseminate customer value with extreme clarity.

6.3. Pull process tasks and outputs based on need, and reject others as wastes.

6.4. Promote a culture in which people pull knowledge as they need it and limit the supply of information to genuine users only.

6.5. Promote process standardization in all bank work.

6.6. Identify repeatable activities and standardize them.

6.7. Immediately organize training in any new standard to ensure buy-in and awareness.

6.8. Whenever possible, select the simplest solution.

6.9. Strongly prefer physical team co-location to the virtual co-location when coordinating work.

6.10. Minimize hand-offs to avoid rework.

6.11. Let information needs pull the necessary work activities.

6.12. Train the team to recognize the internal customer (receiver) and the supplier (giver) for each task. Use the supplier–inputs–process–outputs–customer (SIPOC) model to better illustrate process flow.

6.13. For all critical activities, define who is responsible for approving, consulting, and informing (the RACI matrix) using a standardized tool, paying attention to precedence of tasks and documenting hand-offs.

6.14. When pulling work, use customer stakeholder value to separate value-added from waste.

6.15. Make work progress visible and easy for all to understand.

6.16. Utilize visual controls (not computer screens) in public spaces for best visibility.

6.17. Use a traffic light system (green for good, yellow for warning, red for critical) to report task status visually and ensure that problems are not concealed.

6.18. Follow up written requirements with verbal clarification of context and expectations to ensure mutual understanding and agreement. Keep records in writing, share the discussed items, and do not allow requirements creep.

7. Continuous Improvement

7.1. Promote the idea that the bank should incorporate continuous improvement in its organizational culture.

7.2. Promote complementary continuous improvement methods to draw best energy and creativity from all stakeholders.

7.3. Adopt a culture of stopping and permanently fixing problems when they occur.

7.4. Utilize and reward bottom-up suggestions for solving employee level problems.

7.5. Use quick-response small teams composed of program stakeholders to solve local problems and develop standards.

7.6. Use formal, large improvement project teams to address bank-wide issues.

7.7. Assign responsibility and accountability for reviewing, evaluating, standardizing lessons learned, and implementing required changes.

7.8. Treat any imperfection as an opportunity for immediate improvement and a lesson to be learned. Practice frequent reviews of lessons learned.

7.9. Insist on standardized root cause identification and establish a process for implementing corrective action and related training.

7.10. Develop standards that pay attention to human factors including level of experience and perception abilities.

7.11. Define a process that implements successful local improvements in other relevant parts of the bank.

7.12. Promote standardized skill sets with careful training and mentoring, rotations, strategic assignments, and assessments of competencies.

7.13. Create mechanisms to capture, communicate, and apply experience.

7.14. Identify best practices through benchmarking and professional literature.

7.15. Develop a system that makes imperfections and delays visible to all.

7.16. Use and communicate failures as opportunities for learning; emphasize process problems, not people problems.

8. Hiring

8.1. Hire people based on passion, "spark in the eye" and broad professional knowledge not only based on highly specific skill needs (hire for talent, train for skills). Do not delegate this critical task to computers scanning for keywords.

8.2. Invest in people selection and development to achieve bank excellence. Ensure that the hiring process matches the real talent and skill needs of the bank.

8.3. Include teaming ability among the criteria for hiring and promotion. Encourage team building and teamwork and base rewards on team performance.

9. Planning

9.1. Plan early for consistent robustness and working "right the first time" under normal circumstances instead of dealing with hero behavior in crisis situations.

9.2. Maximize concurrency of independent tasks and tasks that inform each other.

9.3. Carefully plan for precedence of tasks (which task to feed what other tasks with what data and when) understanding task dependencies and parent–child relationships.

9.4. Plan below full capacity to enable flow of work without accumulation of variability and schedule buffers.

10. Suppliers

10.1. Partner with suppliers for the long term.

10.2. Select suppliers that are technically and culturally compatible.

10.3. Outsource and subcontract only work elements that are perfectly defined and stable. Do not subcontract early activities when the need for close coordination is the strongest.

10.4. Clearly communicate to suppliers all expectations, including the context and need and all procedures and expectations for acceptance tests. Ensure that the requirements are stable.

10.5. Invite long-term suppliers as trusted program partners to help the bank add value.

10.6. Involve key suppliers in your planning.

10.7. Work proactively with suppliers to avoid conflicts and anticipate and mitigate program risks.

10.8. Streamline supply chain processes and focus on just-in-time operations that minimize inventory-carrying costs.

Chapter 8

Lean Product Development Flow (LPDF)

This chapter describes the super-efficient LPDF methodology intended for managing bank projects. We estimate that 15% to 20% of employees in medium to large banks are engaged in dedicated projects typically involving 5 to 20 people for several months. This is a significant fraction of bank operation time and thus the method should be of interest to a considerable number of bank employees. LPDF was created as a contribution to engineering in space applications and is adapted here for banking. This chapter has been adapted from a full-length article [Oppenheim, 2004].

8.1 Introduction

The LPDF method is intended for a super-efficient and rapid execution of projects while promoting the creation of the best value. It does not, however, apply to all projects. The limitations are described in the vignette.

> LPDF is limited to projects that involve only mature technologies, low risks, and are understood well enough so that a detailed plan can be created for the project at its beginning.

An LPDF project may involve limited risk or research. Such needs should be identified early and handled outside the project's critical path. Typical bank projects are small enough to perfectly fit the LPDF method and offer strong benefits in schedule, cost, quality, customer satisfaction, bank competitiveness, and importantly, vastly better morale of employees.

LPDF execution is organized as a rhythmic workflow through a series of short and equal duration *takt* periods,* each terminating in a comprehensive meeting called an integrative event. The event is devoted to structured, comprehensive coordination and resolution of all issues that arose during the *takt* period.

LPDF requires solid training (about one day), detailed and competent planning of the LPDF process, and disciplined execution. The preparations include the selection of a core team of managers (or highly competent deputies) of all involved departments and major stakeholders, and training of teams.

Planning involves detailed value stream mapping (VSM)—parsing of a value stream map into equal *takt* periods, and architecting the LPDF team using dynamic allocation of employees if necessary. LPDF also requires excellent leadership modeled after the practices of the chief engineers of Toyota, Honda, and the early US aerospace programs. A project leader must be an expert in the project domain with a good understanding at minimum of first-level interfaces and trade-offs between all major elements. The individual must be an expert project manager and a strong leader. He or she must be skilled in consensus building while remaining focused on the integrity of both the project and the product being designed. The leader is responsible for the entire project, is accountable, and has authority to pursue both technical and business success of both project and a product being designed. Complex projects may require one or more assistant leaders to help the leader in selected technical, project administration, and finance areas.

8.2 Lean Manufacturing: A Useful Refresher

LPDF shamelessly steals some concepts from Lean manufacturing so it is useful to review the basics. In manufacturing, *takt* time denotes the amount of time allocated to each workstation on a moving line for a robust completion of its task so that the entire line can advance one station at a time. It is also equal to the rate at which finished products exit the production line, are synchronized with customer orders, and shipped to customers. Each worker

---

* *Takt* is the time required to complete a task to a common rhythm.

or process must work to a common *takt* time; otherwise pile-ups or gaps occur in the workstations before and after the offending station, and the line must then stop or slow down to catch up.

As customer orders increase, production rates and line speed must increase while *takt* time decreases. This is accomplished by adding resources *up to the capacity* of the system rather than forcing processes to run faster. The capacity must be realistic: No worker should be asked to work faster than the well-tested ergonomic rate set by a combination of worker training, and machine and process optimization. If a task does not meet the ergonomic rate, workers will not be able to complete their tasks and inevitably will produce defects. Flexibility in adding and removing human and machine resources is an important factor in Lean system profitability. *Flow* denotes the uninterrupted or pulsed motion of work pieces at a steady pulse of *takt* time through all processes without backflow or rework.

After more than a century of using production lines in factories, we tend to take them for granted. However, designing a complex production line flow according to the *takt* pulses is very difficult. Implementation requires carefully splitting and balancing of total assembly work among individual aligned workstations or cells, perfecting each process, and providing each worker with adequate parts, tools, training, and ergonomics to make timely and robust completion of any task possible. Numerous references describe this production system, for example, Spear [1999].

The key to success, which is also the key to the LPDF method, is the ability to plan and parse total work into tasks of equal duration. Each task should be small enough to allow its outcome, quality, effort, and cycle time to become predictable.

Lean production is the most efficient method known for flexible delivery of quality products in the shortest possible time, at minimum cost, with minimum in-house inventory and perfect quality. Henry Ford was the first person to line production machines in a sequence and split the standard work among workstations into equal duration tasks. Toyota invented the most advanced Just-in-Time (JIT) system with minimum inventories; a work culture based on teaming, openness, empowerment, trust unmatched by its competition, and an amazing quality system which obviates the need for final inspections [Liker, 2004].

8.3 Overview of LPDF

Figure 8.1 illustrates the LPDF on a project timeline. Project effort begins with a precise value definition. A bank or other organization must understand fully what a project is to deliver before detailed planning can begin. LPDF planning may be impossible if value is poorly formulated, unstable, lacking clarity, incomplete, or prevents comprehensive capture of need or consensus. After the value proposition is defined fully, detailed planning using a value stream map (VSM, Figure 8.1) can be followed.

The horizontal lanes in the figure represent bank departments and major subcontractors participating in the project. Typically, a project involves two to six departments and vendors. The lanes are colloquially called "swimming lanes." The boxes labeled with letters represent individual tasks assigned to bank departments, specific individuals, or major suppliers involved in value creation, for example:

A = Information technology
B = Security
C = Account services
D = Risk
E = Legal

Other letters and participant categories may be added easily. The task boxes are shown in different sizes to symbolize the different amounts of work required to complete the various tasks of the project.

The flow can begin after the VSM (Figure 8.1) is completed. The flow ends with the release of the value deliverables. Between the two ends, flow proceeds as a moving line at a steady pulsed rate.

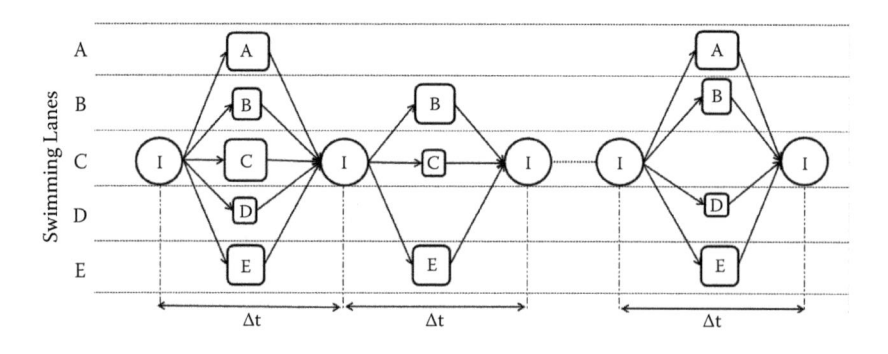

Figure 8.1   Lean Product Development Flow: parsed value stream map.

The flow consists of a sequence of equal *homework* periods called *takt* periods, all of equal duration Δt. Each *takt* period terminates in an integrative event (I). *Takt* periods of very short duration are recommended, typically 2 to 5 days, to expose any issues in real time and enable immediate and effective mitigation while issues are still small and easy to handle. The *takt* periods provide the entire project with a constant rhythm and common disciplined deadlines for all tasks. The ideal LPDF is a steady progress of the value stream through all *takt* periods, with frequent and optimum coordination and minimum waste. Each *takt* period should terminate with an integrative event.

LPDF places few constraints on team architecture, except for the absolute need for the core team to be co-located during value stream mapping and during all integrative events. Employees and major suppliers can be organized into any configuration that makes sense to the core team, including long- and short-term teams, sub-teams, groups, or individuals assigned to the project and dynamically allocated from their home departments in a matrix organization, or individuals such as hired experts and supplier representatives. In matrix organizations, it is important to evaluate department heads and other participants based on the degree of support they provide to the project leader. The core team should consist of the same individuals for the duration of a project; other members can be assigned as needed.

All *takt* periods are of equal duration but, as noted above, do not necessarily require equal effort. Task staffing will vary based on the amount of work needed to complete a task within a *takt* period. Some tasks may need only a single individual, others a small team with a mix of full-time employees, part-time employees, and subcontractors. Some tasks may not be needed in some *takt* periods (e.g., A and D are missing in the second period in Figure 8.1).

To comfortably function in this work environment, all employees should be trained for the organization of LPDF. Although tasks are self-contained by definition, questions about projects frequently arise and should be resolved immediately without waiting for the next integrative event. An employee who has a question should locate the person who can provide the answer immediately and seek the answer without wasting time.

In addition to structured communications during integrative events, informal communications take place constantly. Therefore, all stakeholders should have access to a directory and organizational chart of the entire project team. The infrastructure should be organized to facilitate informal communications, perhaps locating all participating employees in one building or one floor.

As many tasks as possible should be carried out concurrently within a *takt* period. Concurrent execution is the most effective way to shorten overall project time, but it requires detailed planning of the task scheduling, precedence, inputs, outputs, and control points. The shortest possible schedules for projects are conducive to lower costs and higher levels of customer satisfaction and competitiveness. The "Critical Chain" formulated by Goldratt [1997] explains how to estimate tasks without padding. To compensate for accumulating task completion variability, it may be prudent to insert time buffers into the VSM every few *takt* periods [Goldratt, 1977]. The buffers ensure that the overall schedule will be met even if an individual task exceeds its planned duration.

The intrinsically tight schedule of LPDF makes the robust and timely completion of tasks absolutely critical. The project leader should insist that failure to meet *takt* period deadlines will be justified only as a rare exception when no alternative exists. Tasks should be staffed and people trained and rewarded accordingly. The role of the LPDF core team is to provide the resources, coordination, and training required to make the achievement possible. The leader, his or her staff, and core team members should be available for guidance, mentoring, ad hoc training if needed, and general support of workflow improvement.

8.4 Integrative Events

An integrative event is a meeting of the core team at which all current issues and risks are discussed openly and mitigated, and the work comprehensively coordinated, verified for consistency with value proposition, and prepared for the next *takt* period. Unlike the spontaneous communications that occur during *takt* periods, integrative events are scripted. The project leader or an assistant should define the integrative event agenda and structure and lead the meeting. Box 8.1 is an integrative event checklist.

For complex projects spanning several months, one-week *takt* periods are recommended. The optimum *takt* period for projects lasting about a month is 2.5 work days (Monday morning to Wednesday noon and Wednesday noon to end of Friday). For short, urgent projects involving only several hours of work per task, one-day *takt* periods may be considered. It is recommended that an integrative event comprising about 20% of *takt* period time be held at the end of each *takt* period. Table 8.1 illustrates several *takt* periods, and recommended integrative events.

BOX 8.1 INTEGRATIVE EVENT CHECKLIST

1. Efficient review of progress. The leader or assistant leader asks pointed relevant questions of participants and asks *why* often, in a non-confrontational style.
2. Comprehensive coordination of work.
3. Resolution of trade-offs, concerns, issues; if practical, pursue consensus building in break-away sessions involving only needed individuals.
4. Identification, mitigation, and retirement of project risks.
5. Exploration of available options.
6. Optimization and coordination to achieve minimum iterations, efforts, and costs.
7. Deciding whether to reuse knowledge from legacy projects.
8. Involvement of suppliers and other external stakeholders.
9. Reuse of checklists from earlier projects.
10. Discussions and decisions about analyses, tests, and documents that are needed; elimination of those deemed wasteful.
11. Adjustments of VSM, assignment of adjusted work to responsible parties, and allocation of necessary resources.
12. Addressing any and all relevant questions.

Table 8.1 *Takt* **Period and Integrative Event Schedule Recommended for Various Project Durations**

Project Duration	Takt Period	Integrative Event
Several months or longer	1 week	All day Friday
1 month	20 hours: Monday morning to Wednesday noon and Wednesday noon to end of workday on Friday	4 hours: Wednesday morning and Friday afternoon
1 week	8 hours	Last 2 hours every day

In the following material, we assume weekly takt periods; adjustments to the other period lengths are easy and are left to readers. On each Thursday afternoon by a set time (e.g., 3 p.m. at the latest), the project leader and key stakeholders should be notified of any issue that needs to be scheduled for a discussion during Friday's integrative event. All cross-departmental issues, potential delays, potential specification changes, risks, cost variations, and non-conformance situations should be reported to the leader's office as promptly and as efficiently as possible.

Standardized A3 forms (Figure 5.12) are recommended for such notifications as the only attachments to e-mails (see Section 5.14). All project stakeholders should be trained in the use of the A3 forms and discouraged from attempts to write wordy memos, e-mails, and reports. Many employees lack good writing skills and can waste precious project time attempting to write documents that may not fill the need. An A3 form listing only salient bullet statements saves reading and writing time and transmits information concisely. An additional benefit of the A3 is that the form provides a clear and easy-to-catalog record of a project and easy means for sorting the project issues into agendas for integrative events.

If the recipient of an A3 form needs more information, he or she should request it explicitly. On Thursday afternoon after the set deadline time, a staff member in the project leader's office should sort the received A3 forms into an agenda to be followed during the next day's integrative event. The event should continue (if necessary, and hopefully not often spilling into the weekend) until all issues are resolved and all questions addressed so that the next week's schedule is not affected.

It is obvious that the scope of integrative events extends well beyond the frequent practice of status reviews. The leader should frequently ask *why?* The *why* questions will stimulate better decision making and verify correctness of information discussed.

Co-located meetings of the core team (supported by staff as needed) in a common project (or war) room are absolutely critical. Strict policies should prohibit overdissemination of documents intended for the integrative events to prevent team members from being overwhelmed with data. Strict discipline for perfect attendance is recommended. Even one absence of a critical participant may delay an important decision and cause a delay of an entire *takt* period.

8.5 Devising Project Schedule

The total LPDF time (also known as project throughput time, cycle time, or schedule) is a vital component of the value proposition but in practice it is an arbitrary aspect of a project. LPDF time must be decided at the beginning of the value stream mapping effort in a bank for the same reason as for a moving manufacturing line. Ideally, the throughput should reflect the time when the stakeholders need the deliverables or the time needed to beat the competition—not a schedule convenient for the team. In the absence of a stakeholder-set deadline, we recommend the radical step of reducing the traditional legacy-based (or proposal-quoted) throughput time by the fraction of project waste the project management team is ready to tackle. For example, if management estimates that the amount of obvious and easy-to-eliminate waste on a similar project was 20% of the project time or cost, the throughput time for the current project should be cut by that fraction.

Ambitious leadership may favor more aggressive cuts. (After five years of experimenting, Henry Ford realized a 90% throughput time reduction when evolving his assembly line from the former craft production, although it is doubtful that he could have predicted it *a priori*.) The risk of schedule cutting is small; at worst, the schedule may slip back toward the traditional asymptote. In the spirit of continuous improvement, larger cuts should be possible as a bank's experience with LPDF increases. Admittedly, this is a radical and arbitrary approach, but it is no less arbitrary than the current practice of cutting 25% to 50% from the schedule estimate to compensate for suspected padding.

8.6 Mapping Value Streams

Common wisdom calls for good planning at the beginning of a project. Experience-based, competition-motivated, consensus-created streamlined value stream mapping (VSM) parsed into short *takt* periods is the ultimate good plan. The VS must be mapped before the LPDF flow can begin. While subsequent execution permits flexible adjustments of tasks in real time, the adjustments should be used as tactical mitigations of issues rather than poor substitutes for good initial planning.

The VSM must list all tasks that contribute to value, starting with project input requirements and other descriptions of need, and ending with value deliverables. The comprehensive effort of VSM was described in Section 4.3.2. For LPDF use, VSM requires three steps: (1) current state mapping, (2) future state mapping, and (3) parsing of the future state map into *takt* periods.

8.6.1 Mapping Current State

The current state map is a detailed graphical representation of a project plan using current project methodology (before any streamlining). It depicts all tasks (even the wasteful ones), their precedence, and control (approval) points. The current state map is a starting point for subsequent identification of waste and streamlining. If available, a VSM used on a recent similar (or legacy) project showing task precedence and lessons learned is an excellent way to begin developing a current state map.

Good corporate memory is invaluable in this step. Incentives should be introduced to capture and preserve VSMs from past projects along with the various checklists, trade-off charts, and numerous other useful documents. Starting with legacy knowledge is helpful even if only partial information such as a process map of a completed product or a Gantt chart is available. Participation of a high-level manager from the earlier project in the VSM exercise for the current project is highly desirable, particularly for identifying do's and don'ts for the new team.

Each task should be described on a separate task sheet (Figure 8.2) standardized with the following fields:

1. Task number and week of execution (left blank until future state mapping step)
2. Responsible party (name, title, telephone, cell, e-mail, location (also left blank on current state map)
3. Major inputs, each indicating source tasks
4. Major outputs, each indicating destination task and approval or control nodes
5. Brief description of effort and scope
6. Warnings about potential issues, notes, and comments

If possible, each task sheet should be temporarily placed in the best-guessed week in which it was executed on the legacy project or where the task "owner" feels it should go. The idea is to include all tasks, and then iterate their time placements later. Where available, notes should indicate wastes identified for subsequent removal (e.g., the time of waiting for or chasing data, time wasted waiting for signatures, rework, and "reinventing the wheel").

Next, tasks from a legacy project should be tailored and modified to reflect the current project. The precedence of tasks should be determined, usually by iterations. The iterative process may appear messy, but it offers huge payback potential in the future state mapping. From this point on, the effort should be handled by a complete project core team composed of experienced department managers (or competent deputies) representing all

Task Sheet	
Task owner: name, title, office location, office and cell phones, email	
Task ID:	Takt Period:
Inputs:	Sources:
Outputs:	Destination
Description of Effort & Scope	
Warnings & Comments	

Figure 8.2 Task sheet.

major and relevant bank departments, representatives of major suppliers, and the core team leaders (project leader and assistants, if any).

A typical core team may involve three to six individuals. Each core team member should be free to bring along a staff person for help, but the staff member should not replace the core team member and should not make major decisions, negotiate, iterate, or foster consensus.

Brainstorming, negotiations, and iterations are the most productive activities at this stage. A project leader experienced in VSM and possessing good motivational and leadership skills should lead the effort. The focus should be on listing *all* tasks and their wastes, rather than on task or flow optimization, which are handled later during future state mapping.

8.6.2 Mapping Future State

This step has a potential for generating huge returns on investments (ROIs), often measured in project savings of hundreds of thousands of dollars per hours of effort. Therefore, future state mapping should be performed as comprehensively as possible.

The core team may conclude that the project involves one or more uncertainties that may pose risks to the project schedule if left within the main workflow. Each uncertainty should be isolated from the main flow, placed on a separate track, assigned to a separate subteam, and staffed to resolve the uncertainty in time for deployment within the main flow.

The current state map displayed on the walls becomes the basis for iterative waste removal and for improving task concurrency, precedence, and general flow. Experience indicates that some non-value-added activities (NVAs) are obvious and easy to remove; some NVAs and necessary NVAs may require brainstorming and negotiations within the core team, and some may be uncovered only in a future project during the continuous pursuit of waste removal and streamlining.

8.6.3 Parsing Future State Map into Takt Periods

The final phase of VSM is parsing the future state map into *takt* periods. This step and the previous future state mapping step may require iteration together. Again, the entire core team should participate to enable iterative brainstorming and negotiations. The dynamic allocation of employees during different *takt* periods should be addressed at this stage. The parsing may reveal additional opportunities to remove waste and optimize task precedence and flow.

The application of fixed-length *takt* periods is an absolute requirement for disciplined flow, just as a manufacturing line must move forward in equal pulses. All work must be parsed into equal *takt* periods (lasting just short of four days of work to reserve a few hours on Thursday afternoons to report issues to the project leader and for integrative events on Fridays). The parsing must be done by formally splitting larger tasks into smaller ones or by logical splitting of such tasks for reporting purposes. For example, a task inherently longer than the *takt* period (e.g., a multi-week test) can always be logically subdivided into shorter *takt* periods so that the person responsible ("owner") for the task can report during the relevant integrative event that "task number X proceeded as planned during *takt* period number Y" or "the following issues have been identified."

Clearly, in any complex flow involving many stakeholders, unexpected events and uncertainties may require adjustments to the schedule, as occurs on automotive assembly lines. The general attitude of the core team should be to map the best value stream possible and also prepare for flexible handling and mitigation of the changes. Experience indicates that an imperfect plan is better than none.

The role of the project leader is to guide the core team toward consensus on the VSM. The mapping should continue until that goal is met, that is, when every core team member accepts the final parsed VSM and declares readiness to provide the required resources and complete tasks when planned. A detailed value stream mapped into short *takt* periods at the beginning of a project automatically constitutes a detailed project plan and schedule. Theoretically, the subsequent monitoring of project progress may be as simple as checking off task sheets in the VSM displayed on the walls. This reduces the need for complex metrics and costly bureaucracy to monitor progress.

8.7 Project Leadership and Management

Good leadership cannot be delegated or automated. A highly skilled project leader modeled after the Toyota [Sobek et al., 1999], Honda [Clark et al., 1990], and Skunk Works models [Rich, 1994] should lead the entire LPDF project. The leader's job description should specify the ability to *produce the required bank product or service to the satisfaction of stakeholders, within budget and schedule*, and the leader should be evaluated only by how well this goal is met.

The leader must be the sole "owner" of the project, totally responsible, with authority and accountability for the entire project (preparation, planning, concepts, trade-offs, key decisions, coordination, targets, schedules, and budget). He or she should be ultimately responsible for balancing technical success with business case. For relatively short projects, a single leader is sufficient. For complex and lengthy projects, the project leader should be aided by one or more assistant leaders, one of whom may be responsible for project administration and finances.

Box 8.2 summarizes the desirable attributes of the project leader, assistant leader, and administrative assistant.

BOX 8.2 DESIRABLE ATTRIBUTES OF PROJECT LEADER, ASSISTANT LEADER, AND PROJECT ADMINISTRATIVE ASSISTANT

■ <u>Interpersonal skills.</u> Ideally, a good leader, with high degree of credibility, who is free of domineering personality traits, capable of leading and motivating for excellent performance using non-confrontational style. More like a movie director or symphony conductor than a drill sergeant. In frequent personal contact with project employees, without micromanaging. High level of interpersonal skills to guide the team toward consensus during the value proposition and VSM work, when resolving issues during integrative events, and when negotiating with the bank for resources. Ability to draw on team members' competence, experience, and creativity.

■ <u>Education.</u> Preferably a degree in project management (or systems engineering), with significant experience in banking work, or a master's degree or equivalent in banking with several courses in project management (or systems engineering).

■ <u>Experience.</u> Solid understanding of all critical first-level interfaces, trade-offs, and risks. Experience as an assistant leader on at least one successful project. Understanding of frustrations, issues, and solutions experienced on former projects and understanding of bank culture. Most professional years spent rising through the ranks and rotating through major bank departments. Record of lifelong learning, attending professional conferences, and following relevant literature.

■ <u>Freedom of action.</u> The leader of a complex project must have the freedom to select a few assistant leaders to complement his or her expertise, whose loyalties are to the leader, the end customer (i.e., the project), and the bank—and not to his or her home department. The leader alone should evaluate the assistant leaders. The leader must have the freedom to execute LPDF according to his or her own preferences.

■ <u>Focus.</u> Never-ending focus on customer satisfaction, other stakeholders' needs, project value and integrity, and reduction of waste.

- <u>Compensation.</u> Clearly, the leader's compensation should be proportional to the exceptional role he or she plays and the vast responsibilities handled.
- <u>"The most coveted job in the bank."</u>
- <u>Project administrative assistant</u> (needed only for long and complex projects) reports to the project leader. He or she understands and tracks in real time all project costs and provides real-time accounting support to the leader to aid his decision making. The assistant also handles administrative support for the project to free the leader to focus on value creation. However, only the leader balances the technical and business success of the project.

A bank should groom enough leaders to serve all its project needs by supporting their professional growth and education, exposing them to challenging experiences, and rotating them through major departments. Candidates should be selected carefully among the brightest and the most promising employees for their technical and interpersonal skills. Candidates should prove themselves as assistant leaders before they are promoted to project leader positions.

8.8 Project Room

VSM is a complex undertaking even for moderate-size projects. A large war room or project room with ample wall space should be dedicated to each project for its entire duration. The VSM planning effort, all integrative events, and ad hoc meetings should be conducted in this room, with the VSM and project notes conveniently in view.

Computer screens are strongly discouraged; they are too small to project a complete project map and too difficult to see. Wall layout is preferred to electronic implementation, because it enables the core team members to see all task data; brainstorm; and negotiate task parsing, precedence, concurrency, scope, and effort, inputs, outputs, and waste; and finally reach a consensus.

Takt periods should be delineated by vertical lines on the walls throughout the duration of a project to allow easy posting of each task sheet in its designated period. Each task sheet should fit onto an A4 (letter-size) page. The vertical lines should be spaced about 30 cm (12 inches) apart, requiring a room with about five meters (20 feet) of clear circumference for a three-month project. Oppenheim [2004] details the recommended room architecture.

Ideally, a few smaller rooms should be available nearby for break-away discussions. The offices of the project leader, any assistants, and their staffs should be located in close proximity for *gemba* walks. The project room should contain networked computers, printers, projectors, ample writing materials, and a large conference table with enough chairs to accommodate the core team.

8.9 Closing Remarks

Disciplined work execution within short *takt* periods is an important element of LPDF. Compelling arguments favor this approach. If LPDF is not followed as recommended here, the penalty to the project would be less-than-full benefit but no risk to outcome integrity. The resulting penalties in cost and schedule should not be worse than outcomes of recent traditional programs. In other words, LPDF offers potential for radical benefits with no cost or schedule risk beyond those of traditional projects.

LPDF represents an adaptation of Lean manufacturing to a project environment. Over the past century, significant knowledge, experience, and effort have been devoted to the design of flow in automotive lines, and we tend to take the progress for granted. Yet even the best modern assembly lines still suffer from frequent stoppages due to unexpected problems. The first author of this book observed a Toyota line in the NUMMI plant in Fremont, California, recognized as one of the best in the world, stopping several times per hour while assembling a mature model of the Corolla. Local employees confirmed that the frequent stoppages were normal.

This demonstrates that problems are to be expected even after significant planning. Therefore, it would be naïve to expect no problems after implementing LPDF flow. Nevertheless, the significant potential benefits and minimal risks make the method worthwhile. Typical bank projects are small enough to fit the LPDF method perfectly, offering dramatic benefits in time savings, lower costs, enhanced quality and customer satisfaction, bank competitiveness, and vastly better morale of employees.

Glossaries

Abbreviations and Acronyms

6S	Method of organizing work spaces and information storage
aka	Also known as
B&Q	Batch & queue
CE	Concurrent Engineering
CEO	Chief executive officer
CI	Continuous improvement
CS	Current state
CSM	Current state map
DoD	Department of Defense (United States)
EADS	European Aeronautic Defense and Space Company
EdNet	LAI Educational Network
FDIC	Federal Deposit Insurance Corporation
FS	Future state
FSM	Future state map
GDP	Gross domestic product
GE	General Electric Corporation
ID	Identification
INCOSE	International Council on Systems Engineering
IPT	Integrated product team
ISO	International Standards Organization
JIT	Just-in-Time
LAI	Lean Advancement Initiative (formerly Lean Aerospace Initiative and Lean Aircraft Initiative)

LEfSE	Lean enablers for systems engineering
LEI	Lean Enterprise Institute (nonprofit organization)
LEM	Lean enterprise model
LMU	Loyola Marymount University
LPD	Lean product development
LPDF	Lean Product Development Flow
LSE	Lean systems engineering
LSE WG	Lean Systems Engineering Working Group (of INCOSE)
MBA	Master of business administration
MIT	Massachusetts Institute of Technology
MoD	Ministry of Defence (United Kingdom)
NASA	National Aeronautics and Space Administration
NBC	National Broadcasting Company
NNVA	Necessary non-value-added
NVA	Non-value-added
PD	Product development
PDSA	Plan–Do–Study–Act improvement cycle
PM	Project management
PMI	Project Management Institute
RAA	Responsibility, accountability, authority
RASI	Responsible, approving, supporting, informing
RFP	Request for proposal
RNVA	Required non-value-added
ROI	Return on investment
SE	Systems engineering, systems engineer
SPF	Single-piece flow
TBD	To be determined
TPS	Toyota Production System
TQM	Total Quality Management
UK	United Kingdom
US	United States
USAF	United States Air Force
VA	Value-added
VSM	Value-stream map
WG	Working group

Idioms, Colloquialisms, and Foreign Expressions

A3	Preformatted form for reporting and solving issues on international A3 size paper
Agile	Quick and nimble method used for software development and requirement change management
All together	Urgent activity in which all employees participate equally, regardless of position
Au courant	(French) up to date
Back office	Bank operations area not accessible to walk-in customers
Batch and queue	Traditional production system of producing massive batches (inventories) of parts regardless of immediate need by next station; batches wait in queues
Big bang approach	Using all required (or massive) resources
Big picture	Viewing a project as a whole instead of considering individual tasks
Bottom-up	Initiated by workers rather than management
Chinese walls	Symbolic walls between employees and between departments that protect client financial data from inside-information abuse
Fail early–fail often	Iteration method based on trial and error, recommended in early design phases allows quick evaluation of many possibilities or simple prototypes before major costs are expended
Five whys	Asking *why* five (or so) times to find the root cause of a problem; each answer reveals the next layer of understanding; technique is said to require five questions to identify a root cause in a typical modern environment
Front office	Bank area intended to serve walk-in customers
Gemba	(Japanese) "Go to the place of action and see for yourself"
Hand-off	Passing information or item to another person or organization
Hands-off attitude	Business relations attitude of not communicating with business stakeholders

Hejinka	(Japanese) Leveling of workloads over time
Homework	Tasks performed in home departments between integrative events
Hoshin kanri	(Japanese) Refocusing Lean deployment effort on highest priority problem
Integrative Event	Meeting with clear agenda designed to resolve all issues arising during homework period
Ishikawa diagram	Diagram relating a problem to its potential causes (fishbone diagram)
Just-in-Time	System by which a work piece is supplied to the user only when needed where needed in the quantity needed and ready for use
Ju-jitsu	(Japanese) Popular martial art; in Six Sigma terminology, it denotes different levels of training
Kaizen	(Japanese) Small team of local stakeholders tasked to achieve rapid focused improvement of a problem
Kanban	(Japanese) Signal (typically visual) indicating need to resupply
Know-how	Knowing how to get something done
Lean Academy™	Short Lean and Six Sigma course developed by EdNet
Lean Enabler	Best practice to strengthen value and reduce waste, inspired by Lean Thinking
Monument	Machine, tool, or software that is too big, too expensive, and too complex for the needed application and workflow
Muda	(Japanese) Waste
Mura	(Japanese) Unevenness, irregular demand
Muri	(Japanese) Overburden of people or equipment
One off	Unique
Over the wall	Sending specifications to a supplier or stakeholder with no follow up, explanation, or clarification
Poka yoke	(Japanese) Mistake-proofing device
Project owner	Person fully responsible for project success
Reinventing the wheel	Discovering what is already known
Requirements creep	Uncontrollable growth of requirements
Right the first time	Achievement of good results on first attempt

Seiketsu	(Japanese) Standardization (6S term)
Seiri	(Japanese) Sorting or organization (6S term)
Seiso	(Japanese) Sweeping, shining, cleanliness (6S term)
Seiton	(Japanese) Planning for storage of documents and items (6S term)
Shitsuke	(Japanese) Self-discipline to sustain (6S term)
Six Sigma	Continuous improvement method
Spaghetti chart	Chart tracing motions of people or items over a work floor
Takt time (Period)	(German) Time required for a workstation to complete a task to a common rhythm
Visual control	Visualization of some aspect of work on a marker board or large TV screens

References

C. Bogan. *Benchmarking Best Practices*. New York, McGraw Hill, 1994.

H. Bonölken and H. Wings. Lean Banking-Wege zur Marktführerschaft, Von der Konzeption zur Realisierung. Weisbaden, Gabler, 1994.

J. Byrne. Editorial. *Business Week*, June 23, 1997.

W.L. Carter. *Process Improvement for Administrative Departments: The Key to Achieving Internal Customer Satisfaction*. BookSurge Publishing, 2008.

G. Convis. Role of Management in a Lean Manufacturing Environment. SAE International, http://www.sae.org/manufacturing/lean/column/leanjul01.htm

C.J. Corbett, M.J. Montes-Sancho, D.A. Kirsch et al. The financial impact of ISO 9000 certification in the United States: an empirical analysis. *Management Science* 51: 1607–1616, 2005.

J. Cunningham, O. Fiume, and L.T. White. *Real Numbers: Management Accounting in a Lean Organization*. Managing Time Press, 2003.

S. Dalgleish. Probing the limits: ISO 9001 proves ineffective. *Quality Magazine*, April 1, 2005.

W.E. Deming. *Out of the Crisis*. MIT Center for Advanced Engineering Study, 1982.

DoD Total Quality Management Master Plan. US Department of Defense, ADA355612, August 1988.

P.F. Drucker. *The Practice of Management*. Harper & Row, 1954.

M.L. Emiliani. Improving business school courses by applying lean principles and practices. *Quality Assurance in Education* 12: 175–187, 2004.

G. Galsworth. *Visual Workplace, Visual Thinking*. Boston, Visual Lean Enterprise Press, 2005.

J.H. Gittell. *The Southwest Airlines Way*. New York, McGraw Hill, 2003.

E.M. Goldratt. *Critical Chain*. Great Barrington, MA, North River Press, 1997.

Go Lean: Six Sigma Success Stories in the Financial Services Industry. http://www.goleansixsigma.com/lean-six-sigma-success-stories-in-the-financial-services-industry/

M. Graban. *Lean Hospitals*. Productivity Press, 2008.

M. Harry and R. Schroeder. *Six Sigma: The Breakthrough Management Strategy Revolutionizing the World's Top Corporations*. Doubleday, 2000.

I. Heras, G.P.M. Dick, and M. Casadesús. ISO 9000 registration's impact on sales and profitability: a longitudinal analysis of performance before and after accreditation. *International Journal of Quality & Reliability Management* 19: 774, 2002.

C. Hernandez. Challenges and Benefits to the Implementation of IPTs on Large Military Procurements, SM Thesis, Massachusetts Institute of Technology Sloan School of Business, June 1995.

INCOSE. http://www.incose.org

INCOSE Lean Systems Engineering Working Group. http://www.lean-systems-engineering.org

ISO (International Standards Organization). http://en.wikipedia.org/wiki/ISO_9000

A. Jenkins (Ed.). *Lean Management: New Frontiers for Financial Institutions*, McKinsey, 2011.

LAI (Lean Advancement Initiative). http://lean.mit.edu

LAI Lean Academy® Course, Massachusetts Institute of Technology. http://ocw.mit.edu/OcwWeb/Aeronautics-and-Astronautics/16-660January—IAP—2008/CourseHome/index.htm

S. Lasater. *Case Study: Bank of America, a Lean Six Sigma Deployment Success.* Lasater Institute. www.lasaterinstitute.com

Lean Home Building. http://leanhomebuilding.wordpress.com/2010/02/17/creating-the-fishbone-5-why-analysis/

LEI (Lean Enterprise Institute). www.lean.org

J.K. Liker. *The Toyota Way: Fourteen Management Principles.* New York, McGraw Hill, 2006.

H. Malhotra. *Lean Six Sigma at the World's Local Bank.* Process Excellence Network.

B.H. Maskell, B. Baggaley, and L. Grasso. *Practical Lean Accounting: A Proven System for Measuring and Managing the Lean Enterprise*, 2nd ed. Boca Raton, CRC Press, 2011.

R.A. McCormack. *Lean Machines: Learning from the Leaders of the Next Industrial Revolution.* Publishers & Producers, 2002.

H.L. McManus. *Product Development Value Stream Mapping Manual: LAI Release Beta.* Cambridge, Massachusetts Institute of Technology, 2004.

R.L. Millard. Value Stream Analysis and Mapping for Product Development. Master's Thesis. Massachusetts Institute of Technology, June 2001.

M.J. Morgan and J.K. Liker. *Toyota Product Development System.* Productivity Press, 2006.

M. Müller. *Lean Banking, Bankspezifische Ausprägungen, Ökonomische Wirkung der "schlanken" Prinzipien.* Wien, Ueberreuter, 1994.

E.M. Murman, H. McManus, and A.L. Weigel. The LAI experience: introductory Lean Six Sigma curriculum. *Journal of Enterprise Transformation* (accepted for 2014).

E.M. Murman, T. Allen, K. Bozdogan et al. *Lean Enterprise Value: Insights from MIT's Lean Aerospace Initiative.* Hampshire, UK, Palgrave, 2002.

E. Naveh and A. Marcus. ISO 9000 standard and safe driving practices: effects on accident rate in the US motor carrier industry. *Accident Analysis & Prevention* 39, 731, 2007.

NBC. *If Japan Can, Why Can't We?* June 24, 1980.

J. Oehmen (Ed.). *The Guide to Lean Enablers for Managing Engineering Programs.* PMI-INCOSE-MIT LAI. http://hdl.handle.net/1721.1/70495

T. Ohno. *The Toyota Production System: Beyond Large Scale Production.* New York, Productivity Press, 1988.

B.W. Oppenheim. Lean Product Development Flow. *Journal of Systems Engineering* 7, 2004.

B.W. Oppenheim. *Lean for Systems Engineering with Lean Enablers.* New York, John Wiley & Sons, 2011.

B.W. Oppenheim. Improving affordability: separating research from development and from design in complex programs. *Crosstalk Journal*, July–August 2013.

B.W. Oppenheim. Lean as a way of thinking (interview). *Quality Management Journal* (in Polish) 5, 2006.

T. Osada. The 5S's: five keys to a total quality environment. *Productivity*, December 1991.

K. Ozeki and T. Asaka. *Handbook of Quality Tools.* Productivity Press, 1988.

S.M. Paton. Is TQM Dead? *Quality Digest*, April 1994.

R. Reagan. Gwinnett County's Department of Financial Services embraces Lean. *Government Finance Review*, December 2011.

W.H. Schmidt and J.P. Finnigan. *Race without a Finish Line: America's Quest for Total Quality.* Jossey Bass Business and Management Series, 1992.

P.R. Scholtes. *The Leader's Handbook: Making Things Happen, Getting Things Done.* New York, McGraw Hill, 1997.

D.S. Sharma. The association between ISO 9000 certification and financial performance. *International Journal of Accounting* 40: 151, 2005.

R.A. Slack. Application of Lean Principles to the Military Aerospace Product Development Process. Master's Thesis, Massachusetts Institute of Technology, December 1998.

S. Spear. Fixing healthcare from the inside today. *Harvard Business Review,* September 2005.

S. Spear and H.K. Bower. Decoding the DNA of the Toyota Production System. *Harvard Business Review*, January 2006.

A. Stanke. A Framework for Achieving Lifecycle Value in Product Development. SM Thesis, Massachusetts Institute of Technology, 2001.

D.C.S. Summers. *Lean Six Sigma: Process Improvement Tools and Techniques.* New York, Prentice Hall, 2011.

J. Toussaint, G. Roger, and J. Womack. *On the Mend: Revolutionizing Healthcare to Save Lives and Transform the Industry.* Lean Enterprise Institute, June 2010.

C. Uhle. *Lean Banking.* Cologne, Botermann & Botermann, 1993.

J. Wade. Is ISO 9000 really a standard? *ISO Management Systems*, May–June 2002.

A.C. Ward. *Lean Product and Process Development*. Cambridge, MA, Lean Enterprise Institute, March 2007.

I. Wedgewood. *Lean Six Sigma: A Practitioner's Guide*. New York, Prentice Hall, 2007.

I.R. Winner, P.J. Pennell, E.H. Bertrand et al. *The Role of Concurrent Engineering in Weapons System Acquisition*. Institute for Defense Analysis, Report-R-338, 1988.

J.P. Womack and D.T. Jones. *Lean Thinking*. New York, Simon & Schuster, 1996.

J.P. Womack, D.T. Jones, and D. Roos. *The Machine That Changed the World: The Story of Lean Production*. New York, Harper Perennial, 1990.

Index

About the Authors

Bohdan W. Oppenheim, PhD, served as the Lean expert on our team. He has been a professor of systems engineering at Loyola Marymount University in Los Angeles since 1983. He is a recognized global leader in Lean systems engineering and author of an influential book titled *Lean for Systems Engineering with Lean Enablers for Systems Engineering* published by John Wiley & Sons (2011).

Dr. Oppenheim co-led a team of 15 experts supported by a community of 150 practitioners to develop the best Lean-inspired practices for managing complex engineering programs. For this work he received the Shingo Award, the highest honor in the field of operational excellence, INCOSE's Best Product Award, and two smaller awards. This work was later expanded into a joint project of the Project Management Institute (PMI), International Council on Systems Engineering (INCOSE) led by a team based at Massachusetts Institute of Technology on which Oppenheim served as key contributor. The result was a second book on Lean-inspired best practices for managing engineering programs: *The Guide to Lean Enablers for Managing Engineering Programs* (PMI-INCOSE-MIT, 2012) for which the team was honored with a Shingo Award (the second for Oppenheim).

Dr. Oppenheim is the founder and co-leader of the INCOSE Lean Systems Engineering Working Group, the organizations largest working group involving more than 200 members. He also directed Loyola Marymount University's US Department of Energy Industrial Assessment Center. In this capacity, he advised 125 Southern California companies of all sizes and types on Lean productivity matters.

With S. Rubin, Dr. Oppenheim designed Aerospace Corporation's POGO simulator for liquid rockets used by NASA and private industry. He consulted for Northrop-Grumman, Boeing, Airbus, EADS, Telekomunikacja Polska, Mars, Medtronics, the US Coast Guard and the US Air Force, Thales,

TRW, and 50 other firms and governmental institutions in the United States and Europe.

Dr. Oppenheim is or was a member of INCOSE, LAI EdNet, PIASA, ASEE, ASME, ISOPE, NPAJAC, and SNAME. His honors include a Fulbright Award, (2011) IAE fellowship, and the 2008 Best Engineering Teacher award by the Los Angeles Council of Engineers and Scientists. He has been the recipient of almost $2 million in externally funded grants. He is the author of 40 books and book chapters, technical journal articles, and many non-technical articles, books, and TV programs. He also presented 45 workshops, tutorials, and webinars on Lean Enablers and Lean Product Development Flow in Canada, Finland, France, Germany, Israel, Netherlands, Norway, Poland, Russia, Sweden, UK, and the United States.

Dr. Oppenheim was born and raised in Warsaw and has lived in the United States since 1971. He earned a PhD (1980) from University of Southampton in the UK; a postgraduate degree (1974) from MIT; a master's in ocean systems (1972) from Stevens Institute of Technology in New Jersey; and a BS (1970), from Warsaw Technical University. He divides his time between Santa Monica, California, and Warsaw, Poland.

Marek Jan Felbur served as our expert in banking and financial operations. Since 2002, he has served as director for corporate banking at BRE Bank S.A. He was involved in negotiations and bilateral credit agreements for leading consortia and companies including VW AG, Ford, Pfleiderer AG, Mercedes Benz, Orlen, Lotos, Huawei, and Belvedere. He also participated in complex restructuring negotiations for the steel industry and negotiated for multinational banks operating in Central and Eastern Europe to obtain local credit service permits. He is a member of the German–Polish Chamber of Commerce.

Before joining BRE Bank, Felbur worked for 21 years for Polimex-Cekop starting as a sales representative and advancing to member of the management board. He was responsible for privatization and restructuring of the company including takeovers of two companies on the Warsaw Stock Exchange. For eight years, he conducted negotiations, managed finances, and executed 63 successful technology investment projects in the People's Republic of China. He was named a director for trade and marketing and group director responsible for organization, operations, and finance (2000 sales of about 1.5 billion PLN, almost 10,000 employees). Felbur was the CEO of Polimex-Cekop Development and a director and CEO of Media

International Belgrade, a member of the boards of directors of ZREW S.A. and Naftorement and has served on the board of Polish Mint S.A. since 2006.

His education includes a master's in international trade from the Warsaw School of Economics (formerly Main School of Planning and Statistics). He completed managerial courses on company appraisals, capital group management, mergers and takeovers, service on boards of directors, management communications, and Lean in several countries.